Mission in Contemporary Scotland

Mission in Contemporary Scotland

Liam Jerrold Fraser

SAINT ANDREW PRESS
Edinburgh

First published in 2021 by
SAINT ANDREW PRESS
121 George Street
Edinburgh EH2 4YN

Copyright © Liam Jerrold Fraser 2021

ISBN 978 1 80083 020 2

Scripture quotations are from New Revised Standard Version Bible: Anglicized Edition, copyright © 1989, 1995 National Council of the Churches of Christ in the United States of America. Used by permission. All rights reserved worldwide.

The views expressed in this volume are the author's own and are not necessarily endorsed by the Church of Scotland.

British Library Cataloguing in Publication Data

A catalogue record for this book is available from the British Library.

It is the publisher's policy to use only papers that are natural and recyclable and that have been manufactured from timber grown in renewable, properly managed forests. All of the manufacturing processes of the papers are expected to conform to the environmental regulations of the country of origin.

Typeset by Regent Typesetting
Printed and bound in the United Kingdom by
CPI Group (UK) Ltd

To the Scottish Church

'As we believe in one God, Father, Son and Holy
Ghost, so we firmly believe that from the beginning
there has been, now is, and to the end of the world
shall be, one Church ...'

Scots Confession, Chapter XVI

Contents

Acknowledgements

The writing of my first book was a rather solitary affair, with few friends or colleagues to act as dialogue partners. Thankfully, that is not the case with the present work, which has benefitted from discussion with friends and acquaintances over many years.

I would like to thank John McPake, Russel Moffat, Christopher and Hanna Rankine and Joseph Ritchie for their friendship and conversation over the years. I would also like to thank Ally Collins, Josep Martí Bouis, Adam Frisk, Rachel Frost, Benjamin Hodozso, Nathan Hood, Jamie Lockhart, Craig Meek, Kayla Robbins, JoAnn Sproule and Simeon Wilton for their work with Edinburgh University Campus Ministry (EUCAM), and their willingness to explore new ways of being Church. Thanks must also go to various members of the Forge Scotland team for their wisdom and support, and to Jock Stein and David McCarthy for reading and commenting on an earlier version of this book.

I am most grateful to Christine Smith at Saint Andrew Press for being willing to take on this project, and for her patience in its completion. I also wish to thank Mary Matthews for her assistance in finalising the manuscript for publication.

As ever, my final thanks are to my family, and in particular to my wife Samantha. Perhaps when her husband prophesies 'no more books after this one' the Lord will one day fulfil his words.

Liam Jerrold Fraser
Feast of Thomas Becket 2020

Introduction

The summer is over, and we have not been saved. For though we are still standing, we stand at the end of an age, one that will never rise again. The bowl lies broken, the golden cord is snapped, and the aged Church peers through its blinds into a world grown dark, and strange and forbidding.

For in the blink of an eye, the Scottish Church has been undone. Since the 1950s, Scotland has moved from being a Christian to a post-Christian society, with the rate of change accelerating in recent decades. Over the past thirty years, the number of Scots who make their way to worship on the Lord's day has halved, so that 93% of Scots do not attend Church.[1] This is not only the Church's tragedy, but has consequences for all Scots. Community is in decline and mental illness on the rise, with a growing number of Scots no longer knowing who they are or what they are for. The decline is unprecedented, precipitous and real.

This is the reality that we, the last Scottish Christians, must reckon with. Yet reality is hard, and the common responses to it are despair and delusion. The despairing person asks: Why bother doing anything? Why set ourselves up for failure when success is impossible? Isn't it enough that my church will be there to 'see me out'? The delusional person, meanwhile, carves idols of hope for themselves. The statistics aren't that bad, are they? Didn't a Cabinet Minister address our conference? Doesn't the Queen send a representative to the General Assembly each year? Doesn't my daily devotional, or my pastor's teaching, or the latest book on church growth prove that we will soon see exponential growth?

Despair and delusion are powerful, but we must not settle for either. We must learn to see not with the eyes of the cynic, or of the optimist, or even of the realist, but to see ourselves, our Church and our nation with the eyes of Christ. He alone knows the way, for he is the Way.

This book is an attempt to do that, to present the Scottish Church with the depths of our predicament *and yet* to hope in Christ. It does so by offering a comprehensive introduction to the background, context and practice of mission in contemporary Scotland. It provides church members and leaders with a single point of reference, the kind that any missionary might use to familiarise themselves with the new land that they are travelling to. It presents the latest academic research on missional theology, the causes of secularisation, the social, political and spiritual contexts of Scotland and best practice in relation to Christian service, evangelism and public witness. It is not a 'how to' book in the sense of giving the Church a step-by-step guide to engaging in mission, but, like a map and compass, will keep church members and leaders from wandering off track, and point them in the direction they should be travelling.

A work of this kind, however, faces three serious objections: the relevance of a book focused only on Scotland, its multi-disciplinary approach and its utility for the Church.

The first issue is that of relevance. Do we not already have books about the theology and practice of church planting, fresh expressions and community development? Do we not live in a global Western culture that makes national characteristics irrelevant? What is the difference between Glasgow and Gateshead, Dunblane and Detroit?

As we shall see, Scotland is indeed heavily influenced by the general forces of Western culture. Yet Scotland has a unique history, sociology and political complexion that requires its own study. Scottish sociologist David McCrone recounts that when he studied sociology at Edinburgh in the 1960s, he learned about London, Chicago and a host of other Western cities, but came away knowing nothing about what was happening down the road from him. He was studying sociology in Scotland, yet few had made any effort to find out what the sociology of

Scotland actually was.[2] It is much the same with mission. We learn from detailed case studies of church plants in Amsterdam or Sydney, of experiments in fresh expressions in Sheffield and pub churches in Dallas, but know little to nothing about Aberdeen, or Inverness, or Stornoway, or Dundee. One could count the number of works dealing with mission in contemporary Scotland on almost one hand, versus many hundreds from England and thousands from America. With so little knowledge of our nation, we in the Scottish Church are in danger of doing ministry and mission in the dark.

To remedy this, I will seek to develop a contextual missiology for Scotland. Over three decades ago, Will Storrar recognised that if the Church is to reach Scotland it must first *understand* Scotland.[3] Yet we can only truly understand Scotland by *identifying* with Scotland – with its history, its culture and its hopes for the future – just as Jesus did with the law, culture and aspirations of Israel. Participation in, and commitment to, a nebulous Western Protestant culture of mission is not enough. We must enter *fully* into the identity and culture of Scotland if we are to redeem it from within.

In order to do that, however, we must employ every lens and tool at our disposal, thus necessitating a multi-disciplinary approach. In addition to Scripture and theology, we must employ history, economics, sociology, religious studies, philosophy and political theory if we are to understand how we arrived at this point, and how we, by God's grace, might turn a corner.

It is at this point that we must consider a prominent objection to multi-disciplinary studies of this kind. In *Theology and Social Theory*, John Milbank argues that social sciences like sociology are compromised by anti-Christian assumptions due to the beliefs and prejudices of those who first developed them. By ignoring Scripture and the tradition of the Church, sociology – so it is claimed – describes society *as if* God does not exist, and *as if* we do not know his intentions for it. Christians using the social sciences are said to mistake sinful human behaviours for God's will, and lack the resources to critique contemporary society.[4] While he is not a household name, Milbank's fears correlate with those of some evangelicals. Why do we need to turn to secular sources to know what God thinks about our culture? Do we not have his full revelation in the Bible?

While Milbank is correct that we must not mistake what *is* for what *should* be, he overstates his case. The social sciences are not fundamentally different from the God-given senses we use every day. They are ways of looking at society and human beings in a disciplined way, and just as we do not ignore our senses, so there is no reason to ignore the insights of the social sciences and other disciplines. Moreover, it was *evangelicals* who first popularised the use of sociology and demography in the nineteenth century in their attempt to chart numbers of conversions, prove the strength of evangelical influence in society and better understand the role of social forces in preventing people from turning to Christ.[5]

In using such tools, therefore, this work is not doing anything novel or controversial. As long as one has recourse to God's revelation in Christ as recorded by Scripture, one can look at our fallen creation without mistaking it for the new creation. When we discover, for example, that most Scots view their efforts at authenticity and self-fulfilment to be *more moral* than traditional Christian ethics, we are not saying that, theologically or biblically, they are correct. Rather, sociology and other disciplines offer powerful tools for diagnosing the influence of secular forces upon Scotland in general, and the Church in particular.

One of the most important of these insights, and one which we will encounter repeatedly in this book, is the issue of *plausibility*, the way in which certain cultures – both within and outwith the Church – make Christian belief easier to accept, while others make it harder to accept.[6] That is because religious beliefs are not free-floating and abstract, but grounded in cultural practice, in day-to-day social interactions in community. To use technical language, there is a *dialectical* relationship between practice and belief, so that the *right* kind of culture will make it easier for non-Christians to come to Christ, while the *wrong* kind of culture will make it harder. Crucial to the success of the Church in contemporary Scotland, then, is the ability to shape its congregational culture so that its character and activities make faith more, rather than less, plausible.

This brings us to a final possible criticism concerning the utility of this work. Why does the Church need to understand why faith has collapsed in Scotland? Why do we need to understand why our neighbours reject the authority of God, and construct non-religious identities for themselves? It is not understanding that we need, but *action*. We need to find the right worship, the right discipleship structures, the right methods of evangelism and then pray into them, so we can catch what God is doing and follow him!

We do indeed need action, but action without thought is blind. Worse, the wrong kind of action is wasteful and self-destructive. The lack of reference works on mission in Scotland is the equivalent of a doctor prescribing medical treatment without first diagnosing the patient. How do we know if what we are doing is pleasing to God and effective at reaching our neighbours? How can we know whether our missionary activity will bring Scotland back to faith if we don't know why Scotland lost its faith to begin with? How do we know if our fresh expression or church plant will take root and grow if we don't understand why certain beliefs become plausible and attractive to non-Christians?

No – in mission, as in medicine, the first step to treatment is diagnosis. That is why the first two parts of this work deal with the background to mission in contemporary Scotland and its present-day context. Because the majority of Scottish Christians have spent their lives living in Scotland or other parts of the United Kingdom, we tend to think we understand our country. On a great number of levels, there appears to be a shared culture of understanding between ourselves and our non-Christian neighbours. We speak the same language, buy the same things, watch the same programmes and use the same technology. But these similarities mask a divide of feeling, thought and purpose. There is a difference between following Christ and following the popular assumptions of the age. There is a difference between living your lives for your neighbours and for God and living it for yourself or a select number of others. There is a difference between thinking that your life and identity are gifts from God to be realised in relationship with him, and thinking that your life is a project that you can shape in whatever manner you wish. As well as we think we know our nation, in our deepest commitments, we Christians are *different* from our neighbours. While we do not sit by the waters of Babylon and weep as the daughters of Israel once did, we must nevertheless, like them, learn how to sing the Lord's song in a strange land.

Having addressed the most important objections to a work of this kind, we turn now to its structure and content. The book is structured into three parts of three chapters each. Part 1 examines the *background* to contemporary mission in Scotland, exploring the missional meaning of Christian doctrine, historic understandings of the Church's mission and the secularisation of Scotland. Part 2 examines the national *context* of mission in contemporary Scotland, surveying our changed social situation, the growth of Scottish nationalism and the spiritual complexion of Scottish culture. Part 3 then turns to the *practice* of mission, exploring acts of service, new forms of evangelism and fresh expressions and the public witness of the Scottish Church.

The primary argument of this work is that, in a secularised society where Christianity does not benefit from political privilege or advantageous social forces, the Church must create *local cultures of plausibility* to raise the significance of the Church and the credibility of the Christian faith. These local cultures of plausibility will be driven by contextually relevant worshipping communities that integrate service with discipleship and evangelism, and which are supported by a strong – and unified – Christian voice in the public life of Scotland.

This primary argument is supported by a number of others:

• That Christian mission has as its end the re-creation of human beings and the world, a process that is directed and empowered by the action of the Holy Trinity, in whom knowledge, love, self-sacrifice and witness are inseparable.

- The mission of God has a Church, and to the extent that it allows itself to be moved by God to serve and evangelise its neighbours, it is the sign, instrument and foretaste of the new creation.
- That the historic success of Christianity in Scotland was largely dependent on its social functions rather than its explicitly religious activities, and that these social functions gave plausibility and impact to the Gospel message.
- That the decline of Christianity in Scotland is largely the work of social, political and economic change, but that the Scottish Church further weakened its position through faulty theologies, poor structures and disunity.
- That while the Gospel speaks to our deepest needs, the majority of Scots are, as a matter of fact, satisfied with their lot, and largely indifferent to matters of faith.
- That Scottish nationalism has replaced older forms of Scottish identity founded on religion, and that it is state and nation, and not Church and God, that provide the foundations for the collective self-understanding of contemporary Scots.
- That the future of the Church is dependent on communicating a clear, intelligible and orthodox Gospel to both our members and neighbours, and encouraging confidence in, and passion, for Christ.
- That service and evangelism are two interdependent parts of Christian mission. Following the logic of the Trinity, it is by giving ourselves to our neighbours in authentic and loving service that we witness to Christ, and the nature and glory of God are revealed.
- That the Church must adopt new structures and forms of training that decentralise power and authority, and permit experimentation with new forms of worship and Christian community in particular local contexts.
- That the Scottish Church can find a distinct – yet principled – political voice by resisting attempts to silence or ostracise those with unpopular views, and by modelling an alternative ethic in Scottish public life.

- That the Scottish Church is not presented with the choice of lauding or condemning our culture, but affirming what is good in it, passing over what is false, and telling a better story about our needs, desires and aspirations than our society does.

The book concludes by presenting the foundations of a contextual missiology for contemporary Scotland. Central to this missiology is the creation of local cultures of plausibility through the proper integration of worship, service and evangelism, and the sharing of mission between all parts of the Church. This can only be accomplished, however, through the reorientation of Scottish Christianity away from historic – and divisive – marks of the Church focused on structures and doctrinal uniformity, towards those focused on mission, and grounded in the Trinity. The Scottish Church will only become what it is when it accepts that mission is of the essence of the Church, and in accepting that essence, will rediscover its essential unity in Christ. When that happens, our Lord will not only be acknowledged by a declining group of Christians, but will be revealed for what he is: the Son of God, and the King of Scotland.

PART I

Background

I

A Missional Theology

*Man's chief end is to glorify God,
and to enjoy him forever.*

In a work on mission, it is tempting to hurry: hurry into case studies, into analysis and – ultimately – into action. Mission is, after all, a *sending*, a going out, a restlessness with how things are and the taste of what they might be.

Yet mission does not begin with action, nor does it have action as its end. The beginning and end of Christian mission is *wonder*: wonder at the majesty of God's glory, and the worship it gives rise to. It is God's glory alone that provides the existence, motivation, means and end of Christian mission, and if we cannot picture this glory in our minds and experience it in our hearts, we will fail.

This point is sometimes lost, however. Missiology, theology and doxology (worship) are sometimes separated. Missiology deals with practice, theology with thought and belief, and worship with what happens on a Sunday morning. Yet while men and woman separate out, God reconciles, and each of these are three aspects of the one reality that any work on mission must grasp. As such, in this chapter, we do not present a *methodology* of mission, or a *theology* of mission, but a *missional theology*: an account of the Christian faith which shows the missional meaning of its core doctrines.[1] It is only when we approach doctrine in this way that we can understand the missional identity of our God and our Church, and equip ourselves with the analytic tools to properly assess the background, context and practice of mission in contemporary Scotland.

The Trinity: the Origin of Mission

Mission begins and ends with our witness to the majesty of God's glory, and with our deep satisfaction with who he is, irrespective of what he does for us, our neighbours or our Church. God has all life, glory, goodness, blessedness and love in and of himself, and is all-sufficient to himself. His being and nature are beyond all thought, and when we frame him with language, and picture him in our minds, our thought quickly reaches its end, for he is greater than anything that can be conceived. In the presence of the one who is now and evermore, whose place is everywhere, it is not description, analysis and discourse that is right, but wonder, love and praise.

Without his mission to us, we would know nothing of him. Yet through Israel and Jesus Christ, God has revealed himself in history, and in him and through him, we have been given the greatest blessing of all: to know, and be known, by the Living God, the eternal Trinity of Father, Son and Spirit.

In the life of the Trinity, God knows and loves himself eternally as Father, Son and Spirit. In knowing his identity and will, the Father begets the Son. The Son is a witness to all that the Father is. He knows the Father completely, and is in turn known by him. The Son is light from light and God from God, of the same substance as the Father.

The knowledge that the Father and the Son have of each other is not cold or distant but takes the form of love. This bond of love between Father and Son is the Holy Spirit, equal in majesty and worship and substance to both. The Holy Spirit is the Spirit *of* the Father and *of* the Son, for the one who begets and the one who is begotten, the one who wills and the one who is willed, the one who witnesses and the one who is witnessed to are not two but one. The one who witnesses to the self-knowledge and love of the Father and the Son is *himself* a witness: knowing and loving, and being known and being loved, by the Father and the Son in turn.[2]

The knowledge and love of Father, Son and Spirit is not static, therefore, but creative. Each of the Persons *is* only in relation to the other. The Father is Father only of and for the Son. The Son is Son only of and for the Father. The Spirit is the Spirit only of and for the Father and the Son. They witness to each other, give themselves to each other, and in so doing become who they are. The life of God's Triune being, therefore, is one of faithful love and knowledge, which manifests in self-giving and being for the other. In the Trinity, witness, love, knowledge, self-giving and glorification are different aspects of the one divine nature.

This description, of course, is *abstract*: abstracted from Scripture and abstracted from the life of the Church. Yet it is in God's inner life that we discover the logic that animates his mission to the world and the mission of his Church. We see unity and difference, similarity and dissimilarity, community and personhood, serving and being served. In God, however, these are perfectly integrated. Unity arises out of difference and difference shapes unity. Love arises from knowledge and knowledge grounds love. The difference of the divine persons is not a problem, but the very means by which each is constituted. Difference is constructive and unity creative. The divine logic of love and knowledge, service and freedom is complete, realised and perfected.

Creation: the Horizon of Mission

The logic seen in the Trinity also hints at another possibility, however, that God would not only experience difference *in himself*, but create one who is *wholly different* from himself, that he might unite himself with it. Yet if God were to create something wholly different from himself, then, at least initially, the love and knowledge between he and it would *not* be complete and eternal, but partial and temporal. The principles seen in the divine life would still be in play, but they would form part of a *process*, one by which that which is separated from God would come to live in him, and participate in his own divine life. That is what God did when he created the universe.

If God is changeless, the universe is changeable. If God is incorruptible, the world is corruptible. If God is limitless and infinite, the world is limited and finite. The very nature of creation, therefore, shapes God's mission. If God is to unite himself with a creation that is so unlike him, he must find a way of reconciling time and eternity, the infinite and the finite, the perfect and the imperfect. This process of reconciliation moves creation to new creation, from being distanced from God to being integrated into his divine life. This is what God's mission to the world consists of. Mission is not the salvation of individual souls, or even of the Church community alone, but of the whole of creation in all its aspects, a fact that – as we will see in Part 3 – has a fundamental bearing on the scope of mission.

In creating such a world, however, a world that was so *unlike* him, God could be accused of being irresponsible. Yet in the corruption of the world, we see the same logic as we saw in the life of the Trinity. Just as Father, Son and Spirit only exist in relation to each other, so our corruptible world was never meant to exist independently of its Creator. It was created to exist in *communion* with him, receiving all that it lacks from his hand: beauty for brokenness, hope for despair. Without God, *there is no hope* for the imperfect and decaying world in which we live. Yet with God and in God, there is even more than hope: there is life, *eternal* life.

It is God's desire for deepening intimacy with his creation that forms the motivation for his mission to the world. For the great narrative of Scripture is of the God who longs to dwell among his people, that in raising them to participate in his own divine life he might perfect them in every way. Creation, therefore, is only the first stage on the movement to new creation. Creation must be created if it is to be perfected in unity with its Creator. Flesh must be created if it is to be healed, empowered and fulfilled by the Spirit, and humanity must be created if it is to be reconciled to God and participate in the life of the Holy Trinity. When creation and Creator, flesh and spirit, humanity and God are united, the new creation will be realised. We will live in God and he in us. God will be all in all, and in the fulness of love we will behold the face of the Father himself.

The desire of God to perfect his creation by dwelling among it and reconciling it to himself is seen in the very means by which God created. For ours is not a faraway God, a distant deity who creates and sustains at a distance. When God created, when he willed, when he spoke his Word, he created and willed and spoke *through himself*, through the Son. Just as the Son is the perfect witness of the Father, so God created the world to be a finite, dependent, creaturely witness to his beauty, goodness, wisdom and power. The Son is the *logos* – the reason, underlying structure – of the world because, in him, the Father created the world to reflect his perfect being and will, to manifest and point creation towards its proper end and purpose, and prepare it for the time when he would dwell within it for ever. Yet creation was not only the work of the Father and Son, but of the Spirit, who brooded over the waters of chaos. It is the Holy Spirit who, working through the Son, sustains not only living things but *everything*. The Spirit is present at every point of time and space, maintaining the creation created in and through the Word. Yet he not only maintains but *moves*, moves it towards its end – the new creation – so that it resembles more perfectly the likeness of the Son, who is, in himself, the perfect likeness of the Father.

A Holy People

This explains God's motivation and aims for mission. Yet how is this mission to be accomplished? The answer has already been given to us: reconciliation through the self-giving of God.

For human beings are not purely spiritual but *material*. We live as embodied creatures in space–time, existing in human societies with histories and future horizons. If God wishes to unite himself with human beings, to fully give himself for the world so that it might manifest and witness to his glory, he must not only structure, sustain and guide in a hidden way, but enter *into* human history, society and experience itself.

This process began in the first human beings. Humanity is made in the image of God. More precisely, we are made in the image of God's Son. We were created to represent creation to God and God to creation. Humanity is analogous to God in ruling over the earth, tending and nurturing nature and mirroring the life of the Trinity in its social and sexual relations. Because we resemble God in these ways, human beings are worthy of honour, and whoever dishonours another human being dishonours God. Because we bear God's image, we – of all animal life – were chosen by God to be that part of creation through which and in which he would come to dwell ever more closely with his creation.

The creation of humanity, however, gave rise to new problems. For while God already had to overcome time, change and finitude in relation to creation as a whole, with human beings, he also had to overcome *sin*. Human beings were made in God's image and created to be conformed to his Son. Yet because we live in a world of change, finitude and imperfection, human beings are currently only *like* God, and lack his perfection. As such, we routinely prefer our own will to his and hurt ourselves and others. To the extent that human beings are righteous, we cooperate with God. Indeed, as we shall see, when human beings follow God's will, it is correct to say that both God and human beings act *at the same time*. When we do not follow God's will, however, we act alone, and act in sin.

Because the first human beings disobeyed God's will, God called other good men and women to be his partners in the restoration of the earth. God revealed himself to Noah, Abraham and their families, and called them out of cultures whose spirituality was based on idolatry and projection into true worship. These covenant relationships were unconditional and centred on individual people. Yet – following the Trinitarian logic that love shown to one person brings blessing to all – in blessing Noah and Abraham, God blessed *all* people. In setting aside Noah, Abraham and their families as the people of God, as *holy* in his sight, God sought to call *all* nations to himself. In being the recipients of God's grace and self-giving, the patriarchs became witnesses to God, and in the building of the Ark and the binding of Isaac, they – mirroring the reciprocity of the Trinity – sacrificed all they had to give glory to God.

This pattern was fulfilled in the nation of Israel itself. God revealed himself to Moses in the wilderness, and he became a witness to the Living God. Yet with Moses and the Israelites, God would go further. He would not only covenant with his people, but be present among them. In pillared flame and moving cloud, in the Tent of Meeting and the Ark of the Covenant, God gave himself to be with and for his people. Yet this blessing was not only for them but for the world. Israel was made holy by God's presence and the giving of his Law, but only that the nations might be made holy and reconciled to God *through* them. Just as all nations would be blessed through the faith of Noah and Abraham, so the world would be blessed by Israel, who were called to be a holy nation, a royal priesthood.

God stooped low to live in tent and temple, but Israel turned away. Though God sent prophets to preach, rebuke and inspire, Israel was not faithful to the calling to which it was called. Rather than seeing the Law as a means for self-transformation, they saw it as a badge of righteousness that elevated them above those they were elected to serve. Rather than leading the nations to worship of the Living God, they succumbed to the same idols as others did. Neglecting the divine presence in their midst, they exchanged the glory of God for a lie.

The Coming of the Saviour

Yet God had more to give, and the history of Israel would only be fulfilled when God gave not only laws or prophets or even his external presence to his people, but *himself*. Now, the destiny of Israel and the destiny of God's creation would converge in the birth and Incarnation of the Holy One, Emmanuel, God With Us: Jesus of Nazareth. In Jesus, God the Son not only entered into the culture of his people, but into human nature itself. In taking our sinful humanity upon himself, God's self-giving reached a new level of intimacy. He identified not only with the righteous, with those who were – however imperfectly – like him, but with *sinners*, those who were not like him. In Jesus, we see the full realisation of God's mission from creation to new creation, fallenness to righteousness, in the reconciled harmony of humanity and God.

In reconciling God and humanity, Creator and creation in his own person, Jesus *reveals* the identity of God and the identity of humanity. In Jesus, we learn of the love of Father, Son and Spirit, and their mission to save and re-create the world through the inauguration of the Kingdom of God. In Jesus, we also see what perfected humanity looks like, and what our identity and true nature really is. In Jesus, we see that we were created to worship God and become who we were created to be in relation to him: loving, self-sacrificial and truthful. Jesus exposes the lies that humanity has told about God, and the lies humanity has told about itself.

Rather than identifying with all that was considered glorious and valuable by the world – that which the world considered closest to the divine – God chose that which was considered worthless, and weak and accursed by the world. Christ was born to ordinary people, forced into migration and poverty by the evil of the powerful and born in a stable. In doing so, God indicated the future direction and mission of his Church, that it should identify with the poor and suffering, and oppose those who oppress them.

This bias towards the poor and suffering was made explicit in Jesus' teaching and witness concerning the Kingdom of God. The Kingdom of God is not something built by human greatness – whether through strength, wisdom or missional strategy – but something we perceive, enter into, inherit and receive.[3] It manifests itself in the world through that which is good but is held of little account. It is in the world, but not of it. In the first great commission given to his followers, Christ taught that the Church should feed the hungry, clothe the naked and heal the sick, for when they do these things, they do it for him. He ate with, and befriended those, who were spurned by God's people. He gave his company, wisdom and love to the unlovable, that they would become beloved. At the dinner table, at the well, and as he preached and healed, Jesus transgressed barriers of purity, ethnicity and law to enable those who had ears to hear, and eyes to see and hearts to receive to become children of God: to know and love the Living God, and to be known and loved by him.

Yet Jesus came not only to reveal but to *accomplish*. For though he had taken flesh, he had not experienced the deserved fate of flesh and blood in a sinful, godless world: judgement and death. In Jesus, God took upon himself the fate of all humanity, entering into death, damnation and hell itself to reconcile and overcome that which was most opposed to him. The Holy One of Israel became the hated Man of Sorrows, spurned and rejected not only by Gentiles, but by his own people of Israel. God surrendered himself to the petty rulers of the day, and entered into that which was dark, and ugly and God-forsaken, and there manifested his glory, the glory of the only-begotten Son of God, full of grace and truth. For in giving himself fully, going as far as he could for the love of his creation, God overcame the barriers of sin and death and judgement that separated humanity from him. On Calvary's hill, atonement was accomplished, and the reconciliation of God and humanity, perfection and imperfection, law and grace was completed.

Yet the atonement was not an end in itself, nor was its meaning understood by those who witnessed it. For three days, God's mission to creation appeared to have ended in failure. Satan rejoiced in the greatest of all crimes: the murder of God himself. Yet the weakness of God is stronger than human strength and his foolishness is wiser than human wisdom. On the third day Christ rose again in glory, having preached to the souls in captivity, and broken the chains of death and nothingness. In the resurrection, Christ, *in his own person*, became the new creation and the realised Kingdom: the locus of eternal life, joy, freedom and blessedness. In the resurrection of Christ, humanity and the material world *themselves* were raised up, made to participate in the very life of God. In entering into human flesh and raising it from the grave to the heavens, God's self-giving perfected, restored and glorified humanity. In this movement of self-giving, we see that creation was never intended to exist apart from God, but always in him, receiving from him all that it lacks. The world was not completed on the sixth day of creation. It was completed when Jesus rose from the grave.

Even in the splendour of the resurrection, however, where Christ, the first fruits of the new creation, displayed the victory of God over all that opposes us, God was not yet finished. For the new creation and the realised Kingdom were just that: displayed in Christ *only*. The rest of creation – sun and moon, stars and planets, animals and plants – beheld his glory in silent witness, yet only from afar. For this reason, Christ ascended to the Father, from whose side he would intercede as Great High Priest, bringing the cries of creation before the throne and directing the governance of the world so that all things might work together for good.

The Church of the Mission of God

Christ's intercession before the throne of God, however, could only be effective in ordering events, people and things in a providential, external and general way. His influence over *the heart* – over human feelings, thoughts, desires, motivations and actions – was still limited. To reach all of humanity, therefore, God had to fill *part* of humanity with his own Spirit, so that through them, he might complete the movement from creation to new creation, and God might be all in all.

To that end, before his Ascension, Christ charged the disciples with the second of their great commissions: *to make disciples of all nations*. On the night before his arrest, and most powerfully on the great day of Pentecost, Christ did a new thing: he formed the Church, the community of the new creation, through the gift of his Holy Spirit. This Spirit was not something less than God, *but God himself*. By receiving the Spirit, the disciples became fully united with the risen and ascended Christ, and – through that unity – began to manifest the power of Jesus in and through sinful humanity. God's Spirit changed the disciples, allowing them to change the world. From this point onward, the disciples became *apostles*: ones who are *sent* by their Lord to deliver his message, and further his mission. Just as Jesus had ministered in the flesh, so the Church, by his Spirit, now ministered. Through their preaching, service and martyrdom, they – empowered by the Spirit, and participating in the life and mission of the Holy Trinity – became witnesses to Christ and the Father. The mission of God, founded in eternity, had created *a Church* in the midst of the world.

This Church – as defined by the Council of Nicaea – is one, holy, catholic and apostolic. This Church is not the creation of men and women – a mere human institution – but the creation of the Lord himself, the family and household of the Living God. Its unity, holiness, catholicity and apostolicity are not primarily the work of human beings but of the Holy Trinity: of the Father who wills it, of the Son in whom it lives and of the Spirit by whom it is empowered.

The Church's identity as one, holy, catholic and apostolic should not be interpreted as static, therefore, but dynamic and charismatic. Its identity is *dynamic* because it is only insofar as the Church is united with Christ, filled by the Spirit, and doing the will of the Father that it is the Church. The Church's identity is *charismatic* not in the narrow sense of belonging to the Charismatic or Pentecostal traditions, but in the original sense that it receives the gifts it needs to undertake its ministry and mission to the world through the empowering of the Holy Spirit. If it is united with Christ in faith then his Spirit flows into it, producing gifts such as teaching, pastoring, prayer, service and prophecy. When it receives the Spirit, the Church is clothed in power from on high, enabling it to accomplish things that no eye has seen nor mind comprehended.

Insofar as it lives in Christ and receives his Spirit, the one, holy, catholic and apostolic Church becomes the *sign, instrument and foretaste* of the new creation.[4] In it, humanity sees what it was created to be: loved, forgiven, reconciled and restored. In it, the world to come becomes present, Christ coming from the future to hallow the community and raise it to heaven. Yet having been changed by Christ, so Christ changes the world through it. Its ministry is *Christ's* ministry, its mission is *his* mission. When its leaders preach, Christ preaches. When its members forgive, Christ forgives. When it baptises or celebrates the Lord's Supper, Christ baptises and celebrates. It is Christ's Body, and all who believe are members of this Body, becoming the hands, feet, eyes and ears of Christ in the world. Through the ministry and mission of the Church, the Kingdom or reign of God is manifested, and where the Kingdom is, there the new creation begins to take root. Salvation, therefore, is not individualistic or private, but communitarian and public. Salvation takes place in this world: seen, accomplished and lived out in, and through, the Church.

For these reasons, the Church exists in two dimensions. On the one hand, it exists in an immediate relationship to God, through which it is created and maintained. Christ reigns in it, and everything good that happens in and through it is his activity. On the other hand, the Church exists in space–time, and is subject to the same physical and social forces as anything else. It is this dimension of the Church that allows it to act in history and cooperate in God's mission to the world. To the extent that it allows Christ to reign in it, the Church draws closer to what it – and humanity – were created to be. To the extent that it does not recognise his reign, it becomes more and more susceptible to the physical and social forces that affect fallen humanity, and will – like all flesh – wither and die. Because of its sin, and because creation is not yet new creation, the Church is therefore sign, instrument and foretaste of the new creation in a *provisional* or *incomplete* manner only. The Church – like all flesh – is forever tempted to rest in its own strength. Yet precisely as it rests in its own strength it loses its strength. As it rests in its own wisdom, or the wisdom of the age, it becomes foolish. As it ceases to witness to Christ, it loses all significance.

Culture: the Context of Mission

Being one, holy, catholic and apostolic, the provisional sign, instrument and foretaste of the new creation, the first Christians set about transforming the world. As the creation of Christ and the Spirit, who were sent as witnesses to reveal the Father through the redemption of fallen humanity, so the Church was sent into the world to witness to, and glorify him, through mission.

Heeding the commissions of their Lord to serve the least and make disciples of all nations, the first members of Christ's

Church shared their possessions, fed the poor, rescued orphans and tended the sick. They built schools, trained men and women in the Scriptures and preached Christ at home, work and in the marketplace. The love of the Trinity was replicated in the Church's service to its neighbours, and the knowledge of Father, Son and Spirit was replicated in its evangelism. Service and evangelism, love and knowledge went hand in hand, and just as the witness of Christ to the Father achieved redemption, and just as the witness of the Spirit to Christ empowered the disciples, so the witness of the Church reaped a rich harvest. By declaring the worth of slaves, women and outcasts, and recognising their God-given charisms and ministries, the Church ennobled thousands, robing them with sacred destinies, and winning them for Christ.

Yet precisely because their mission was to the world, the first Christians were confronted with the challenge of how to relate to the cultures and contexts they found themselves in. They knew that the Father creates and rules over all things. They knew that the Spirit was present in their hearts and at every point of space–time, and was moving all things to be conformed to the likeness of the Son. Yet the world did not, as yet, display the power of the Father, the movement of the Spirit, or the likeness of the Son. It was a world of partial light and partial shade, of practices that were sometimes good, sometimes evil and sometimes neutral. These difficulties lay at the heart of the early Church's reflections, as they attempted to discern whether food sacrificed to idols, reverence for the Emperor, military service and cultural forms honoured or dishonoured God, whether they furthered the Kingdom or hindered it. As we shall see, this problem continues to trouble the Church to this day.

Due to the distinct stances they took in relation to culture and politics, the loyalty of Christians to the Empire was suspect, and persecution – sometimes official, sometimes popular – broke out against the Church. Thousands were killed, tortured and terrorised, and the unluckiest – in imitation of Christ – became subject to cruel and humiliating deaths. Yet by rejecting opportunities to recant, maintaining their faith to the end and displaying kindness and forgiveness to their killers, the first Christians witnessed to Christ, and through their faith and courage, gave glory to the Father. More and more high-born citizens converted to the faith, and Christianity eventually gained official sanction under Emperor Constantine. Against all odds, Christ had conquered Caesar.

Being concerned with the great truths of Trinity and Incarnation, and the desire – seen in the desert fathers and mothers – to serve Christ perfectly, the early Church did not have reason to consider the same questions of mission that concern us today. They lived in a political, social and spiritual context very different from our own, and one in which such questions did not arise. As the Church moved from being a persecuted minority to a privileged majority, however, and as it spread throughout Europe and later the world, it began to be confronted by questions that the early Church did not address or fully resolve.

The most important of these questions are those with which the rest of this work will be concerned:

- What is the exact relationship between the mission of God and the mission of the Church?
- Is it possible for the Church to bring about the new creation, or can only God do this through direct supernatural power?
- What is the aim of the mission of God? Is it to make people happy and healthy or to bring them to faith? If both, what is the relationship between the two?
- In what way should the culture of the Church mirror or be distinct from the culture of its host society?
- Are there some cultures that are simply toxic to faith?
- Does God only work through the Church, or also through society? If he works through society, does he work only through Christians, or through non-Christian people and institutions too?
- What is the proper relationship between the mission of God and the state? Should the Church seek state support for its work, or should it reject any form of power?

- Is the unity of the Church essential for mission, or is it secondary?
- Are churches 'successful' because they are faithful, or do they succeed for reasons unconnected to faith?

These are the questions that would be played out in the history of Scotland, as Christians sought to plant and grow the Gospel in their land. While these questions would sometimes be creative, their unresolved nature would have serious implications for the witness and mission of the Scottish Church, leading to centuries of conflict, confusion and missed opportunity. It is to that story that we now turn.

2

The World That Was

The question of why Scots no longer go to church is closely related to the question of why they went to church to begin with.[1] That question is connected to what has been called the 'parish state': the way in which the Church of Scotland's religious role in society was enhanced by a range of political, social and economic functions that made it central to the lives of most Scots.

Reference to the Church of Scotland in this context may seem surprising. Why privilege the Church of Scotland over other denominations? What does an institution that faces one of the worst rates of decline in the world have anything to teach us about effective mission? These questions would be legitimate if the Scottish Church had always been what it is now: a set of denominations sharing the basics of a common faith but enjoying little cooperation. Yet that is a relatively recent phenomenon. For centuries, there was only *one* Church, and even after the Reformation, the Church of Scotland was the dominant Christian force in society until the mid-twentieth century. Due to its decisive position in Scottish history, the Church of Scotland shaped the ministry and mission of *all* the Scottish denominations, and it was the Kirk's mistakes – above all others – that resulted in the kind of secularisation we now find ourselves with. This is not to say that other denominations did not make important contributions to mission, however, and reference will be made to the Scottish Episcopal Church, the Roman Catholic Church, the Secession Church and the Baptist Church throughout this and following chapters. Indeed, it was denominations outwith the Church of Scotland that were often the pioneers of methods and mindsets that would become normative in later times, while the Church of Scotland remained wedded to models of Church that had grown redundant.

In this chapter, we examine how the Scottish Church understood its ministry and mission to the people of Scotland from its formation until the industrial revolution. Three themes important for later chapters will emerge in the course of this survey: the close integration of religious, political and economic power through the parish system, the dependence of Christian faith upon government support and the social power of the Church, and the absence of what we would now think of as mission from the marks of the Church. The last point is crucial, for 'mission' during the period from the Reformation to the industrial revolution largely consisted in conversion from one Christian tradition to another. While we sometimes believe we have moved beyond these days, as we shall see, we still live with the legacy of yesteryear. For that reason, no account of mission in contemporary Scotland can be complete without an account of the world that was.

The Scottish Church

Living as we do in the fragmented and declining world of the twenty-first-century Church, it can be easy to forget three important truths: that the Scottish Church is a product of mission, that it was once united and that it once dominated society.

While Christianity was probably first introduced to Scotland during the period of Roman occupation, the first sustained evidence of Christian communities can be dated to the fifth and sixth centuries. Small groups of monks would set out from an established Christian centre and travel – often in danger of their lives – into pagan lands where the Gospel had not yet been proclaimed. At centres like Whithorn and Kirkmadrine, Christian communities were planted that, in turn, would plant other communities. Around a rhythm of daily worship, these small Christian centres – sometimes known as the 'Celtic Church' – devoted themselves to education and service, their moral example and advanced technologies winning pagan rulers and their subjects to the faith. Later, these communities of prayer, learning and mission – the most famous of which was Iona – not only planted Christian communities throughout Scotland, but throughout Europe. To this day, the *Schottenkirchen* – churches and monasteries founded by Irish and Scots – of Germany and Austria bear witness to the success of these missionaries.

As Christianity took root in Scotland, and as more pagan rulers were won for the faith, the Church became favoured with great wealth and power. The relationship between the Church and political rulers was advantageous for both sides. With wealth, political patronage and armed protection, the Church gained the power to extend the Gospel throughout Scotland. By planting and maintaining churches, political rulers demonstrated their piety, and the Church taught rulers' subjects that they were God's appointed leaders, who were to be listened to and obeyed.

The growing convergence of spiritual and worldly power, taken with improved communication between Scotland and the rest of Europe, led to the incorporation of the Celtic Church into the Western Catholic Church from the seventh century onward. These developments had important implications for mission. First, they led to the Church in Scotland becoming, at times, an ancillary of regional warlords and later the Crown, denting its ability to speak truth to power. Second, the regularisation of Scottish Christian communities through parishes and dioceses under Catholic bishops stunted local initiative, and focused missional attention within more limited geographical areas. While society was undeveloped and sparsely populated this system worked well, yet it set a precedent that was inappropriate for later contexts. Third, parishes were maintained through a sometimes complex financial arrangement, whereby lands and incomes were levied in partnership with the Crown or local landowners. This made the Church dependent on the powers that be, while also – on occasion – leading to resentment among the local population. These developments increased under the reigns of Malcolm III and his successors, and continued until the end of the high medieval period.

The *Ecclesia Scoticana* – the Church of Scotland, for there was only one Church at this time – not only provided legitimacy for the Scottish Crown among its own subjects, however, but in relation to other monarchs and the Papacy. In resisting the attempt of the Archdiocese of York to bring the Church of Scotland under its jurisdiction, and through its repeated requests to the Pope for a Scottish archdiocese, the Scottish Church made it harder for English monarchs to subjugate Scotland. When doubts over the Scottish succession provided an opportunity for King Edward to appoint his own puppet ruler, the Scottish Church eventually swung its support behind Robert the Bruce as an independent Scottish King. This support gave rise to one of the founding documents of Scottish identity: the Declaration of Arbroath. The Declaration of Arbroath is the first developed articulation of Scottish nationhood, and presents the case for King Robert and an independent Scottish crown. Yet the Declaration of Arbroath is a petition to *the Pope*. The Declaration argues that Scotland exists because Jesus Christ *wills* Scotland to exist. This is proven by his appointment of Saint Andrew as its patron saint, and the granting of his relics to the nation in the town of St Andrews. From its inception, therefore, the Scottish Church was not simply one institution among others, but was the primary means of legitimation for the nation's existence. As Storrar notes, therefore, the very foundation of Scottish nationhood and distinctiveness is Christian in character.[2]

Reforming the Nation

This medieval settlement was transformed, however, by the event which, above all, would determine the future of Scotland: the Reformation.

The Scottish Reformers believed that the Roman Catholic Church had adopted doctrines and practices that were unscriptural, sinful and which endangered the souls of their fellow Scots. Rather than the liturgy of the Mass and the authority of the Catholic hierarchy culminating in the Pope, the Reformers located the identity of the Church in three 'notes' or 'marks': the true preaching of the Word, the right administration of the sacraments and discipline rightly administered.[3] These marks focused the Church's identity upon uniformity of doctrine, practice and – to a lesser extent – polity and structures, and would have important implications for the future of mission in Scotland.

In addition to its spiritual consequences, the Scottish Reformation of 1560 hastened a range of political, social and economic changes that would, in time, give rise to three other factors decisive for the future shape of ministry and mission in Scotland: Christian disunity, the close association of Protestantism with political Unionism and the creation of the parish state.

While Knox and the Scottish Reformers believed that they were restoring the true Catholic Church in Scotland, the repudiation of Papal jurisdiction and the Mass by the Scottish Parliament of 1560 severed Scotland from Rome, and created a divide between Protestant and Roman Catholic Scots that has persisted for over four centuries. Roman Catholics were deprived of their places of worship, priests were arrested and sometimes killed and Roman Catholics often had to hide their faith for fear of persecution. Christian disunity was not confined to Roman Catholics and the Reformed, however, but would soon extend to divisions among Protestants themselves. For the majority of the Church of Scotland, the rejection of the Roman Catholic hierarchy also entailed the rejection of bishops. James VI's desire to unify Scotland and England through a united – episcopal – church therefore gave rise to conflict between Episcopalians and Presbyterians, with both parties taking turns to persecute the other.

While adopting different approaches towards bishops, the Reformation ensured that both Scotland and England would be Protestant. Protestantism provided the foundation for the Union of the two nations, and one of its most important ongoing justifications. It allowed Scotland and England to differentiate themselves from their Roman Catholic European enemies, and allowed the Union to persist even in the midst of other tensions between Scotland and the British state, most notably over patronage. After centuries of association between the Church of Scotland, the British Crown and the Union, Presbyterianism in Scotland came to be firmly associated with Britishness, something that would prove significant in the twentieth and twenty-first centuries.

The last effect of the Reformation relevant to the shaping of mission was the creation of what has come to be known as the parish state.[4] The parish state was the social, political, economic and religious context that persisted in Scotland from the late seventeenth to mid-nineteenth centuries, and in diminished forms until the mid-twentieth century. It represented a unique religious settlement between the Church of Scotland and the British state, one based on what was known as the doctrine of the Two Kingdoms.

The doctrine of the Two Kingdoms held that spiritual and temporal power were distinct but overlapping.[5] The Church should directly control those things that touch upon religion, such as worship, moral discipline, schooling and poor relief. Likewise, the civil magistrate, acting under the authority of the Crown, should directly govern those matters that touch upon the outward, worldly life of all, such as defence, trade, taxation and infrastructure. As such, the Church and its members should be subject to the law and the direction of magistrates insofar as these did not endanger religion and morals. Yet the magistrate, and even the Monarch themselves were, in turn, members of the Church like everyone else, and were subject to its teaching and discipline. This meant that while the magistrate might rule the outward aspects of life, *every part of society* had to conform to the faith taught by the Kirk. The belief that the Gospel should shape every aspect of society became an abiding aspect of Reformed Christianity in Scotland, and marked it out from other Protestant traditions in Britain and Europe. It was this belief that gave rise to the astonishing encounter at Falkland Palace in 1596, when the Presbyterian leader Andrew Melville rebuked King James IV as 'God's sillie vassal', reminding him that:

there are two kings and two kingdoms in Scotland. There is Christ Jesus the King and His kingdom the Kirk, whose subject King James the Sixth is and of whose kingdom he is not a king, nor a lord, nor a head, but a member.[6]

Things were not quite as clear-cut as Melville maintained, however. Although the Kirk aspired to have its spiritual jurisdiction fully recognised by the state, this jurisdiction would be financially dependent upon landowners and the Crown. Moreover, while focusing on religion and morals, the Kirk nevertheless performed a variety of other functions that we would now associate with local government. Thus, while the doctrine of the Two Kingdoms was clear in theory, in practice, it was necessarily confused.

This confusion would contribute to centuries of schism, war and infighting. Through the Bishops' Wars and the Wars of the Three Kingdoms, Scotland was convulsed by different interpretations of the relationship between Crown and Kirk. In the midst of these struggles, the Reformed vision of a godly commonwealth based on the doctrine of the Two Kingdoms found expression in the National Covenant of 1638, and the Solemn League and Covenant of 1643. These documents expressed the desire of a substantial proportion of the Scottish population to be a covenanted people, a nation which – in direct analogy to the Israel of the Old Testament – entered into a binding contract with Christ to be a holy nation and a royal priesthood. For as long as episcopalianism received royal support, this vision for Church and state could only be realised in a piecemeal and inconsistent way. With the accession of William and Mary, and the legal establishment of Presbyterianism, however, the Church of Scotland could advance its aim of bringing all of Scotland under the rule of Christ, and creating a godly, covenanted nation.

With the establishment of Presbyterianism, the parish state assumed a more stable form. From the late seventeenth to the mid-nineteenth century, the Church of Scotland was central to the political, social and economic life of most Scottish communities. One's first encounter with the Kirk would be within days of one's birth, receiving baptism from the minister and the recording of one's name in the parish register. The First Book of Discipline's commitment to universal education meant that most children were educated in the Kirk's parish schools, where the *dominie* – school master – was employed by the Church, and was sometimes even the minister himself. Children not only learned to read, write and count but learned the Westminster Shorter Catechism, discovering that their chief end was to glorify God and to enjoy him for ever. The paying of the *teinds* (tithes) in cash or kind, and the working of the minister's glebe by parishioners, meant that the Established Church was placed at the centre of a complex weave of economic practices.

Attendance at Church was not only – or even primarily – a matter of spiritual need, but a sign of social respectability and standing. In the agricultural, semi-feudal society of early-modern Scotland, food, money and even public order were often in short supply. Everyone had to do their duty and pull their weight, because the life of the entire community depended on it. This economic uncertainty had moral and religious consequences. It gave rise to 'scarcity values', values that limited personal freedom and choice, and emphasised moral conformity and social control. If one made the mistake of not attending church, or of conducting oneself in a scandalous manner, one would find oneself before the Kirk Session and the community on a Sunday morning. An account of one's behaviour would be asked for, and discipline administered as a mark of repentance.

In this older Scotland, sex, in particular, had to be carefully policed. Because of its intrinsic connection – before reliable contraception – with procreation, sex was essential not only for the continuation of families, but for labour and the retention of wealth. Promiscuity and pre-marital sex increased the number of destitute children, contributed to the loss of female labour through childcare duties and accelerated the dispersal of family wealth. These concerns lay at the heart of the historic condemnation of pre-marital sex in Scotland. By teaching the importance of sexual purity and disciplining offenders, the

Church held an important social role as the enforcer of the morals of scarcity, and was seen as indispensable to good order and public safety.

A less contentious aspect of the Church's social control was the role it played in compelling Scots to provide for the upkeep of the poor. This was the original purpose of that ever-present feature of the church service, *the collection*, which was also supplemented by grants from local landowners and the Crown. If one should have the misfortune to fall on hard times, one would be faced with the elders of the local Kirk Session, who – as the administrators of poor relief – would decide if one was worthy of aid. Churchgoing and good morals proved one's worthiness, and were therefore important means for procuring material help.

Churchgoing also displayed one's loyalty to the prevailing social and political order. The local laird would almost always have his own loft or pew in a prominent part of the kirk, and would be able to see which of his tenants were, and were not, present in church. The royal coat of arms would often be displayed on the outside or inside of the kirk, and the pulpit would be used for the reading of government proclamations. All of this signalled one's participation in the prevailing Protestant establishment.

In this way, while the doctrine of the Two Kingdoms meant that spiritual and temporal power were theologically distinct, for all intents and purposes, Church and state were socially, economically and politically indistinct. Loyalty to the Crown and social order meant loyalty to the Kirk, and loyalty to the Kirk meant loyalty to the Crown and prevailing social order. In a time when there was little legislation – the courts primarily operating through unwritten common law – and when government was smaller and more remote from everyday life than it is now, *the Church* was what most people thought of when they thought of the state.[7] Indeed, during periods of Scotland's past, it was sometimes the only effective agent of public order.

The social, economic and political position of the Church gave it great power over the lives of Scots, and kept the social significance of the Christian faith at high levels. Scots no doubt entertained sceptical or heretical thoughts. Yet given the Kirk's centrality to the spiritual and material life of the nation, such ideas would rarely be shared or discussed openly. In this, we see a key lesson for mission in contemporary Scotland: *spiritual plausibility is related to social significance*. If the Church meets real social needs, or features in day-to-day social interactions, then its significance and plausibility will be higher. If it does not, the Church will struggle to make the Gospel heard.

Mission and Control

Having examined the social, economic and political context of the Church in pre-industrial Scotland, we will now explore how its ministry and mission operated within that world. Before we can do that, however, we must first examine Reformed understandings of ministry in more depth.

As we saw earlier, the Scottish Reformers recognised three marks of the Church: the true preaching of the Word, the right administration of the sacraments and discipline rightly administered. This Reformed approach towards ministry was developed in contradistinction to two other branches of the Christian family: Roman Catholics and Anabaptists. Against the Roman Catholic Church, Reformed theologians came to believe that ministry was *evangelical* rather than *sacerdotal*. It was by hearing and believing God's promises in the preached Word – and not by receiving communion, absolution and other sacraments from an episcopally ordained priest – that one was saved. Yet if salvation required the preaching of God's Word, it was essential that those preaching knew and understood that Word correctly. Protestant ministry therefore required a higher level of education than was commonly thought necessary for Roman Catholic priests. In opposition to certain strands of Anabaptist thought, however, the Reformed continued to believe that ordination was a normal prerequisite for teaching. Rather than baptised believers assuming the responsibility for preaching the Gospel as their talents and desires led them, Calvin believed that lay preaching led to disorder in the body of the Church, and the corruption of God's Word.[8] Baptism alone was not enough.

This rejection of lay ministry also rested on Calvin's marginalisation of the so-called 'extraordinary ministries'. In Ephesians 4:11, Paul appears to recognise five different offices of ministry: apostleship, prophecy, evangelism, pastoring and teaching. In the *Institutes*, however, Calvin argues that the ministries of apostles, prophets and evangelists were limited to specific eras: the prophets to the time of the Law, and the apostles and evangelists to when the Gospel had to be planted and communicated for the first time. In light of our contemporary context, however, it is interesting to note that Calvin acknowledges that God had, in fact, raised up these extraordinary ministries afresh in his own lifetime during the Reformation, and that – should they be required – God could raise them up again.[9]

The two remaining 'ordinary' ministries recognised by Calvin – pastoring and teaching – are further qualified. Calvin considers that pastoring, in some senses, encompasses all other ministries, leaving the teaching ministry to be fulfilled by what would come to be known in Scotland as the doctors (theologians and Bible scholars).[10] As such, in Scotland, ministry became almost totally identified with that of the pastoral ministry. What forms of service remained for the non-ordained were largely found in the eldership, an office whose role in direct ministry and mission was limited.[11] For these reasons, in the Reformed theology of ministry, 'the priesthood of all believers hardly plays any part at all'.[12] It is the pastor or minister, called by God and admitted to the congregation, who builds up and preserves the health of the Body through the preaching of the Word. As the Second Book of Discipline puts it, 'Pastors, or bishops, or ministers, are they which are appointed to particular congregations and kirks which they rule by the word of God and over which they watch.'[13] Ministers *rule* over their congregations by the Word of God, a rule which is the preserve of those who are called, trained and appointed to do so. This applied also to the Sacraments. The sovereignty of the Word meant that no-one should baptise or celebrate the Lord's Supper without also being called, admitted and ordained. The authors of the First Book of Discipline are explicit: 'Neither judge we that the sacraments can be rightlie ministered by him in whose mouth God has put no sermon of exhortation.'[14] Word, sacrament and church authorisation belong together.

These theological principles decisively shaped the Scottish Reformers' attitudes towards ministry and mission. As apostleship had ended, there was no need to plant churches anywhere and everywhere, but, rather, focus on established churches. As prophecy had ended, there was less reason to listen to the direct prompting of the Holy Spirit and a great deal of reason to focus on the text of Scripture and the education of ministers in universities. As almost everyone was a Christian, and as no-one could be trusted to talk about the Gospel without education and training, dedicated evangelists were also unnecessary or undesirable. The result was that ministry became equated with a small group of educated men, something that a small minority did on behalf of – and towards – a larger, less educated majority.

Just as what we would now understand as evangelism was almost always associated with preaching by parish ministers, so too was what we would now call missional service identified with education and poor relief. Given these theological principles, and their institutionalisation in the parish system, mission as we now understand it did not feature in the minds of most Church leaders. When mission *was* mentioned more explicitly, it was almost always viewed in apocalyptic terms. In the frontispiece of the Scots Confession, for example, the Scottish Reformers inscribed these words from Matthew 24:

> And these glad tidings of the kingdom shall be preached throughout the whole world for a witness to all nations, and then the end shall come.[15]

Here, the Reformers displayed their belief that the propagation of the Gospel in Scotland and abroad would herald the end of the world. As it was a work of *eschatology* – something done by God at the end of time – full evangelisation was something that was primarily the work of Christ, not his Church. Certain events in human history – for example, the Reformation itself – could be a sign of the end, but only God could bring it about. In the same way, the Directory of Public Worship of the Westminster divines instructs the Church 'To pray for the propagation of the gospel and kingdom of Christ to all nations; for the conversion of the Jews, the fulness of the Gentiles, the fall of Antichrist and the hastening of the second coming of our Lord.'[16] Once again, evangelism is closely connected with the end of the world, rather than something that should be a routine and normal part of the Church's work.

Despite this, the seeds of other possibilities already lay within the Scottish Church. The chaos of the Bishops' Wars and the Wars of the Three Kingdoms gave rise to a covenanting tradition which, by necessity at first, adopted a number of practices and attitudes that would later be emulated by others. The inability of the Reformed faction during the mid-seventeenth century to worship freely in episcopal-controlled churches resulted in the creation of *conventicles*: outdoor preaching and communion services that were sometimes related to parish ministry but were often not. When the majority of covenanting elements were absorbed back into the parish system of the Church of Scotland at the Glorious Revolution, these practices entered into the folk memory of the nation, giving precedent for later innovations.

Political and social changes would soon require the Church of Scotland to adopt more sustained alternatives to the parish system, however. The first factor leading to this change was one that might appear strange to the modern reader: the continued existence of Roman Catholics and Episcopalians.

In the immediate aftermath of the Scottish Reformation, Roman Catholicism was generally weak and covert, and the General Assembly did not devote serious effort to eradicating it. Following their theological principles, they believed that what they viewed as error and superstition would be eradicated through the planting of Reformed ministry in every part of the country. This changed, however, with the growth in Roman Catholic missions, and the political consequences of the Glorious Revolution. While Jesuits had undertaken missionary activity in the later sixteenth century, the first sustained post-Reformation Roman Catholic mission to Scotland took place in 1619. From 1694 a more coordinated approach was taken under the new Vicars-Apostolic for Scotland, and Roman Catholicism began to make limited inroads. Taken with Scotland's – and later Britain's – continual warfare with Roman Catholic European powers, Roman Catholic Scots were not only viewed as people who honoured the Pope and favoured the Mass, but those who owed allegiance to a despotic foreign power who could make them commit any crime. This negative political perception also extended to Episcopalians in the later seventeenth and early eighteenth centuries. After the Glorious Revolution and the establishment of Presbyterianism, the presence of Christian communities whose bishops maintained loyalty to Stuart monarchs who threatened to incite rebellion or invade the country was problematic to say the least.

These developments led to the first Reformed domestic missions. The first Christian initiative bearing the name of 'mission' in Scottish history came in 1707, with an Act of the General Assembly 'for the suppressing of Popery'. This act made provision for the recruitment of 'fit and able young men' to be sent 'in mission' to debate and refute Roman Catholics in the Highlands and Islands.[17] This was followed two years later in 1709 with the establishment of the *Society in Scotland for Propagating Christian Knowledge* (SSPCK). SSPCK was the first domestic missionary body in post-Reformation Scotland, directed towards the conversion of the Highlands and Islands to Reformed Christianity. Establishing what would become a common trend within Scottish *overseas* mission, the SSPCK's primary strategy for evangelisation was education. The children of the non-Reformed would not only be taught in a context that precluded tainted languages such as Latin and Gaelic, but would be taught the Westminster Shorter Catechism, thus securing both their religious and political allegiance.[18] While the SSPCK – and the related workers of the King's Bounty – began to lose impetus towards the end of the eighteenth century, its use of lay catechists and missionaries provided an important precedent for future domestic mission, a legacy living on in the lay missionaries of nineteenth- and twentieth-century Kirk.

In addition to this government-backed Reformed mission came that which arose from the evangelical revival. The revival began with the innovative preaching of George Whitefield and John Wesley, and quickly spread throughout England. Evangelicalism – sometimes defined by its focus on conversion, activism, the Bible and the Cross[19] – affected ministry and mission in a number of ways. The deeply personal nature of evangelical piety, which called upon the individual to submit themselves totally to Christ, led to a changed understanding of what it was to be a Christian. A Christian came to be seen less as someone who attended church and more as someone who had a *personal* conviction of the truth of the Gospel, and had surrendered their heart to Christ. In addition, an emphasis upon a personal relationship with Jesus weakened denominational identity and loyalty, and the connection between nation and Church. The reason for this was simple. If the most important thing in the Christian life was one's relationship with Jesus, then the unity of the Church, and the interrelation of Church, state and nation were secondary.

The most important effect of evangelicalism for mission, however, was its emphasis upon personal conversion, and – following from this – the desire of evangelicals to bring others to faith. In this, evangelicals were not only focused – as the Reformed tended to be – upon converting Christians to the *right kind* of Christianity, but upon bringing everyone into a living relationship with Jesus, unhindered by parish boundaries and ecclesiastical structures. As Whitefield famously put it: 'The world is now my parish.'[20]

In the short term, the evangelical revival appeared to do little to change Reformed attitudes. When George Whitefield came to preach in Scotland in the mid-eighteenth century he was denied entry to almost all Church of Scotland pulpits, and was shocked by the attitude of the Secession Church, which – having left the Church of Scotland – demanded that he only preach in *their* churches and nowhere else. Nevertheless, succeeding generations of the Secession Church, the Relief Church and their offshoots began to recognise that multiple denominations created two new realities: religious choice and religious competition. This – when added to their lack of a recognised parish structure – made these denominations congregational and attractional by default, and pushed them from the late eighteenth century onward into a more missional mindset.

Being emboldened by the evangelical revival and with the Secession and Relief Churches showing the way, more Christians began to explore the possibility of domestic mission outwith the parish structures of the Established Church of Scotland. While the activity of Methodists on Shetland is better known, the most important of these innovators were the Haldane Brothers. The Haldanes were wealthy elders of the Kirk, who – given their evangelical sensibilities – were concerned that the Kirk was failing to reach substantial sections of the population. They used their wealth to form the Society for Propagating the Gospel at Home, and recruited and trained what would become known as the 'Haldane Preachers': men trained in the Bible outwith Divinity Schools, and sent to areas of perceived need. Needless to say, the Kirk was not pleased with the Haldanes' innovation. In 1799, the General Assembly issued a 'Pastoral Admonition' to the entire nation, which decreed that no-one should listen to the Haldane Preachers or invite them to preach.[21] Such was the perceived threat from itinerant bands of non-ordained and non-university educated evangelists.

Conclusion

In this chapter, we have seen how the Church's ministry and mission in the early-modern period took place in the context of the parish state. This, taken with a Reformed theology of ministry focused on the three notes or marks of the Church, meant that ministry was largely the preserve of ministers. Mission as we now understand it was fulfilled by the minister's preaching, celebration of the sacraments and catechesis, along with the Church's administration of poor relief. The Church's centrality to the life of Scotland meant that, in many respects, it *was* the state, and this social and political position not only allowed it to teach Scots the truth of the Christian faith through worship and schooling, but greatly enhanced the plausibility of the faith.

Given today's fashionable dislike for 'Christendom' and the 'Constantinian Church', readers may baulk at this conflation of spiritual and temporal power, and the coercion and occasional persecution that went with it. Yet while this situation no doubt gave rise, at times, to unchristian practices and hypocrisy, the enculturation of Christianity in Scotland bore much fruit. No matter one's definition of Christianity, there can be little doubt that there was a higher proportion of genuine Christians in early modern Scotland than there is today. Indeed, the Church was so successful at evangelising Scotland that a significant proportion of the population voluntarily entered into a National Covenant with Christ himself. Such was the power of God in early-modern Scotland.

Whether it furthered the mission of God in Scotland or not, the close relationship between Church, state and nation that brought the Church many advantages would soon be undone by the same social, political and economic forces that propelled it to power. It is this story, the story of *our* times, to which we now turn.

3

The Secularisation of Scotland

In the last chapter, we examined the Scottish Church prior to industrialisation. We saw that the place of the Church in society was based not only – or even primarily – on what we would now understand as its religious duties, but its role in schooling, social care, the local economy, politics and the preservation of social respectability. In short, the significance and plausibility of Christianity – and in particular the Church of Scotland – was heavily dependent on government support and social forces. All of these aspects came together in the *parish*: an ecclesiastical entity, but one with close ties to the state and landowners.

We will now examine how this 'parish state' was undermined between the late seventeenth and mid-twentieth centuries by two key factors: church schism and economic affluence. These changes would bring about the *secularisation* of Scotland, the process by which Christianity changed from having high levels of importance in Scottish society to having low levels of importance. This occurred on a number of levels and at different speeds: first economic, then institutional, then social. When social secularisation occurred, so too did the secularisation of the minds and hearts of the majority of Scots.

In charting the progress of secularisation in Scotland, it is not being claimed that Christianity in Scotland will one day be wiped out. This was the assumption of earlier schools of secularisation theory, yet is both empirically and theologically incorrect. Neither is it claimed that *only* schism and affluence brought about secularisation. A wide number of causal factors were involved. Yet it is argued that schism and affluence played a decisive role and that because of them, the importance and plausibility of Christianity has been massively eroded in

Scottish society. Because of secularisation, there is no way back to the world that was.

Schism and Choice

The first cracks in the authority and social position of the Kirk came just a few decades after the establishment of Presbyterianism with the Scottish Episcopalians Act 1711. This Act relieved Scottish Episcopalians of the worst aspects of legal discrimination. Yet it also meant that a section of the population was now exempt from the full discipline of the Church of Scotland. If toleration for Episcopalians guaranteed the continuing existence of at least two denominations in Scotland, the Church Patronage Act – also enacted in 1711 – ensured the creation of many more. This Act reintroduced the controversial right of heritors to present a minister of their choosing to a vacant church, leading to increasing tension between Church and state.

In and of itself, this change may only have resulted in formal protest and occasional disobedience. Yet patronage coincided with the decline of traditional agricultural communities and the growth of industry. Industrialisation is relevant to the story of secularisation in Scotland for four reasons. First, as people moved to work in mills and factories, they left behind the customs and obligations of the past. The burgeoning cities permitted anonymity and newfound freedom. Workers did not have to go to the parish church, but could attend a church of their choosing, or, in some cases, no church at all. Second, rapid expansion in some areas, and depopulation in others, created difficulties for a system of ministry that required an act of Parliament for the creation of new parishes. The Established Church struggled to set up a presence in some areas, creating an opportunity for smaller denominations to take the initiative and plant congregations in under-churched regions. Third, industries such as weaving and later mining and heavy industry increased the importance of skilled working-class labour, and created new working-class cultures that had their own identities and political interests. Industrialisation created social and political tensions that could not be reconciled through worship in the parish church, and prompted Scots to seek forms of Church that supported their independence from elites and their upward social mobility. Lastly – and most importantly for the future – industrialisation created the economic and technological conditions for both personal affluence and the welfare state, factors that would prove decisive in the twentieth century.

While the presenting issues may have been theological, these social and economic factors provided the impetus for a number of schisms from the Established Church. First came the Secession Church in 1733, and later the Relief Church in 1761. Both secessions benefitted from growing animus against social elites controlling the religious beliefs of the people. Even though the nobility and landowners might control other aspects of a person's life, they could not determine or direct their relationship with God.

As more people left the disciplinary authority of the Kirk, its control over Scottish society became weaker. Of greater importance to the future story of mission in Scotland, however, was the *choice* that multiple denominations created. This proliferation of denominations coincided – and strongly overlapped – with the growth of evangelicalism. Evangelical piety was itself a response to the changed economic and social condition of society. The traditional agricultural economy of Scotland required close integration between social classes, and gave rise to a Church that was communitarian, inherited and shaped by one's social obligations towards peers and betters. An industrial economy focused on factories and commerce, and set in contexts that were urban and often anonymous, made this level of social cohesion and obligation impossible, and gave greater reign to personal identity and conscience. These developments gave rise to new forms of mission. Evangelicals were at the forefront of evangelising the poor and 'civilising' them through Christian values, a process that often meant socialising them into an alternative middle-class evangelical culture.[1]

There can be no doubt that industrialisation, in and of itself, resulted in the dechurching of significant numbers of Scots. Yet as Brown has argued, the Scottish Church remained remarkably strong during the nineteenth century. Denominations of all stripes adapted to the new urban conditions through evangelistic missions, Gospel-hall rallies, cheap Christian literature and highly organised contingents of visitors and lay missionaries. While some stayed away, the Scottish Church was surprisingly effective at reaching the working classes, exploding the myth of the 'godless cities' and 'heathen' working class.[2]

Nevertheless, the evangelical and missionary mood of the age met its limit in the continuing problem of patronage, and the inability of the Westminster Parliament – which putatively protected the Church of Scotland – from understanding the perilous position the Kirk was in. When Thomas Chalmers and other evangelical leaders of the Kirk attempted to explain to the British Government the right of congregations to call a minister of their choice, they were met with a mixture of disbelief and scorn. Chalmers' vision of a renewed godly commonwealth, overcoming the divisions and evils of industrialisation through church building, evangelism and Kirk control of social services received limited state support. Theological and political resentment against patronage and elites increased, until approximately 40% of the ministers, and perhaps half the members of the Church of Scotland, seceded to form the Free Church of Scotland.

Schism and Secularisation

Of all the factors leading to the secularisation of Scotland, the Disruption was one of the most important. As one commentator has put it, 'The Reformed vision of Scotland as a godly nation, where kirk and people were one, *died* on 18 May 1843, at the Disruption of the Church of Scotland.'[3] The Disruption severed the connection between the Church of Scotland and Scottish identity, hastened the breakup of the parish state and brought about institutional secularisation, one of the key catalysts for the secularisation of wider society.

While Chalmers and his colleagues 'went out' in the belief that the Free Kirk would preserve Scotland's Reformed heritage, convert the nation and – when the Kirk eventually collapsed – win the support of the state, they were mistaken. The loss of a significant part of its ministry and membership, along with a corresponding reduction in funds, meant that the Kirk could no longer adequately staff and finance the schools, colleges, hospitals and other services it was responsible for. The result of this division was the takeover by the state of institutions and social roles that were historically the preserve of the Kirk. In 1845, poor relief was transferred from Kirk Sessions to elected poor-law boards. This not only reduced the Kirk's social significance in relation to poverty and unemployment, but also further dented the power of Kirk Session discipline, which was, at times, premised on a Session's ability to withhold aid. In 1852, religious tests for non-theological University positions were removed, setting the scene for the divorce of the Kirk from higher education. From 1843 onward, but culminating in the 1872 Education Act, the Kirk and Free Kirk gradually gave up control of their schools to the state, something which the Kirk, with depleted resources, was generally happy to do. This movement from key social services being administered by the Church to being taken over by the state, is the *primary definition of secularisation*. In Scotland, this process was not the result of atheist philosophies, anti-Christian government policy, or any other external factor, but the disunity and infighting of the Christian Church.

In these developments, we encounter an important causal issue: that factors which at one time do not give rise to a decline in faith do so at a later time. As Brown notes, while poor law and education were removed from the direct control of the Kirk and other churches, parish ministers and elders of the Kirk routinely served on the new poor-law and education boards, thereby maintaining their control, albeit in a new form. These new forms of control were dependent, of course, on the continuing social importance of ministers and churches. Yet as Scotland secularised, the lack of sufficient legal or institutional safeguards made it relatively easy to shift public policy concerning schools, poor relief and social care to *exclude* churches and religious considerations. In the non-denominational

Protestant worship that took place in state schools, the Kirk may have *believed* it was getting an excellent deal. After all, Protestant worship continued, and Protestant identity was inculcated without any financial cost to the Church. Yet, not for the last time in the Kirk's history, this confidence in the abiding Christian character of Scottish society would prove short-sighted and disastrous.

This is seen in three theological developments that would prove important for the future *internal* secularisation of the Scottish Church: the distinction between Kirk and Kingdom, the growth of biblical criticism and the decline of Calvinism. While the distinction between Church and Kingdom was not new, it was given a new interpretation by Robert Flint. Flint was part of a wider European movement – encompassing Strauss in Germany, Renan in France and Jowett in England – that sought to revisit Christ's self-understanding through a new – supposedly 'objective' – rereading of the Gospels. When Flint did so, he believed he had discovered that the purpose of Christ's ministry was not to found a Church, but to inaugurate the Kingdom of God. The Church could point to and further the Kingdom, but it was only ever a tool for doing so. From this basis, Flint went on to develop a new understanding of God's providential control not only of the Church but of the state, culture and public institutions. In Flint's interpretation, God furthered his Kingdom through these creaturely means as much as – or perhaps even *more* than – the Church. He wrote:

> The Church is not the Kingdom of God and these elements of social life, in separating themselves from the Church, have not separated themselves from the Kingdom of God; nay, by the very act of rejecting the control of the Church they set aside the mediation of the Church between them and the Kingdom of God and secured for themselves, as a portion of their independence, the right of standing in immediate contact with the Word and the Kingdom of God. Before their independence they were related to the Kingdom of God only through their connection with the Church; now, since their independence, they may justly claim to be portions of the

Kingdom of God, each one of them as much a portion of it as the Church itself.[4]

While a cursory reading of this paragraph might view it as a continuation of the doctrine of the Two Kingdoms, and its belief that the Church did not have to govern every aspect of social and political life, it actually represents a dramatic departure from that position. In the traditional Reformed doctrine, while the Church's direct governance was restricted to certain areas of life – traditionally termed 'spiritual' – *every member of society* and *every institution* had to be ordered in accordance with the teaching of the Kirk. While the magistrate had a divine mandate – within limits – to rule, that rule was not *independent* of the Church, but was shaped and formed by it in a variety of complex ways. Flint argues, however, that the magistrate and – crucially for later developments – what we would now call civil society, relate to God *directly*, without the mediation of the Church. Even more strongly, and as he states explicitly, they maintain their relationship with *God's Word* independent of the teaching and preaching of the Church. That means that they can forge *their own* interpretations of God, the good and the spiritual, without recourse to the Church.

By posing the relationship between Kirk, Kingdom, state and society in this way, Flint made it easier for the Church to do two things. First, it became easier to believe that the Church did not need to exert influence over the state or society in order for God's Kingdom to be realised. Indeed, if they relate to the Word of God directly, they may follow Christ's will more closely than his Church, showing *the Church* the way. Second, if the coming of the Kingdom is not dependent on the Church, then it is not too difficult to believe that the Kingdom is largely unconnected to the Church's core activities of worship, teaching and the celebration of the sacraments. By becoming Professor of Divinity at Edinburgh and ultimately Moderator of the General Assembly, Flint was able to influence many thousands of ministers and elders. His ecclesiology would, in the course of the next 150 years, come to exercise a decisive influence over the ministry and mission of the Church of Scotland in particular, and the traditional denominations more generally.

Contemporaneous with the growth of this form of political and cultural theology was biblical criticism. While Calvin and the majority of the Christian Church had long recognised that Scripture was written by human beings under the direction of the Holy Spirit, biblical criticism sought to study Scripture as if it were any other set of ancient documents.[5] When this was done, scholars believed they discovered inaccuracies and inconsistences. While this began as 'faithful criticism', over the course of the twentieth century, the Divinity Schools in which ministers were trained would become increasingly secularised in terms of their personnel, teaching and financial arrangements. The result of this was that growing numbers of men – and later women – were trained to believe that the Scriptures at the heart of the Christian faith, and which form the basis for the missional theology outlined in Chapter 1, were, at least in part, *untrue*. This was then communicated to congregations in subtle and not so subtle ways, weakening the faith and commitment of members, and their willingness to engage in – often taxing – missional activity.

The final theological development from this time that hastened the internal secularisation of the Scottish Church was the decline of Calvinism. While Calvinism reached its last peak in the middle decades of the nineteenth century, the effect of biblical criticism, Kirk and Kingdom theology, scientific advances and growing affluence led all of Scotland's major Presbyterian churches to pass Declaratory Acts distancing themselves from the Westminster Confession and Reformed orthodoxy. As Bruce says, a Calvinist theology that stresses the omnipotent and inscrutable will of God over all things is plausible in a society where one has little control over one's life, but makes less sense in a society growing in wealth, choice and personal autonomy.[6] The decline of Calvinism need not have contributed to the secularisation of the Scottish Church. Yet it led directly to a decline in *discipleship* – the intentional development of personal faith – within the Church of Scotland and other Presbyterian churches. For centuries, Scottish youths had been schooled in the Westminster Shorter Catechism, which by means of questions and answers on a wide range of theological topics gave most people in Scotland a basic understanding of the faith, and a common religious culture. The decline of Calvinism led to neglect of the Catechism, which meant that an increasing number of church members became dependent only upon sermons and personal Bible reading for their faith development. Over the decades, this would lead to a large yet nominal membership that was, at times, barely Christian, further undermining the strength of the Scottish Church.

The Kirk Resurgent

Despite the hopes of the Free Church that the Established Church would wither and die, the Kirk began to recover members as the nineteenth century progressed. Scottish churchgoing probably reached its zenith around the turn of the twentieth century, at the same time as a new convergence of Protestantism and political Unionism.[7] This was made possible by the British Empire, which became the largest and most powerful empire in history, and which used religious language, imagery and ritual to justify its success.[8] Scotland, and particularly the West of Scotland, became one the key industrial drivers of Britain's expansion, and was therefore economically and politically integrated into Britain in an unprecedented way. As Green argues, for many – and perhaps most – people, religion was something that was simply a part of being British. God, Providence, Queen Victoria, the Empire and Christian rituals were a mutually reinforcing whole, where to be Scottish was to be Presbyterian, British and loyal to Crown and country.[9] Only the Victorian age could have given rise to hymns such as *Land of Hope and Glory*, *I Vow to Thee My Country* and *Onward Christian Soldiers*.

The brutality of the First World War led to a loss of faith for some, along with the revelation that the fighting men of Britain were not as religious as Church leaders had sometimes thought.[10] Nevertheless, military conscription, taken with Irish immigration, the Easter Rising and the creation of the Irish Free State, helped to shore up the relationship between Kirk, Union and Empire for decades to come. The reunion of the United Free Church and Church of Scotland in 1929 was facilitated by a common Protestant and Unionist identity that set itself against both socialism and Irish Roman Catholics. While often shying away from its excesses, this expression of Protestant and Unionist identity within the Kirk found popular support in resurgent Orangeism, Old Firm football rivalries and political movements such as Protestant Action. This form of popular – and largely working-class – Protestant culture, often centred on heavy industry, would become an abiding feature of life in Scotland, and Protestant and Unionist identity would play an important role in maintaining church membership, especially in the West, until the end of the twentieth century.

The close integration of Church, state and national identity was also augmented by the advent of the welfare state. For the first time in history, Scots had full existential security. No longer did anyone have to fear illness or unemployment or homelessness, for the state would look after them from cradle to grave. New churches were built to serve burgeoning housing estates, with the Kirk often being successful in reaching the unchurched. In one new council estate, it was initially reported that 30% of the population had no existing church affiliation, but through visitation, community events and youth clubs, this percentage had dropped to 18.3%.[11] Communitarian values, church planting and a desire for a return to normality and traditional certainties handed the Kirk its largest ever membership of over 1.3 million in 1956.[12]

While the welfare state represented the culmination of centuries of Christian influence in Scottish society, few considered the effect that this existential security would have on faith. For if the needs of Scots were fully met, would they still have need of a Saviour? For those who had eyes to see, there were already signs of the collapse to come. In his study of the Scottish churches in 1959, Highet calculated that of the Kirk's impressive membership, only 21.4% were in church on the Sunday he surveyed. By comparison, over 90% of the membership of some other denominations were in attendance.[13] This suggested that the Kirk was inflated by a nominal membership with low levels of commitment and faith. A decade later in 1969, Peter Sissons was commissioned by the Kirk to undertake a more detailed study into church membership and attendance in Falkirk. His findings confirmed Highet's, while also adding significant detail about the dynamics between Kirk and nation. When Church of Scotland members were questioned about their faith, he found that, for the overwhelming majority, Christianity was one and the same thing as morality and respectability. Respondents were resistant – and even offended – by the notion that there might be a significant distinction between a Christian and a non-Christian and considered that duty, competency and professionalism were more important qualities in church office holders than personal faith or sound doctrine.[14] This reaction is not surprising when one considers Sissons' discovery that only 13% of Kirk members primarily attended church for worship, with the overwhelming majority attending for more mundane reasons.[15] In contrast to this, members of small – more sectarian – denominations viewed personal faith as very important, and were noted by Sissons to use more Christian expressions and concepts in their responses.[16] In concluding his report, Sissons noted that while smaller churches had developed cultures and patterns of discipleship that were successful in socialising their members – particularly their young – into faith, the Church of Scotland relied on wider social forces to recruit and keep members, and had no effective way of socialising its young past the point of adolescence. In doing so, he summarised the Kirk's dilemma: its successful integration and inculturation into Scottish society meant that it was at the mercy of social forces in a way that other churches were not.

This picture of Scottish church life is confirmed by Brown's oral histories. They tell the stories of adults in the post-war years who went to church out of duty and conformity, and of young people who attended church youth groups and Bible studies despite having no real faith.[17] At its best, the Kirk could be a centre of community, civic values and genuine Christian love. At its worst, religious and social conformism could become stifling, judgemental and irrelevant to life in twentieth-century Scotland. Sadly, for many Scottish children in the post-war era, Church and Sunday school were little more than 'memorials to their parents' history' which the young were forced to endure.[18]

Permissive Consumerism

By the 1950s, the Church of Scotland was, in many aspects, the strongest it had been for centuries. Incorporating the majority of its former schismatic elements, enjoying peak membership and significant social influence, and basking in the glow of Second World War communitarianism and welfare socialism, it was a time of renewed confidence and hope. Yet, largely unknown to its minsters and members, all of the *necessary* conditions for its imminent demise had been met. Its social roles in education, poor relief and healthcare had been taken over by the state. It had become politically and economically – if not legally – disestablished. It had abandoned important elements of discipleship, trained its ministers in Divinity Schools where the inspiration of Scripture was questioned, and had adopted a cultural theology that taught that the nation and state could fulfil God's will independently of the Church. It drew a significant part of its support from a conflation of Protestant and Unionist identity that made it vulnerable to political change, and possessed a large – yet often nominal – membership. All that was needed was for the *sufficient* conditions of welfare security and affluence to alter the causal function of these factors. This would give rise to a new culture of consumerism, permissiveness and self-authenticity that would precipitate the decline of the Kirk and, in turn, effect the secularisation of Scotland.

In the poem 'Annus Mirabilis' from *High Windows* (1974), the poet Philip Larkin reflected that sexual intercourse in Britain had only really begun in 1963. While it is doubtful that the Scots ever fully yielded to the sexual excesses of the permissive society, the *anni mirabiles* of the 1960s marked a watershed in Scottish religious life. The 1960s have been heralded as 'marking a rupture as powerful as that brought about by the Reformation'.[19] They saw a paradigm shift in individuals' relation to society, the state, organised relation and to themselves, and were the pivotal decade in the story of British secularisation.[20] Brown has recently put forward a compelling argument about the role of women in this process. Women had always been the bedrock of the churches. Christianity allowed women to earn respectability for themselves and their children through marriage, baptism, modesty and good works. Yet due to increased financial independence from the 1950s and 1960s onward, women adopted new self-understandings, and no longer sought to safeguard their respectability through church-going, marriage and family. This not only had an effect on women themselves but upon the socialisation of their children into the faith, leading to a wholesale collapse in the social significance of churches.[21] While there is much truth in Brown's thesis, as we shall see, the causal connections he identifies are not as he supposes. Rather than changes in female identity being the primary catalyst for the collapse of religion in Scotland, these changes were only one among others, and, properly speaking, were more an *effect* of secularisation than its cause. On the contrary, as McLeod notes, if we wish to look for a primary cause, we should seek it instead in *affluence*.[22]

The full effects of consumerism had been kept in check until now by a lack of dwelling space, the prevalence of a heavy-drinking culture that consumed disposable income, the cost of healthcare and the cost of consumer goods. The result was that people spent much of their time with their neighbours: socialising, gossiping and playing games.[23] New housing developments, however, gave the majority of Scots their own space. This was particularly marked among the young, who rather than sharing rooms with parents or siblings had greater freedom to develop their own tastes and style, papering their walls with posters and magazine clippings, as well as – increasingly – engaging in sexual activity. In addition, this newfound luxury led to an accelerating decline in community interaction. Put simply, with more space, more possessions and less material need, the importance of other people and communities for security and practical aid declined. While this had negative effects on all the churches, the Kirk – being founded on a geographical parish model, and relying largely on social forces for the recruitment and retention of members – was particularly vulnerable.

The result of welfare security, affluence and consumer choice was the creation, for the first time in Scottish history, of the possibility of non-religious identities, the structure of which we shall explore in more detail in Chapter 4. The first to fully imbibe this new possibility were the young. They had not been as fully socialised into the ethic of scarcity as their parents had been. From 1938 to 1958, real earnings for 15–25 year olds rose by 50% and the greater affluence of their parents meant that many could remain in the parental home – newly enlarged – and devote almost all their income to the latest consumer goods. This gave rise to new youth cultures centred on fashion and music, cultures which rejected the scarcity values of the pre-war generations.[24] This was particularly damaging for the Kirk, which – as Sissons noted – struggled with the socialisation of young people around the time of adolescence. Because of its poor discipleship structures, the Kirk could offer little alternative to contemporary youth culture, so that – for most men and women coming of age in the period 1950–70 – faith would remain something firmly associated with childhood, and had little to offer their adult selves.

In his comparative study of world economies, Inglehart sees these two key developments – welfare security and affluence – as key drivers in the secularisation of society. Central to this movement is the transition from 'scarcity values' premised on survival, to 'post-materialist' values based on wellbeing and self-fulfilment.[25] As we saw in the last chapter, when wealth is scarce and there is little or no welfare, community bonds and personal discipline must be high. In particular, sex must be carefully policed to avoid unsupported children, mothers draining resources and conflict among men. For these reasons, in previous centuries, the Church had an important social role as the enforcer of the morals of scarcity. Yet this logic also explains the growth of promiscuity and pre-marital sex. As Offer has noted, rates of pre-marital sex and illegitimacy in Britain in the twentieth century followed economic affluence very closely, because an abundance of wealth meant that unwanted and illegitimate pregnancies posed less of a threat to families and the social order. Crucially, this trend began *before* the advent of reliable contraception. Contraception – and in particular the pill – acted as a catalyst to this process, but it was not itself the cause.[26] In short, affluence led to a direct change in morality, and removed the need for traditional scarcity values connected with the Christian Church.

This cultural drift resulted in the secularisation of two areas in which the Church still had an important social function: spirituality and emotional support. New Age spirituality first burst into the imaginations of the Scottish public with the Beatles' trip to India, yet was soon seen closer to home in the occult, alternative therapies and practices such as meditation and yoga. While adopted by only a few, New Age spirituality marked a more widespread democratisation and individualisation of religion, with each person free to explore their own personal connection with the divine in whatever way felt right to them.[27] This undermined the authority of institutional religion, leaving the Church irrelevant to the spiritual journeys of most people. Perhaps more serious, however, was the growing irrelevance of the Church's pastoral care. In centuries past, the minister and elders were the only source of emotional support apart from one's family and friends. Yet the 1950s and 1960s saw the growing popularity of psychology and counselling. Psychologists such as Eysenck and the Scot R.D. Laing became minor celebrities, their adherents claiming that their methods were more effective than traditional Christian pastoral care. While the Kirk had an overlooked role in the development of therapeutic practices, and while many of its ministers and elders adopted elements of psychology and counselling into their activities,[28] rather than securing the position of the Kirk, it only seemed to underline the irrelevance of Christian faith for emotional wellbeing.

The changing nature of social life did not go unheralded. When the BBC was founded in 1927, its ethos and aims were explicitly Christian and evangelistic. The coat of arms of the Corporation – seldom used today – feature the motto 'Nation shall speak unto nation', an allusion to the new age of reconciliation and friendship foreseen in Isaiah 2:4 and Micah 4:3. Even more surprisingly in today's post-Christian context, all of the Corporation's activities were dedicated to the glory of Almighty God, with a Latin inscription to this effect being placed at the entrance to Broadcasting House.

As the 1950s progressed, however, the Christian identity of the BBC began to recede. While criticism of Christianity had been largely censored prior to this period, Margaret Knight's plea for Humanism in 1955 signalled a new opening for non-religious identities. This trend reached maturity under the Director-Generalship of Hugh Greene (1960–69), who intentionally commissioned programming that questioned the establishment and traditional ethics. Shows such as *That Was The Week That Was* satirised clergymen and the Church, and BBC programming began to feature increasing violence, sexual promiscuity and swearing.[29] As we have seen, for a large proportion of the population, faith was wrapped up in their sense of British identity, so that to be British was to be Christian. The BBC's questioning of existing beliefs and norms had an important role not only in legitimising alternative viewpoints, but in actively undermining the identification of Christianity with British values. This gave permission for the people of Scotland to adopt new narratives and concepts by which to make sense of their lives.

At the same time as the BBC was abandoning its support for the Christian faith, artists and musicians were reinterpreting the meaning of Jesus. This trend largely started with Rice and Lloyd Webber's *Jesus Christ Superstar* (1970), followed closely by the American *Godspell* (1970/71). In both productions, Jesus is re-envisioned as a flower-power hippie, challenging the establishment with his parables, wisdom and counter-cultural lifestyle. It is noteworthy that in both musicals Jesus dies but is not resurrected, his spirit living on instead in the community he left behind. The conjunction of the Gospel with contemporary rock was also seen in songs named 'Jesus' by the Velvet Underground, Cat Stevens and Queen, among others. These offerings were revisionist and sometimes mildly critical, yet not without admiration for the person of Jesus. Indeed, the rediscovery of Jesus by 1970s musicians could even be sincere and transformative, as seen in the genuine – if short-lived – conversions of David Bowie and Bob Dylan. This interest in Jesus was largely the result of artists raised in Christian households and cultures attempting to reinterpret Christ in the context of the permissive society. Yet it was also reflective of genuine sadness for the world that had been lost, and fear of the culture of sex, drugs and moral anarchy introduced by the revolution of the 1960s.

Far darker than these artistic interpretations, however – and one, importantly, set in Scotland – was Anthony Shaffer and Robin Hardy's film *The Wicker Man* (1973). The story tells the tale of police sergeant Neil Howie, who travels to the remote Scottish island of Summerisle to investigate the disappearance of a young girl. Sergeant Howie, a devout Episcopalian, is shocked to discover that the island's populace, under the direction of the local laird Lord Summerisle – played by Christopher Lee – have converted to a form of neo-pagan sun worship. In a famous scene, Sergeant Howie, happening upon the ruins of the island's kirk, asks the local handyman where the island's ministers are. With his face framed against a ruined cross, the man replies sarcastically 'Meenister?' before walking away in laughter. The film ends with Sergeant Howie being burned alive as a sacrificial offering to the sun god, while the island's pagans sing and dance around him. The social commentary is not far from the surface: Christianity is dead, and the people of Scotland have gone pagan. Yet even here there is ambivalence, for Howie's death is a *sacrificial* one. The Christian in this story is a *literal* scapegoat for the failure of the community's harvest and economy, and, before his death, Howie warns Lord Summerisle that the people will quickly realise that their new faith is hollow, and will sacrifice him in turn. Christianity may be dead, but the new gods offer little hope either.

While Scottish Christians were being burned alive on the big screen in the 1970s, on the ground, the post-war enthusiasm of the churches was starting to wane. Scottish Episcopal Church expansion began to grind to a halt, with many of its church extension charges folding by the end of the twentieth century.[30] While the Roman Catholic Church in Scotland had experienced near-continuous growth for the past 150 years, from the 1970s numerical decline began to set in, not averted by the reforms of the Second Vatican Council or the jubilant scenes of the papal visit in 1982. While the Roman Catholic Church's growth had always been largely organic – that is, based on childbirth – it had always benefitted from adult conversions, especially when a Protestant or non-Christian married a Roman Catholic. Yet in the changed context of a secularising Scotland, one Roman Catholic commentator in 1979 could claim that adult conversions would play 'no significant part' in the further development of the church.[31]

From the 1950s through to the 1990s, the Church of Scotland continued to lose members at a precipitous rate. While the Kirk's demise was largely down to the factors already identified, it was accelerated by two demographic and congregational factors unique to Scotland. Due to the duplication of church buildings at the Disruption, the Church of Scotland had thousands of small congregations in half-empty sanctuaries. This meant that many lacked the critical mass to maintain their buildings and to staff required offices, robbing them of time and energy for mission. This factor of the 'empty church' has been identified by Robin Gill as being important for the story of British secularisation, and it is likely that the Church of Scotland's churches were often emptier than their English counterparts.[32] Added to this were the effects of post-war population redistribution and the building of new estates. Some who had been moved from inner-city slums to new housing developments maintained their connection with the city-centre churches they left behind, leading to a lack of support for church plants in housing estates. A far greater problem, however, was the collapse of community in new housing areas. With many estates lacking public assets and utilities due to poor planning, and with the absence of settled relationships, the new estates, in many situations, did not have the social capital to support a thriving parish church. This era also coincided with the contraction and collapse of heavy industry, and the working-class Protestant culture that went with it. By the mid-1980s, when John Harvey looked at the estates of Scotland, he wondered whether he was seeing 'the end of the Protestant race', who had lost their jobs, their identity and the social foundation of their faith.[33]

For as long as Scotland remained without a Parliament, however, the Church of Scotland did retain one last social function: a forum for Scotland's voice within the Union. As Scotland lacked a legislature, the General Assembly functioned as a surrogate Parliament, where the state of Scottish society could be articulated and debated. This role reached its climax during the 1980s, when after hearing Mrs Thatcher's 'Sermon on the Mound' – which contained the famous line 'there is no such thing as society' – the Moderator of the General Assembly presented Mrs Thatcher with a copy of the Kirk's recent report on poverty, refuting much of her argument. As Brown has noted, many leading members of the Kirk during this period developed a particular form of 'nationalist welfare socialism', lobbying local and national government for a better deal for the poor, and increasingly agitating for greater representation through a devolved Parliament.[34]

In spite of occasional protests against the Westminster Parliament, however, the conflation of Protestant and Unionist identities meant that the Kirk was still strongly associated with Britishness. While the Kirk's support for devolution might be read as separatist in nature, as Kidd has argued, it followed a centuries-old logic that sought to preserve Scotland's identity and voice *within* the Union. Indeed, while the leadership of the Kirk became increasingly liberal and even socialist in orientation, polls in 1964 and 1986 revealed that 74% and 45% of commissioners to the General Assembly voted Conservative.[35] The result of this was that the Kirk – and Protestantism more generally – never became, as happened elsewhere, a vehicle for political nationalism, and did not benefit from a growth in support for the Scottish National Party. The waning political relevance of the Kirk was sealed with the opening of the new Scottish Parliament. Remarkably, few within the leadership of the Kirk made any analysis of the effect that the opening of the Parliament might have on the position of the Church of Scotland,[36] and the early hopes for a new yet equal relationship between Kirk and state did not develop.

Conclusion

In this chapter, we have examined the breakup of the parish state in the wake of church schism, industrialisation and the expansion of the state. The result of these changes was that the Scottish Church – particularly the Kirk – lost almost all of its social functions. This was not fatal so long as Scots were limited by poverty and poor consumer choice. Yet this changed with the coming of the welfare state and growing affluence, factors that – while good in themselves – meant that, for the first time in history, non-religious identities and lifestyles became possible.

To say that today's Scotland is 'secular' is to say that the majority of Scots no longer look to Christ and his Church to show them who they are or what they should do. It means that the government does not attempt to enforce or propagate Christian belief and practice, but allows Scots to follow their own spiritual course.

At the end of this long process of social change, yet still living in a world that is the object of God's mission, we are faced with a paradox. God created the world, is present at every point of space–time and has created a Church that has been instrumental to the development of almost every part of Scottish life. Yet the Scots do not recognise their God, and do not listen to his Church. These two realities – the omnipresence and omnipotence of God, and the secularisation of Scotland – must constantly be kept in mind, for if we forget either one of them, we will misunderstand ourselves and our time.

PART 2

Context

4

Social Context

In Part 1, we examined the background to mission in contemporary Scotland. In Part 2, we now examine the contemporary context that this background has given rise to. The present chapter begins that analysis by examining the social context of Scotland: how people live their lives and interact with each other on a day-to-day basis. We will discover that welfare security, affluence and consumerism have allowed the creation of new secular identities that privilege authenticity and personal freedom over community and traditional morality. With unprecedented wealth, technological sophistication and developed medical and psychiatric treatments, Scottish society is successful in meeting the needs of most of its citizens. Yet the persistence of poverty and inequality, and confusion over the meaning of freedom and authenticity, leave a growing minority of Scots dissatisfied with life. This affords the Church an opportunity to tell a better story about selfhood and freedom, pointing Scots not to consumerism but to Christ.

Throughout the second part of this book, it must be borne in mind that, in an introductory of this kind, all we can do is describe the broad contours of Scotland's *national* context. Every local and regional context is different, and will be more or less affected by national social trends depending on history, geography and culture.

General Context

A Scot born in 2015–17 can hope to live 81.1 years if they are female and 77 years if they are male. Life expectancy in the last

35 years has risen 5.8 years for women and 7.9 years for men. Nevertheless, Scots continue to have the lowest life expectancy of any part of Britain.[1] This is largely due to deprivation. In Glasgow, for example, men and women living in Bridgton can expect to live 14.3 and 11.7 years less than their counterparts in Jordanhill, proving that inequality really does kill.[2] In 2018, the average Scot earned £563.20 per week, slightly below the UK average.[3] In addition, 20% of workers in low-paid jobs are victims of in-work poverty, often resorting to foodbanks and other forms of aid.[4] Worryingly, poverty appears to be increasing after a long period of contraction,[5] a situation exacerbated by the effects of the coronavirus pandemic.

Between 1961 and 2011, the number of single-person households in Scotland rose from 14% to 37%, making this the largest group of any type of occupancy.[6] At the same time, the proportion of households containing three or more persons more than halved. In addition to growing affluence and a desire to have one's own – ever-increasing – personal space, this change is also the result of the rising age of marriage, marital breakdown and the growing proportion of elderly Scots. The latter factor is once again related to economics. In times past, it was expected that elderly relatives would be taken into the family home, often with one or more family members spending their time caring for them. Yet the welfare state, individualism caused by affluence, and the need for adults to work in order to finance their lifestyles mean that there is less ability or need to care for the elderly in family homes. In addition, the ever-advancing age of elderly relatives means that they live with complex medical needs that families lack the capacity to meet.

Related to the expansion of smaller households is the greater geographical mobility of Scots. The majority of Scots move home at least once every ten years, with a surprising 34% doing so every four years.[7] This means that there is much less time to put down roots and establish relationships in one's community. Indeed, given the transitory nature of today's society, many Scots would not expect to know their neighbours. The desire for affluence, taken with economic mobility and decreasing expectation of community, have led to the phenomenon of the commuter estate and dormitory town. Thousands of people live next to each other without any expectation of ever forming close relationships. Car ownership, and the existence of economic and social activities elsewhere, mean that Scots can usually live their lives without being too involved with their neighbours.

It goes without saying that this social and economic reality has had a devastating effect on community. In 2015, 73% of Scots felt that they were not very involved or not at all involved in their local community, leading to 22% feeling that they did not belong in that community. A lack of involvement in one's local community contributed to 48% of Scots feeling that most people could not be trusted, although it is notable that one's trust in other people increased with one's engagement in the community. Nevertheless – and something that the Church should not overlook – the majority of Scots *do not* feel isolated or cut off from wider society, and half of Scots have either volunteered with a charity or engaged in some kind of social action.[8] Importantly, this sense of involvement increased during the coronavirus pandemic.[9] Nevertheless, Scots' volunteering will often be outside their local neighbourhood, which – taken with time spent at work and in leisure pursuits elsewhere – means that community is now more associated with chosen networks than geographical proximity.

The shadow side of increased mobility, independence and affluence for some, however, is loneliness for others. The most isolated of Scots are the elderly, or those suffering from medical complaints that separate them from wider social life. Among those medical issues is poor mental health and wellbeing. In 2014/15, 20% of the Scottish population reported one or more symptoms of depression, up from 14% in 2008/9. Likewise, 12% of the population in 2014/15 had two or more symptoms of anxiety, compared with 9% in 2008/9. What is more concerning, however, is the unequal nature of these symptoms. One of the groups most likely to experience poor mental health are young women aged 16–24, whose wellbeing is, on average, significantly lower than any other age group.[10]

Another striking figure is the effect that poverty has on well-being and mental health. Those in the most deprived areas are twice as likely to present with mental health problems than those in the least deprived areas.[11] These chronic problems no doubt contribute to Scotland's unenviable record as the drug-death capital of Europe.

While we are divided by a common geography, often living cheek by jowl with people we will never know, we are nevertheless united in our separate homes by a common culture of entertainment, encompassing film, television, streaming services and music. As we saw in Chapter 3, the advent of mass communication was an important factor in the transmission of new non-religious identities, and the ethos of the permissive society. The insertion of promiscuity, same-sex relationships and transgenderism into television soaps and dramas, along with high-level discussions of these issues in news bulletins and panel shows, gradually increased the tolerance and empathy of Scots towards alternative identities and lifestyles. This experience helped to produce a common culture centred on equality and personal rights. In addition, this common culture of entertainment helps to ameliorate the isolating and dehumanising aspects of contemporary culture, and preserves public support for the status quo. We may feel alienated from everyone and everything, but if we can binge-watch *Game of Thrones* or *The Crown* then we can get through the week without erupting into anger, or sinking into existential despair.

In summary, then, Scotland is, in general, a contented place to live, and most people are able to navigate their way through life without irreparable personal breakdowns or spiritual crises. Yet that is only part of the story, for it is primarily the rich and privileged who are able to navigate their way through life in this way. The deprived face significantly worse life-outcomes, and are less likely to have achieved the success and independence that society promises us.

Yet the group that, in a different way, has been most adversely affected by contemporary social and economic forces is the Christian Church. The changed social context of Scotland has devastated models of ministry based on geography, especially the Church of Scotland. In addition, it has lowered levels of trust in society, and destroyed the community relationships that are necessary for the transmission of the Gospel. Greater than even these changes, however, is the change it has effected in our very identities, and what we think it is to live a good life.

Self and Economy

Statistics can only ever tell us part of the story. They represent behaviour, experience and relationships in numbers and percentages, quantifying these complex realities and making them easier to grasp. Of greater relevance to mission in contemporary Scotland, however, is how it *feels* to live a secular life, what it is like to experience day-to-day life without God. Remarkably, there is little in the missional literature that deals with this issue. It is usually taken for granted that people would be better off with faith, and contemporary society is only discussed to cite its problems and underscore the superiority of Christianity. Yet if contemporary society were *that* bad, would not more people be coming to faith? When we examine contemporary existence in more detail, centred as it is on personal freedom and consumerism, we see that while the majority live without God in the world, they do not live without hope. On the contrary, even if it is ultimately wrong, our society has been largely successful in enabling people to live happy lives without Christ. At the root of all of this are three factors: the organisation of life along *national* rather than local lines (known as *societalisation*), the way in which our activities are not limited to physical space but, through technology, now take place across many different times and places (known as *dislocation*) and, finally, the *consumerism* that underlies this reality and is furthered by it.

In order to understand why the decline of faith would be linked to these changes, we need to consider what Peter Berger has called *plausibility structures*. In short, in order to be plausible or believable, Christianity requires daily face-to-face social interactions to confirm the importance of the Church and the self-evident nature of its beliefs. If one lived in early eighteenth-century Scotland, one would have no doubt about the importance of the Church and the self-evident nature of Christianity. As we saw in Chapter 2, much of the ordering and support of society took place at a local level *through* the parish church, and most Scots would spend the majority of their lives within a relatively small area. In such a situation, everything would have confirmed that Christianity was true and that the Church was an important institution to be part of.

At the end of the process recounted in Chapter 3, however, very few of the plausibility structures of Christianity remain in Scotland. Education, social security, healthcare and punishment of low-level crime – to cite only some of the local church's former functions – have been stripped from it, and are now the responsibility of the state. Society is no longer organised locally by the Church but nationally by the state. The result of this is that the Church *really is* irrelevant to the lives of the majority of Scots, who have not had serious reason to think about the Christian faith for a number of generations.

It is not only societalisation and the breakdown of community that makes faith implausible, however, but the related issue of *dislocation*. In previous centuries, one would generally have to be in close proximity to someone in order to communicate with them, or to buy or exchange goods with them. One would have to be physically present in order to go to work, and would not be able to act in more than one time zone at once. Now, however, one can work from home thousands of miles from one's colleagues, can buy goods from the other side of the world, can have more communication with relatives on another continent than with one's neighbours, and be 'present' in a number of different places and time zones simultaneously. One's relationships, work, shopping and identity are no longer integrated and centred on *the local*, but separated out in myriad ways. For a faith like Christianity that is based on long-term relationships in community, centred on a geographically and physically distinct place, the dislocation of activities and identities is deeply problematic.[12]

Closely related to societalisation and dislocation, yet more serious than both, is *consumerism*. Consumerism is a culture based on the acquisition of goods and services and the lifestyles they support. As we saw in Chapter 3, while consumerist elements had been present in the British economy for centuries, it became normative when the majority of the population grew wealthy and independent enough to self-define through their possessions and lifestyles. While consumerism has been long maligned by the churches for its greed and selfishness, it is neither greed nor selfishness that is the greatest threat to the Church, but the *choice* and *independence* that affluence and consumerism bring. They allow the majority of the population to follow their own desires and goals without fear of being ostracised by the community, and hence economically threatened by it. This marks a decisive break with the past, when individuals were economically integrated into small geographically bounded communities, or reliant on family or community connections for work and security. Today, personal wealth and increased social and economic independence allow individuals to seek their own personal wellbeing and self-fulfilment *as* individuals, without thought for tradition, community or family. In short, because circumstances allow people to more or less do what they want, they *will* do what they want.

The move from the discipline of a subsistence existence based on family and community to individual freedom, wellbeing and self-fulfilment gives rise to new forms of personal identity and self. At the heart of contemporary identity is the notion of *authenticity*: that individuals must be faithful not to God or to others, but to themselves and their own perceived desires and characteristics.[13] Rather than making us who we are ,and being the very foundations for freedom, this way of thinking often views tradition, family and society as *constraints* on freedom, constraints we must push against if we are to be true to ourselves. As such, contemporary selfhood denies that there is one single human nature, or that there is one single purpose to life. To use Sartre's language, human beings *exist*, but their essence, nature or purpose are left undefined.[14] Indeed, this absence is what makes freedom possible, for if human nature were fixed – by genetics, biology, nature or God – then the domain of human choice would be severely reduced.

Being liberated in this way, Scots increasingly experience life as an eternal present of possibility. The past may still be drawn upon as part of the self-narratives of individual people and – as we shall see in Chapter 5 – in a highly selective manner as the basis of national identity. Yet, for the most part, the past – and with it the traditions and morals of yesterday – is something to be ignored, and plays little role in the day-to-day decision-making of Scots. The past is not wholly irrelevant, however. It continues as useful foil for the morals of today, a realm of prejudice, superstition and ignorance that – through the progressive enlightenment and virtue of society – we are perpetually leaving behind.

This form of identity and selfhood is not without difficulties, however. While endless possibility can be exhilarating, it can also be anxiety-inducing, dispiriting and anti-social. This form of self-identity can become selfish and narcissistic, harming wider society and, paradoxically, itself. It is also the case that there is an important – some may say *fatal* – contradiction at the heart of contemporary selfhood. Scots do not simply *find* themselves to be individuals, but are *told* that they are individuals: told by businesses and the state that they are unique, different and free to do what they want in relation to sexuality, gender, fashion and religion. The fact that individualism and selfhood are *politically and socially encouraged* in Scottish society makes contemporary selfhood paradoxical. On the one hand, Scots have greater autonomy than ever before. Yet with the growth of the state and the omnipresence of social media, they have never been more exposed to social pressures, pressures that – without the buffering that comes from family, education and self-reflection – mean that much 'individualism' is highly conformist and illusory.

It is at this juncture, however, that Taylor identifies what is sometimes lost in Church discussions of modern identity and selfhood: the *moral* claim that underlies it. It is not simply that individuals are more likely than they were before to seek their own self-fulfilment, but that it is widely believed they are *justified* in doing so, that self-actualisation is the *right* course of action for *all* people. As Deneen argues, this is because liberalism – the dominant ideology in today's West – teaches that personal freedom is the greatest good. Indeed, in its struggle against Arab dictators or Islamist terrorism, the Western world explicitly fights in the name of *freedom*, raising this autonomous, self-fulfilling selfhood into a key marker of Western moral superiority.[15]

The luxury of personal freedom and self-actualisation, however, is wholly dependent on widespread affluence and consumerism, and would not exist without it. According to Zygmunt Bauman:

> Individual needs of personal autonomy and self-definition, authentic life or personal perfection are all translated into the need to possess and consume, market-offered goods ...[16]

As such, while there is truth to the long historical genealogy of modern selfhood that Taylor presents in *Sources of the Self*, when examining the story of Scotland, we encounter little evidence of these forms of self among the general population before the 1950s and 1960s.[17] While this way of living may have been possible for intellectuals and other classes of people with the time or wealth necessary to think progressive thoughts, it was the advent of welfare security and affluence that enabled the transition of the majority of the population from a subsistence morality focused on community obligation to a morality of personal authenticity focused on the individual. In short, then, as Donnelly notes, the cultural revolution of the 1960s 'was less about sexual freedom and psychedelia and more about high-street spending ... consumption was important because it offered more people than ever before the choice to buy themselves identities and lifestyles.'[18]

Being free to choose whatever identity and lifestyle they wish, and in a context in which the Church has lost its social significance, it is not surprising that the majority of Scots do not choose a religious lifestyle. Why would I need to know my identity in Christ if I can successfully fulfil my identity through my friends, family and lifestyle? Why would I take up my cross to suffer as his disciple when I can volunteer for a local charity, or simply enjoy my big-screen television, designer handbags and new car? Why bother?

Here Lies the Body

This outlook does not only extend to faith, however, but to traditional morality founded on Christian principles. Today, moral authority does not come top-down from God or a ruling elite, nor from bottom-up through social conformity. Rather, it is being perpetually renegotiated through public discourse, government and institutional action and personal self-interpretation. The result of this is that – even if they did believe in him – Scots would not view God's existence as a reason to obey him. Their lives are their own, and what they do with those lives will be determined by them alone.

One outcome of these moral changes is a new attitude towards gender and sexuality. As we have seen, sexual choice was an important aspect of the move to non-religious identities from the 1960s onward. The result of the social changes brought in by welfare security and affluence, taken with advances in contraception, meant that there was less risk of unwanted pregnancy. If unwanted pregnancy did occur, the child could either be terminated through abortion or supported through the generous provision of the welfare state.[19] The result is that sexual activity before marriage has become almost universal. According to a recent Pew Research study, only 13% of Britons polled believed that pre-marital sex was unacceptable, with the remaining 87% considering it acceptable or not a moral issue at all.[20] Christian arguments in favour of abstinence, not surprisingly, make little sense to non-Christians, and are often lost on young Christians themselves. To this day, Scotland has one of the highest rates of early sexual activity of any developed nation. This is particularly the case among poorer girls and children who live with only one parent.[21] Despite this, the number of teenage pregnancies in Scotland continues to decline, a trend that is in part due to an increased preference for abortion among under-eighteen-year-old Scots.[22]

One outcome of changed attitudes towards sex are so-called 'dating' apps such as Tinder and Grindr. These apps make commitment-free sex with strangers easy, despite studies showing that they have negative effects on almost everyone who uses them.[23] Tinder and other dating apps are successful because they are a perfect expression of consumerism, and the sovereign choice of the individual. Christian morality, which stresses the inherent value of sexual activity, and its proper location within monogamous marriage, makes little sense to consumerist sexuality. If I want to enjoy sex with other people, and they want to have sex with me, what's the problem? Why do I need to have a long-term relationship before I can have a good time? The fact that this attitude extends consumer choice to *human beings*, treating them as interchangeable sexual playthings, is neither here nor there for many people.

A more high-profile example of the apparent clash between Christian ethics and contemporary culture is seen in the case of same-sex sexual activity. In decades and centuries past, when men and women felt same-sex attraction, the majority – knowing that society viewed it as wrong, and believing that it was condemned by Scripture – would have tried to ignore their feelings. They would have gone on to marry or, alternatively, have lived their lives alone. In economies dependent on procreation and the transmission of wealth through marriage, same-sex relationships were unwanted and potentially destructive. Yet in an age of abundance, where wealth production is no longer dependent on family and immediate community, this is no longer an issue. In a society where authenticity is viewed as an important moral virtue, people are viewed as courageous and virtuous for being true to their feelings, identities and sexual preferences. When celebrities or politicians leave their partners after coming out as gay or lesbian, society does not condemn them for breaking their vows or abandoning their children, but applauds them for their bravery. For many, these are the moral heroes of our time, valiantly challenging the norms of society to become who they truly are.

It is not only consumer products, services and experiences that are used to develop and sustain a particular narrative of selfhood, then, but intimate relationships. Viewing this positively, contemporary Scots recognise the need for other people in order to fulfil themselves. They recognise that consumer products and one-night stands are not enough to achieve self-actualisation, and that the love and companionship of others is crucial. It is this need that underpins the moral claim for the equality of same-sex relationships in contemporary Scotland. How could abstaining from sexual activity with the person I love make me a happier or better person? Human beings complete each other, and why should I, as a gay, lesbian, bisexual or trans person, not have the same right to fulfilment as everyone else? In a culture founded on equality and personal choice, what right do you have to tell me I am bad or sinful because I love someone you disapprove of?

This attitude extends to our bodies. The body is no longer a place over which society has jurisdiction and control. It is under the authority of the individual, who can use and do with their body almost anything they wish. This contemporary understanding of the body can have positive outcomes. The Me Too movement, which started in the wake of allegations against Harvey Weinstein, saw hundreds of thousands of women share harrowing stories of sexual abuse, with many reporting that they felt frozen, or somehow compelled to give in to the unwanted sexual advances of powerful or aggressive men. Our society's emphasis upon personal autonomy and integrity means that more women are finding the courage to call out exploitative and predatory behaviours, something that the Church should support and endorse.

More generically, a new emphasis upon personal control of the body means that it has become more and more a vehicle for self-expression, a blank canvas upon which the individual can write. Consumerism allows us to dress in whatever way we wish, whether it be preppy, sexy, goth or anything else. Advertisements tell individuals to be themselves in all their uniqueness, while – somewhat ironically – selling them a limited range of identities and styles. Everyone in our society is an individual, because it is profitable for the market if they are like that.

A more controversial example of the desire to shape our bodies according to our felt identities comes in transgender issues. The number of transgender people in Scotland is likely to be at least 0.5%,[24] with increasing demand for gender-realignment surgery among both children and adults in recent years.[25] This has given rise to widespread media attention and debate, with a corresponding raft of measures being adopted or proposed by the Scottish Government to defend the rights of transgender people. This political debate will be looked at in more detail in Chapter 5. One of the more obvious social effects of the growth in transgender identities in Scotland has been its effect on language. In businesses, public institutions and university campuses, Scots not infrequently wear name badges with their preferred pronouns (he/him, she/her, they/them etc.). This has led to an increasing number of public figures and commentators being accused of 'misgendering', when – by mistake or design – they fail to use the preferred pronouns of another.

We see here the progressive movement of the self's authority from feelings and thoughts, to the body, and then into the social world, with even language itself being transformed by the will of the individual. Christians may be tempted to dismiss such phenomena as 'political correctness gone mad'. Yet this underplays the immense social significance of these phenomena, and runs the risk of the Church failing to understand its own context. If same-sex relationships, transgenderism and other social changes were simply the result of political propaganda or parliamentary fiat then they would have little power. Yet they do have power, and this power rests not on some conspiracy among the ruling classes, but deep economic, social and existential changes that neither the Church, the government or civic society are in control of. Authority in matters of identity and sexual activity has passed from the control of the community, the Church or the state to individuals, and – failing the economic collapse of the market that sustains them – the genie cannot be put back in the bottle.

Self, Freedom and Shame

As authority in relation to personal identity and sexuality have passed from community, Church and state to the individual, so the power of shame and ostracism in relation to these activities has become increasingly weak. As we discussed earlier, in previous centuries when there was no police force, little state control and low affluence, social control through shaming was an important way of preserving public order, food supplies and human life itself. Yet in twenty-first-century Scotland there is less need for shame, especially in relation to matters that do not threaten the stability of society. Adultery, for example, is a grievous sin worthy of social disapproval. Yet the rates of adultery in Scotland are not sufficient to destroy society. Also, in an age when the preservation of family property through marriage is not as important as it once was, women are – thankfully – less likely to be shamed into looking and behaving in a certain way to maximise their chance of procuring a husband.

These economic and social changes have given rise to the body positive movement, where women – and to a lesser extent men – are encouraged to like their body as it is, in all its good and not so good points. Magazines, advertisements and news items are increasingly filled with stories of 'plus sized' – read normal-sized – models and celebrities encouraging their followers on Instagram to be #bodypositive. This is a welcome development, and harmonises well with Christian teaching on the goodness of creation, God's love for us and the placing of his image in all people. Yet while expectations upon women have lessened in some respects, they have increased in others. In the past, one would have been exposed to a fairly limited range of bodies and fashions, and one's lack of wealth and opportunity would have lessened one's expectations of emulation. Yet with greater affluence, social mobility and the power of mass-media advertising, perfection seems within reach, which makes *falling short* of perfection that much harder to accept.

The body positive movement, and a desire to be free from social disapproval, also have a much darker side, however. For while an Instagram picture of a women showing off her imperfections in her underwear may be rather tame, amateur pornography and sensationalist programmes broadcast on national television are not. Recent years have witnessed an explosion in 'DIY porn', where women – and sometimes men – set up explicit webcams in their homes in order to earn money from viewers, or take pornographic photos of themselves and post them online in the hope of becoming a model for an adult site. There are, of course, economic reasons for this activity, yet it is legitimised as an expression of feminism, and of women's desire to be free from shame. A more public example of this is found in the proliferation of programmes on mainstream television such as *Mums Make Porn*, *Naked Attraction*, *Naked Beach* and *Sex Tape*. The premise behind these shows is much the same: it is wrong for us to be ashamed of our bodies or our 'natural' sexual activity, and so ordinary people must remove their clothing or engage in sexual activity before the nation in order to demonstrate their liberty.

While the Church should rightly reject these programmes, it should not ignore the strong spiritual and moral tone that accompanies them. For at their heart is a desire for freedom: freedom from shame, from guilt, from fear, and a wish to find acceptance and love. They bear witness to the desire for a dignity and value that cannot be tainted by human beings. In all their fallenness, they point to a longing for the unconditional love of God, and the righteousness won for us on the Cross. Yet this desire for unconditional value and acceptance is shaped by a culture whose understanding of how acceptance and love are won is opposed to that of the Gospel, and the participants in these programmes and activities are blind to how their shame, and their desire for acceptance, are exploited and used by a market that takes their weakness and uses it for its own profit and gratification.

The popularity of shows such as *Sex Tape* – in which couples film themselves having sex so that 'sexperts' can offer them advice on how to save their relationship – introduces a final social trend relevant to Christian mission: therapy and counselling. As we saw in Chapter 3, the Church's pastoral care has been almost totally supplanted by medical, psychiatric and counselling therapies designed to restore the mental wellbeing of Scots. Counselling and other forms of therapy have two functions. First, they provide the emotional triage of consumer society, helping those for whom the security and affluence of contemporary life are not sufficient to prevent anxiety and depression. Second, they are an important accompaniment to the contemporary experience of selfhood. Counselling facilitates the individual's transition from a damaged self-understanding – usually following trauma – to a new one, through a re-narration of their lives using language, image and story.[26] Crucially, these treatments are not premised on any faith commitment, and – while faith may be discussed in these therapies – the methods and approaches themselves do not involve theological considerations of any kind. This in itself is significant, for if a person can understand themselves, and face any life trauma without reference to God, then faith is irrelevant or, at best, just one choice among others.

Counselling and other therapeutic practices also risk mistaking spiritual or existential problems for medical ones. At their worst, purely medical understandings of mental distress may ignore the personal and social contexts of anxiety and depression, medicalising and pathologising that which is not pathological. The existence of accessible counselling and psychiatric services, and the methods they use, mean that Scots are increasingly unlikely to view their mental ill-health in theological or spiritual terms, but will understand them as purely medical. Indeed, this tendency has most likely *increased* of late due to high-profile campaigns to end stigma around mental health, which are premised on the claim that mental illness is directly equivalent to physical illness. In short, when Scots are feeling down or anxious, the overwhelming majority will turn to antidepressants and counsellors, and not their local pastor, minister or priest.

Conclusion

In this chapter, we have surveyed those elements of the social context of Scotland that are most relevant to the mission of the Church. We have seen how affluence and geographical mobility have given rise to a reduction in the importance of community, making it harder for the Church to build and maintain relationships. We have also seen how inequality, and the anxiety and despair created by personal autonomy, have a dramatic effect on the physical and mental wellbeing of Scots. This provides an opportunity for the Church to affirm what is good in our culture – a yearning for dignity, freedom, and one's true self – while pointing it towards the God who alone can meet its deepest needs.

The social context of Scotland, however, is only one aspect to the life of our nation. In order to understand the salience, shape and dominance of these social beliefs and practices, we must understand the *political* context to which they give rise, and which, in turn, shapes and directs them.

5

Political Context

Human beings are social animals, and because of this, they are *political* animals. While in popular thinking politics represents a narrow set of interests and activities centred on Holyrood, Westminster and local councils, in fact it encompasses a much wider range of practices. That is because politics is the way in which *power* is used in human relationships and cultures, encompassing the enforcement of belief, the legitimation of values and the suppression of opposing views. As we live in a time of great change, no account of the context of contemporary Scotland could be complete without an analysis of how power is used to promote some beliefs and practices and to marginalise others.

We begin by tracing the construction of an 'imperial religion' in Scotland, built upon the twin pillars of Protestantism and Unionism. This served as Scotland's religious and political identity for centuries, yet in the course of the twentieth century began to give way to an areligious form of Scottish nationalism. This new form of political identity, taken with secularisation, has had serious repercussions for the place of Christianity in public life, restricting the political influence of the Church, and setting many conditions for its involvement in schools, hospitals and other institutions. In the political context of contemporary Scotland, it is Parliament and law, and not Church and morality, that safeguard the national self-identity of Scots. Nevertheless, the desire for a better, fairer Scotland provides an opportunity for the Church to be an agent of change, witnessing to the new creation that God is bringing into the old.

Imperial Religion

As we saw in Chapter 2, Scotland's rejection of Roman Catholicism at the Reformation and its adoption of Reformed Protestantism was an important factor in facilitating union with England. Reformation removed Scotland from its alliance with France and other continental powers and created, for the first time, the possibility of a *United Kingdom* of Great Britain. With the Union of the Crowns in 1603, James VI set about creating a new British identity, with Protestantism at its heart. If the Stuarts believed in Union for largely political reasons, Scottish Presbyterians believed in it for largely religious ones. After the execution of Charles I, a number of Church of Scotland ministers made the journey to London for the Westminster Assembly, whose motivation was to establish Reformed uniformity across Britain, rejecting episcopacy and prayer book for ever.

The Restoration of Charles II in 1660 ensured that all Scotland could achieve was 'Calvinism in one country',[1] a situation ratified by the Establishment of Presbyterianism by William and Mary. While political Union with England in 1707 seemed, at first, to endanger Presbyterianism, the Treaty of Union preserved the Kirk's constitutional position and it was never again threatened with an episcopal takeover. The Treaty of Union laid the foundation for two features of Scottish religious identity that would last for centuries. The first was the *shared Protestant identity* of Britons, united in their rejection of the Papacy and the European powers that followed it. Yet the second was equally important: that Scottish identity was *distinct* from that of England due to its Presbyterian Church, with its own distinctive doctrine, government and worship. For centuries to come, Scottish self-identity would pivot on these two features: *unity* with England through a shared Parliament and Protestant faith, but *distinction* from England through its unique institutions and traditions, the most important of which was its Established Presbyterian Church.

These features of Scottish self-identity found further expression in the opportunities provided by the British Empire.

Empire offered ambitious Scots a way to escape from their traditionally poor country. Engineers, civil servants and soldiers sailed from Scotland to every corner of the world, establishing expat communities – often with a Presbyterian Church – wherever they went. After the lifting of the Kirk's opposition to overseas mission, missionary endeavour became an important part of Presbyterian Scots' understanding of their Church and their purpose in the world. This missionary activity was possible due to Scots' participation in the Empire, which afforded them unprecedented access to non-Christian indigenous people. Empire created strong ties of loyalty to the Union among Scottish Protestants, a loyalty and identification whose symbol was David Livingstone: explorer, missionary and Protestant Scot.[2] The Empire was central to Scottish identity and – after Protestantism – was the single greatest factor securing Scotland's place in the Union.[3]

This conflation of Scottish, Christian and British symbols into an 'imperial religion' reached its apogee in the First World War and its aftermath. The Church of Scotland was patriotically supportive of the war, and 200 ministers signed up as chaplains in its early stages.[4] As patriotism and religious zeal gave way to resignation and despair, however, the churches forged the final expression of imperial religion. This imperial religion persists to this day, seen in war memorials and Remembrance commemorations across Scotland.

There were three stages to this. The first was the creation of Remembrance Sunday as an important feature not only of national life, but of the *Christian year*. In the context of a Christian act of worship, civic and armed-forces leaders would gather to offer their gratitude for victory and mark the sacrifice of their fallen comrades before God. The Cross, rather than a unique event marking the *end* of violence, became a symbol of the sacrifice of the fallen, who – just like Jesus – had laid down their lives for their friends.[5] A second move was the burial of the Unknown Warrior in Westminster Abbey. The solemn action of laying this young man to rest near the door of the Abbey, in the hinterland between the spiritual and secular worlds, was a poignant symbol of the Church's role in interpreting and articulating national grief. The final expression of imperial religion was the erection of war memorials in every village, town and city across Scotland. These memorials allowed ordinary Scots to remember the dead and reconnect with their shared sense of British identity, the two-minute silence every Armistice Day turning all of Britain into a sacred space.[6] These memorials – and the ritual associated with them – stand as tangible reminders of the imperial religion that animated Scotland for centuries, bringing together Union, Empire and Christianity in a potent expression of British national identity.

Secular Nationalism

As imperial religion reached its apex around the time of the First World War, new political currents were developing that would make this Protestant and British identity increasingly alien to many Scots. These currents would coalesce in the growth of Scottish nationalism.

The first development that hastened the growth of nationalism in Scotland was increasing English control over political and economic life in Scotland. By 1906, over half of Scottish MPs were actually *English*, and lived South of the Border. Hastened by government centralisation during the First World War, Scottish banks and heavy industry passed into English ownership, with five Scottish railway companies passing out of Scottish control between 1918 and 1923 alone.[7] Scots appeared to be getting weaker and more marginalised in their own country, a humiliation compounded by gaudy, romanticised images of their nation as an idyllic pleasure ground for wealthy tourists from the South East of England.

Reacting against the anglicisation of Scottish society, and tartan-clad depictions of their people, a new rank of Scottish intellectuals, artists and writers sought to rediscover an authentic Scottish identity. For example, Hugh MacDiarmid railed against the elites who had sold out Scotland, the 'politicians, divines, professors and teachers' who were nothing more than 'the toadies and lickspiths of the English Ascendency'.[8]

MacDiarmid's reference to *divines* – Protestant clergy – was not accidental. There was an anti-Presbyterian stamp to many Scottish Renaissance figures, and men like George Scott-Moncrieff sought to rebel against the Protestant-Unionist status quo by converting to Roman Catholicism. The group's rejection of the so-called 'Kailyard Style' was, after all, the rejection of a genre in which ministers and the Church of Scotland played a prominent role.[9]

As long as the forces that held the Union together – Protestantism and the economic benefits of Empire – were strong, there was little prospect of nationalism entering the mainstream. Yet the factors that brought Scotland together with its Southern counterpart soon came to unravel, and support for the Union with them. The price of victory against Nazi Germany was massive national debt, and a new dependence upon the United States. The diminished economic power of Britain was equalled by a growing anti-colonial movement throughout the world, and Britain would see almost all of its colonial possessions slip away from it. While this brought autonomy to millions of people, it took away many of the economic opportunities that Scots had benefitted from for centuries, and removed one of the central rationales for the Union. Britain's diminished position on the world stage was matched by the collapse in Scotland's historic Christian faith, a process of secularisation that we examined in Chapter 3. The loss of Scotland's Protestant faith, which was the original foundation for the Union, removed yet another feature of a shared British identity.[10]

While Protestantism and Empire were entering into decline, there came the discovery of North Sea oil. At a time of increasing losses in heavy industry, this resource offered Scotland a new economic lifeline. Yet the 'black, black, oil' was a resource that Scotland would have to share with Westminster. This gave rise to the famous It's Scotland's Oil campaign of the Scottish National Party (SNP), which brought the party a growing public profile. The discovery of North Sea oil also coincided with the election of Margaret Thatcher in 1979, a premiership that would see a material change in Scotland's relationship with the rest of Britain. Rather than following the 'post-war consensus' of full employment and social housing, Thatcher sought to hasten the demise of Scotland's unprofitable heavy industries, halt construction of social housing and allow existing tenants to purchase their homes. The result of these actions was the destruction of working-class communities across the nation, and growing civil resistance to Westminster. The Thatcher era had two consequences for the role of the Church in the politics of Scotland. First, in hastening the demise of heavy industry, Thatcher irreparably damaged Protestant and Roman Catholic working-class cultures, which were centred on Celtic and the chapel for Roman Catholics, and Rangers, Freemasonry and the Orange Order for Protestants.[11] Second, the loss of heavy industry destroyed the main constituency of the Labour party, removing the primary rationale for the party's existence. This left the political field open for a new kind of Scottish political party.

It is in this context of industrial decline, ruined working-class culture, increasing secularisation and residual sectarianism that the SNP's narrative of a Scotland united in the bonds of nationhood, and continuing the communitarian welfare socialism of the post-war period, has gained traction. On the one hand, the SNP can speak to post-industrial communities whose traditional working-class culture of gala days and brass bands have been taken away from them, and who are in search of a new identity.[12] On the other hand, it can speak to the middle classes who – following the logic of liberty inherent in liberalism and consumerism – wish to push freedom, equality and choice as far as they can go, even to the point of denying that human beings have an inherent nature. Nationalism offers the possibility of a new political movement that supersedes the old conflicts between socialism and capitalism, Protestant and Roman Catholic, a politics for the *new Scotland* that unites Scots around the one thing they have in common: Scotland itself.

Scotland: the Promised Land

We misunderstand the appeal of nationalism and its relevance to the decline of Christianity if we consider it only in political or economic terms. For at the heart of Scottish nationalism – whether related to the SNP or not – are two powerful *narratives*, both quasi-religious in nature: first, that the nation *unites* while other identities *divide*; and second, that self-belief in Scotland and the Scots will allow the nation to usher in a new and better world.

The idea of the Scottish nation performs a unifying function in two ways: first, by *transcending* existing divisions and, second, by granting a *new form* of common identity. The transcending of social and religious division is particularly important in a Scottish context long marked with schism and sectarianism. In previous centuries, the churches served as the primary agents for unity and identity in Scotland, whether this be Roman Catholic or Protestant. Yet while faith created unity within these religious groups, it also became a source of conflict between them. Whatever the merits of these forms of religious identity, because of the changes recounted in earlier chapters, religion can no longer perform this unifying function for the majority of Scots. The result of this is that as religion has declined in importance as a source of unity and identity, so the role of national pride has increased.[13] As McCrone puts it, 'Just as religion had been losing its force as a key emblem of identity and political behaviour, so nationalism grew in importance.'[14]

As we saw in Chapter 3, the development of the modern state in Scotland was a direct result of the conflict between competing churches.[15] This experience brings Scotland into the same position as other Western societies, which have had to adapt to the breakdown of common beliefs and practices through new political identities and institutional forms. As Fukuyama says, 'Modern liberal democracies are heirs to the moral confusion left by the disappearance of a shared religious horizon.'[16] If modernity has led to a massive fracturing in social life, then nationhood brings citizens together around the one thing they have in common: their country, and the institutions that represent it.[17] The unity brought about by this civic nationalism is, as Berger reminds us, the optimum kind of unity available in the contemporary world, for it provides a base level of commonality while allowing for the pluralism that is inevitable when individuals enjoy high levels of affluence.[18] Scottish identity gives individuals who live in a disenchanted and post-Christian world a sense of purpose, direction and even destiny. I am Scottish, and my identity lies in loving my country and advancing the interests of my people.

Much like the imperial religion of old, in providing Scots with a sense of unity, identity and purpose, Scottish nationalism can perform similar social and psychological functions to religion. This is because, as Durkheim argued: 'Religion is, above all, a system of ideas by which men imagine the society of which they are members and the obscure yet intimate relations they have with it.'[19] While Christians tend to think of their faith as a relationship with *God*, Durkheim is correct that there is much more involved to faith than this. Christianity, after all, provides a range of rules and principles for how to relate to non-Christians, the government and the world, with different theologies giving different accounts of these relations. It is much the same with national identity. Nations are 'imagined communities', where individuals picture their relationship to their neighbours, their land and to outsiders through the use of images, concepts and objects. Examples from Scotland would be the Saltire, the Highlands, the thistle and documents such as the Declaration of Arbroath. The bonds of nationality, in short, are *spiritual*. They are *immaterial forces* that name, unite and animate us.[20]

At its most extreme, the nation – through its transcendent, eternal and reconciling role – becomes a kind of surrogate god. As Eagleton puts it:

the nation, like the Almighty himself, is sacred, autonomous, indivisible, without end or origin, the ground of being, the source of identity, the principle of human unity, a champion of the dispossessed and a cause worth dying for... The nation is incomparably greater than any individual, rather as God transcends his own Creation; yet it also lives at the core of personal identity ...[21]

Yet if the nation can perform a similar function to the concept of God, this god requires a church to interpret and enact its will. It is here that *the state* enters into view. The state represents the nation just as the Church represents God, discerning the will of the nation just as the Church attempts to discern the will of God. This representation and discernment, however, is only one part of its role, for having discerned the will of the nation, the state must *realise* it.

This brings us to the strong *eschatological* tone of contemporary Scottish identity. The use of the word 'eschatological' – which relates to the final perfection of the world in the new creation – might seem surprising. How could there be a *theological* thrust to *secular* politics? Yet just like socialism and other political movements before it, strains of Scottish nationalism represent an attempt to perfect society, not through *divine* action, but through human action alone.

There are four elements to this eschatological project: a reassessment of human nature and potential based on the rhetoric of Enlightenment, a belief in the Scots as a just and communitarian people, the use of critical theory to 'expose' inequalities and the use of the state to correct these inequalities through law.

The first element in the eschatology of contemporary Scottish politics is an affirmation of the goodness of human nature, and the power of human potential. While in Christian theology the Church works with God to extend his Kingdom and bring in the new creation, it is ultimately *God* who perfects the world, while human beings, at best, participate in what God does. This has given rise to an element of scepticism in Christian doctrine generally – and Scottish Calvinism in particular – regarding the ability of human beings to substantially improve themselves and their world. As Beveridge and Turnbull relate, Calvinist scepticism regarding human nature has been a prevalent theme not only within Scottish theology but also in philosophy and literature, and was the default position of most Scottish thinkers until the early twentieth century.[22] Yet this questioning of human potential is distasteful to a culture founded on authenticity and affirmation, and is certainly not suitable as a vehicle for a secular eschatology. For that reason, Scottish nationalism has looked for other voices in Scottish history that support its vision of a renewed Scotland. While writers such as David Hume and Adam Smith were not as sanguine about the ability of human beings to improve themselves as is popularly thought, *it is* the case that Scottish Enlightenment thinkers were sometimes more optimistic about the possibility of human progress than some of their Calvinist forebears. For that reason, the Scottish Enlightenment has been raised to a new level of importance in the narratives and rhetoric of contemporary Scots.

Enlightenment plays a number of different roles in contemporary Scottish discourse. As Craig argues:

> The notion of the Scottish Enlightenment has not only fundamentally changed the understanding of Scottish history since the 1960s, but has played a crucial role in the redefinition of modern Scotland's conception of its contemporary identity – and, therefore, of its possible future.[23]

Enlightenment provides a specific – and highly selective – historical foundation for modern Scotland. This foundation is closely connected with reason and the secular, despite the fact that – as Craig notes – it ignores the richness of Scotland's theological thought and practice, privileging the irreligious Hume against almost the entire Scottish tradition.[24] This selective historical narrative relates, of course, to Scotland's *contemporary* identity as a non-religious, 'rational' nation that seeks to live in the real world and not the make-believe world of faith. The rhetoric of Enlightenment gives *purpose and hope* to the activities of contemporary Scots, promising that they can understand themselves and their world better, and improve Scotland through their own efforts. It provides Scots with a positive, life-affirming view of themselves as a small but noble people, being yeast, salt and light to a world beset by inequality, injustice and ignorance. In contrast to 'Old Scotland', which is sometimes seen as suffering from a crisis of confidence,[25] the Scotland of today – represented by its Parliament – has a resurgent optimism for the future.[26]

A belief in the identity of the Scots as a just and fair people forms the second part of this eschatological vision. This develops long-standing Reformed themes of the Scots as a covenanted, godly nation, but pushes them in a secular direction. An early example of the Christian roots of Scottish egalitarianism is found in the First and Second Books of Discipline. They taught that God's will for Scotland was egalitarian and communitarian. He forbade the rich from flaunting their wealth through clothing and jewellery; he stressed the duty of the community – represented in the Kirk – to care for the poor and destitute; he supported the quasi-democratic right of congregations to call their own minister; and wanted every child to be given the opportunity of schooling, no matter their level of wealth or background.[27] As Craig notes, these values and principles have not died, but now take a different form:

> As Scotland is no longer a culture dominated by God, nowadays redemption mainly takes a secular form ... It is about us once again building the New Jerusalem.[28]

One example of this in recent years is the repackaging of St Andrew as a secular, and not a Christian, saint. Despite his obvious religious significance, the Scottish Government's Scotland.org website makes no reference to the one thing that Andrew would have considered important about himself: that he was a follower of Jesus. Instead, Andrew is depicted as a good Humanist who was kind to people, and fought against social inequality.[29]

This is where the third element of contemporary Scottish eschatology comes in: the use of critical theory to expose inequalities. Critical theory analyses society in terms of power structures. It believes that powerful groups use their influence to grant themselves privileges, but that, because power is finite, the granting of privilege to one group leads to a lack of privilege for others. A recent example is the Black Lives Matter movement. The historic privilege and power of whites in Scottish society led to the enslavement and economic exploitation of Africans. Even when slavery ended, it was followed by centuries of discrimination and marginalisation. Critical theory exposes these structural inequalities, and thereby provides tools for addressing them. Political discourse in Scotland frequently turns to this mode of analysis, primarily in relation to gender, sexuality, race and religion.[30]

Critical theory can also give rise to what has been termed *identity politics*. Identity politics has its basis partly in critical theory, but more fundamentally in the collapse of shared meaning and social bonds following the demise of Christianity in Scotland. Society expects a lot of individuals. People exist, but have not been taught their purpose. They find themselves with little connection to their past, their traditions or their communities, and yet are tasked with discovering themselves and finding meaning in life. As such, they are forced to turn to the few 'objective' characteristics that remain, among which are gender, sexuality and race. The discovery that a person's true identity consists in these things, and that certain identities are oppressed by others, means that self-identity is politicised, and individuals are brought into common cause with others to challenge privilege and transform society. This politicised self-identity gives meaning, purpose and apparent certainty to an otherwise horizonless world, yet pushes, of course, in a secular direction. Rather than seeking to remake Scotland into a godly commonwealth where sin is eradicated, contemporary Scots set their sights on the secular sins of inequality and discrimination.[31]

Belief in the goodness and potential of human beings, taken with communitarian values and critical theory, are not enough, however, to remake Scotland into the secular new creation. It is here that the Scottish Parliament and the Scottish Government come into view. As Sutherland argues, the creation of the Parliament and a host of new Scottish institutions has been essential for the transformation of Scottish self-understanding over the past twenty years.[32] They provided an opportunity to begin Scotland at 'ground zero', creating a new forum to determine who the Scots are and what their purpose is.

The Scottish Parliament has moved the nation from the old Christian Scotland to the new, secular and pluralist Scotland in two ways: by *signalling* the changed nature of Scottish society through its procedure and rhetoric, and by *legitimising* new beliefs and lifestyles through legislation and government action. This discussion began as soon as the Parliament was created. Significantly, the *first debate* in the Scottish Parliament was whether each parliamentary session should begin with Christian prayer, and the first act of the Parliament was to begin each session with a Time for Reflection, featuring a range of speakers from religious and non-religious traditions. This shift from Scotland's traditional Protestant identity to one that was pluralist and secular was also seen in the Kirking of the Parliament. In the first year of the Parliament's life, this service was conducted as a Christian service by Gilleasbuig Macmillan, Minister of St Giles' Cathedral. Yet in following years it became a multi-faith event, manifesting the religious changes that had overtaken Scottish society.

If the Scottish Parliament and Government signal their commitment to a free, pluralist and secular state through a range of symbolic gestures, they also *legitimise* and *promote* secular pluralism through legislation and direct governmental action. During some parts of our history, freedom has been conceived of in a negative way: that if the state and other people leave the individual alone then they are free. This conception of freedom, however, is relatively abstract, and generally safeguards existing privilege and power. One of the changes that has occurred in the shift from a subsistence to a post-materialist society is a new understanding of what freedom is. If the purpose of human life is to maximise happiness through authenticity and self-realisation, then there are situations in which the state must intervene to ensure that society recognises, protects and even celebrates personal identities.[33] This *positive* understanding of freedom, one that recognises that freedom can only be realised through state and collective action, is the one that has been most at work in Scottish politics in recent years. This role of the state is articulated by Weeks:

> Through its role in determining legislation and the legal process it constitutes the categories of the permissible and the impermissible, the pure and the obscene ... The state can shape through its prohibitions and punishments. It can also organize and regulate through its positive will and functions, and influence through its omissions and contradictions.[34]

This role in defining and redefining what is socially acceptable was seen early on in the life of the Parliament with the repeal of Section 28 of the Local Government Act 1986. Section 28 prohibited the 'promotion' of homosexuality in state schools, including the notion that it was an acceptable form of family relationship. This was followed in 2004 with the Civil Partnership Act, which allowed same-sex couples to enter into a new form of legal union recognised by the state. A decade later, the Scottish Parliament passed legislation allowing same-sex couples to marry. This redefinition of the permissible also extended to the recognition of non-religious marriages, with Humanist marriages being permitted in Scotland since 2005.

The public recognition, defence and propagation of LGBT+ values has been seen more recently in the Scottish Government's support for Time for Inclusive Education (TIE). TIE will see the history of LGBT+ people and gender theory being taught to every Scottish pupil from primary school onward. More recently – and controversially – the SNP administration has passed plans to radically change the legal recognition of gender. Rather than gender being a genetic and biological reality, or one premised on socially recognised criteria built up over centuries, under the proposed Gender Recognition Reform Act it will be possible for an individual to self-declare their preferred gender as long as they live as that gender for a short period of time.

The fact that the SNP are willing to accept serious political conflict over the issue of transgender rights is a signal that, while this may be the presenting issue, it is only a shibboleth for a much deeper debate about the ability of individuals to define reality, and receive social and political recognition for their identities. Following American narratives about a 'liberal elite' enforcing their progressive values upon ordinary, common-sense people, some Scottish commentators have interpreted these legislative changes in a similar vein. Ordinary Scots are wary of the LGBT+ agenda, so it is claimed, and following this trajectory will only lead to moral, spiritual and cultural ruin.[35] While sections of the Scottish population continue to dislike same-sex relationships and a progressive approach to transgender rights, there is overwhelming public support for much of the LGBT+ agenda.[36] Rather than being the top-down fiat of a liberal establishment, the legal and political recognition of non-traditional and non-religious identities flows from the 'deep logic' of authenticity and self-realisation that also led to the demise of Christianity in Scotland. As Bruce says:

> That the churches are now minority interest groups rather than the conscience of the nation is not the work of some secular agent that has cheated them. It is a consequence of their inability to retain the allegiance of the population.[37]

The shifting allegiance of Scots is seen in the proliferation of that most contemporary of symbols: the Rainbow Flag. First designed by Gilbert Baker in San Francisco in 1978–9, the flag has become an international symbol of LGBT+ rights. In its role as a symbol for progressive values, the rainbow flag offers an important insight into the transition from the old Christian Scotland of yesterday to the new Scotland of today. The Rainbow Flag now adorns everything from office lanyards to Marks & Spencer sandwiches, from the logos of banks and insurance companies to the traffic lights of Scottish towns during Pride marches. This is because the Rainbow Flag, and support for LGBT+ organisations, are *means of legitimation*, directly analogous to the role of the Church in old Scotland. By affiliating with LGBT+ organisations, and making financial contributions towards them, the Scottish Government and businesses demonstrate their moral standing, and gain the respect – and sometimes cash – of Scots.

The Rainbow Flag signifies more than an admirable desire for equality, and solidarity with LGBT+ individuals and groups, however. To the majority of Scots, it signifies support for a post-materialist culture of authenticity, self-realisation and personal freedom, where all people – no matter their sexuality, gender, belief or race – can live happy, loving, meaningful lives, free from the judgement and control of others. It symbolises the belief that individuals themselves are the best judges of how to live their lives, and that the community and state exist only to protect their rights and enable them to realise their identities. In connecting the struggle for equality with the pride that *all* individuals should have in their identities, LGBT+ groups have understood and harnessed deep currents within Scottish and Western society. On an intuitive level, heterosexual Scots understand that the question of *their* freedom – from tradition, from the community, from the Church, from God – is closely implicated in the freedom of LGBT+ people, and that they stand and fall together.[38] The Saltire may represent the national and political identity of Scotland, but the Rainbow Flag represents its values.

The old Scotland of Church, Union and Empire is dead, and the new Scotland of pluralism, secularity and Humanist optimism has taken its place. In secular and pluralist Scotland, the nation takes on many of the functions of God, while state, law and civil society take many of the functions of the Church. The state and civil society interpret the will of the nation and enforce this will through law and public policy, promoting certain beliefs and practices while marginalising others.[39] Scotland has changed, and there is no going back. As Scots Makar Jackie Kay expressed it in her poem 'The Long View' to mark the twentieth anniversary of the Scottish Parliament:

Scotland itself is my country
And twenty years on, my country has changed!
I remember it once being a country I ran from,
In those days, you felt unwelcome.
You passed. You pretended. You kept your mouth shut
Unless you sang sing if you're glad to be gay, sing if you're
    happy that way ...

And now – look – Old Scotland is no more.
Gay men kiss at the Parliament's door.[40]

In the media, and in much of civic society, the Church continues to be viewed as a remnant of 'Old Scotland', tossed
aside, in the words of Philip Larkin, like an outdated combine
harvester.[41] None of this is to say, however, that nationalism
is incompatible with Christian belief, or that nationalism is
inherently anti-Christian.[42] Rather, it is to say that Scottish
nationalism is largely areligious, and is unlikely to result in a
resurgence of support for the Church. It also does not mean
that the aspirations of the new Scotland cannot converge
with those of the Church. After all, the prevailing political
ideology of Scotland is a *secularised* one, one that derives from
the Christian hope of a new creation. As such, despite the
areligious nature of contemporary Scottish politics, the Church
has the opportunity to tell a different, and better story about
progress, activism and our common aspirations for Scotland.

Religion and Public Policy

In order to complete our survey of the political context of modern Scotland and its relevance for mission, we must look at how
contemporary politics directly impact the work and witness of
the Church. The first issue to consider is what has been called
'Scotland's shame': sectarianism. Just as the Section 28 debate
started within a year of the Parliament's life, so a national conversation regarding conflict and discrimination between Protestants
and Roman Catholics dominated the early years of devolution.
The debate was launched after an infamous speech by Roman
Catholic composer James MacMillan at the Edinburgh Fringe
in 1999. MacMillan claimed that sectarianism against Roman
Catholics was still pervasive, and that the government and civil
society were burying their heads in the sand about it. While a
subsequent Scottish Government report found that the problem
of sectarianism was more one of perception than reality, the
issue of sectarianism coloured the Scottish public's perception

of religion.[43] Rather than being a source of social unity and morality, the sectarianism debate, and the subsequent Offensive Behaviour at Football Act 2012, ensured that religion came to be seen as a source of conflict and division. This, as Walker notes, was useful for the early Parliament. The existence of sectarianism legitimised devolution, for it demanded that Scottish solutions be found to Scottish problems.[44]

A negative public perception of Christianity is seen also in the ongoing debate over Roman Catholic schooling. The accession of Roman Catholic schools into the state sector in 1918 was a major success for the church, securing this distinctive aspect of Roman Catholic mission to Scotland while relieving the church of its financial burden. While 'Rome on the Rates' may have been offensive to some Protestants, the Church of Scotland – and occasionally other Protestants – continued to benefit from the new education system through representation on the education committees of local councils. This educational settlement – reflecting centuries of development – has come under increasing pressure from Humanists and secularists, who argue that the presence of state-funded Roman Catholic schools and unelected church representatives on education committees is an example of religious privilege. While the Roman Catholic school sector is unlikely to lose its funding in the short to medium term, a number of Scottish councils have openly debated rescinding places for appointed church representatives.

Another example of the effect of current political trends on the mission of the Church is the shifting complexion of religious observance in schools. As we saw in Chapters 2 and 3, Christianity has been an integral part of Scottish education for centuries. This is reflected in the Education (Scotland) Act 1980, which makes religious observance a statutory requirement for all Scottish schools, and grants the Church a potentially important role in schools and education. Since then, however, the secularisation and pluralisation of Scottish society have continued apace, and successive government circulars and guidance have progressively reinterpreted what religious observance means within non-denominational schooling. According to one piece of recent guidance, religious observance is defined as:

Community acts which aim to promote the spiritual development of all members of the school's community, and express and celebrate the shared values of the school community.

Importantly, 'spiritual development' is not fully defined in the guidance. As such, the Scottish Government gives headteachers wide discretion as to how they interpret their statutory obligations.[45] This delegation of decision-making produces wide variation in practice, with some schools openly embracing the Church and its leaders and others maintaining a strictly secular and even slightly anti-religious ethos. As Pirrie argues, this local contextualisation ensures that the contemporary secular values of autonomy and personal spirituality predominate, rather than the original – Christian – intention of religious observance as a communal act.[46]

If the Scottish Government affords schools wide discretion as to how they provide religious observance, the situation is different within the National Health Service (NHS). The NHS employs Christian healthcare chaplains across Scotland from public funds, and has developed a sophisticated framework for articulating and practising spiritual care within the healthcare sector. According to the most recent NHS guidance on spiritual care, 'It is widely recognised that the spiritual is a natural dimension of what it means to be human, which includes the awareness of self, of relationships with others and with creation.' Spirituality, here, is distinct from – yet not incompatible with – religion. As the guidance goes on to state:

Spiritual care is usually given in a one to one relationship, is completely person centred, and makes no assumptions about personal conviction or life orientation.

Religious care is given in the context of shared religious beliefs, values, liturgies and lifestyle of a faith community ... Spiritual care might be said to be the umbrella term of which religious care is a part. It is the intention of religious care to meet spiritual need.

Among the basic spiritual needs that all people have, according to the guidance, are the need to find meaning and purpose in life, the need to express feelings honestly and the need to give and receive love.[47]

On the one hand, the creation of these guidelines and the employment of healthcare chaplains from public funds represents the state's commitment to spirituality – and even Christianity – in public institutions such as hospitals. On the other hand, some may feel uncomfortable with government defining what are, and what are not, acceptable expressions of spirituality and religion.

What is certain, however, is that NHS healthcare chaplaincy is in line with what the public at large perceive of as 'normal' religion and spiritualty. This perception has two effects. First, forms of Christianity that were commonplace even two or three decades ago are now seen as inappropriate and immoral.[48] Examples of this include cases where individuals have lost their jobs as a result of praying with members of the public, or giving them devotional material. Yet second, and more intriguingly, these traditional forms of faith are not only seen as being immoral by the public, but *unchristian*. These features came together in the case of rugby players Israel Folau and Billy Vunipola. After comments and posts spanning a number of years, in which Folau repeated the historic Christian teaching that marriage was between one man and one woman, and that gay and lesbian people risked judgement if they did not repent, Folau was sacked by the Australian Rugby Union, while Vunipola was disciplined for 'liking' his comments on Facebook.[49] The ensuing media controversy was noteworthy for the number of non-religious commentators who not only thought that Folau and Vunipola were wrong, but that they did not represent 'true' Christianity. Statements and actions by Christians in the public sphere not only risk being rejected as wrong, therefore, but contrary to the teaching of Jesus and the Bible.[50]

The desire of the state and civil society to police speech that is considered hateful or offensive can also be seen in the changing fortunes of the crime of blasphemy. Blasphemy was the crime of making offensive or defamatory statements regarding

God or the Christian faith. Due to the secularisation of Scottish society, blasphemy has long since ceased to be punished, because God – for most Scots – is no longer considered sacred and worthy of protection. But the idea of the sacred and its protection has not disappeared. That is because the idea of 'the sacred' does not only relate to religion, but to *anything* that is set apart from everyday life, and deemed to warrant special veneration. One example would be the war memorials examined earlier. Increasingly, however, it is the individual and their identity that are deemed sacred, inviolable and worthy of protection, with Scots law safeguarding the honour of the individual and their identity as once it did God.[51]

This creates difficulties for Christians who hold traditional views on sexuality and gender. The Asher case in Northern Ireland saw a Christian bakery taken to court for failing to bake a cake that promoted same-sex marriage, and Christian Unions and Pro-Life student groups have been disaffiliated or shut down on university campuses for challenging contemporary mores.[52] In other examples, Franklin Graham recently saw his bookings in stadiums and theatres cancelled across the country, and Destiny Church had an event pulled from the Usher Hall in Edinburgh. It is noteworthy that in both cases Christian clergy campaigned to have these events cancelled. It is clear, then, that free speech – whether it ever existed – is now increasingly curtailed in Scotland, a reality that the Church must keep in mind when engaging in mission.

While it would be incorrect to say that Christians face persecution or serious discrimination in today's society, *it is* correct to believe that public institutions and civil society increasingly set limits to the Church's actions. The rights of freedom of conscience, expression and assembly have been weighed in the balance with those of sexuality and gender and found wanting. This creates dilemmas for Church leaders, who must make theological and strategic decisions as to what they wish to say – or not say – in a public setting. Accepting the rules of civil discourse can bring greater access to public institutions, funds and the respect of secular commentators. The question, however, is whether this access is worth the price.

Conclusion

In this chapter, we have examined the political context of contemporary Scotland, witnessing how the state tolerates some aspects of Christian belief and practice while marginalising others. As we saw, public perceptions of Christianity have changed significantly in the course of the twentieth and twenty-first centuries. Scotland has moved from a country animated by faith, Unionism and imperial identity to one in which secularity, pluralism and civic nationalism reign. While Scotland may have lost its faith in Christ, it preserves Calvinism's desire to remake society, leading to the adoption of progressive values based on equality and freedom. The preeminent symbols of new Scotland are the Parliament and the Rainbow flag, which can now be found in every public institution and business. If churches are to engage in public life they must adopt a socially acceptable form of faith and spirituality that is supportive of – or at least acquiesces to – the prevailing order, or else risk social ostracism and further marginalisation.

Nevertheless, the desire for a better Scotland, one in which people are treated with equality and dignity and in which our environment is protected and safeguarded, provides an opportunity for the Church to proclaim God's desire for a re-created world. God wants Scotland to become the best it can be, and the Church can affirm this aspect of contemporary culture without being drawn into divisive constitutional debate. Indeed, by not only *arguing* for a better Scotland but *manifesting* it in concrete communities of faith, the Church can – at its best – model what Scotland dreams of becoming.[53]

6

Spiritual Context

In this chapter, we turn to that aspect of contemporary Scotland that is most directly relevant to the mission of the Church: its spiritual context. We shall see how the changes recounted in previous chapters have effected the virtual collapse of churchgoing in Scotland, with a corresponding decline in Christian belief and practice. We shall also examine the widespread indifference to religious questions that this decline has given rise to, as well as the spiritualities and belief systems that have taken the place of orthodox Christianity. We shall conclude with an account of the *Christian* context of Scotland, charting the development of a 'new sectarianism' between Christians, and the prospects for liberal and conservative Christianity in contemporary Scottish society.

Change and Decay

Before we are in a position to analyse our spiritual and religious context, we must first examine Scottish Christianity in numbers.

The statistical information available to us reveals long-term decline in religiosity, whether this be reckoned in terms of church membership, church attendance, affiliation, participation in religious rituals or belief.[1] In the Church Census of 1851, somewhere between 40% and 60% of the Scottish population attended Sunday worship. In 1999, however, it was only 8%. In 1900, 50% of British children went to Sunday school, but by 1998 it was only 4%.[2] In 1930, the Kirk baptised 44% of all Scottish children, but by 2010 it baptised only 7%. Just after the Second World War, 84% of Scottish marriages were religion- or belief-based, while by 2017 only 40% were, with the Humanist Society of Scotland taking the largest share of these.[3]

The 2011 Census and 2016 Scottish Social Attitudes Survey reveal a nation in which a slim majority still identifies with the Christian faith in some way. In 2011, 53.8% of Scots identified as being Christian: 32.4% identified as Church of Scotland, 15.9% identified as Roman Catholic and approximately 5.5% of Scots identified as 'other Christian', which includes everything from Quakers to Reformed Presbyterians. The most significant feature of the 2011 Census, however, is that those who identify as non-religious now comprise 36.7% of the population, up from 27.6% in 2001. This is particularly significant for the Church of Scotland, which lost approximately 10% of its affiliates in the same period, suggesting that the growth of non-religion has been largely at the expense of the Kirk. Through immigration from Eastern Europe, the Roman Catholic Church maintained its affiliation rates between 2001 to 2011, but not in terms of marriages and baptisms, which show a downward trend.[4] Despite their sometimes high public profile, non-Christian religions comprise only 2.5% of the population, with Islam – at 1.4% – being the largest non-Christian religion.[5]

While these statistics give us a picture of overall religiosity and non-religion in Scotland, there are important regional differences, reflective of particular histories and contexts. While the national average of non-religion stands at 36.7%, this rises to 46.3% in Fife, 45.4% in Shetland and 45.2% in Midlothian, with Aberdeen City claiming the crown for the least religious part of Scotland at 48.1%. The highest concentration of Roman Catholicism in Scotland is to be found in the industrial areas of Greater Glasgow, where 37% of the population in Inverclyde and 27.3% in Glasgow City are Catholic. Importantly, this is higher than Glasgow's Church of Scotland affiliation, which stands at 23.1%. The Church of Scotland's highest rates of affiliation can be found in the largely rural areas of Argyll and Bute, Dumfries and Galloway, Angus and the Hebrides and Orkney, where Kirk affiliation all stand at over 40%. Worryingly, the Kirk's lowest affiliation rates are found in Glasgow, Edinburgh and Aberdeen, Scotland's most influential centres of finance, media and culture.[6]

We gain another insight into Scottish religiosity when we turn to church attendance. In the most recent Scottish Church Census, an astonishing 44.3% of the population of Eilean Siar were found to attend Sunday worship, the highest in the country. Approximately 10% of the population attended church in Glasgow and Inverclyde, while in Scotland's capital only 6.5% ventured out to worship. Unsurprisingly, the lowest church-going population was that of Aberdeen City, where only 5.7% went to church. Even in the Aberdeen region, however, there were differences, with a higher rate of 8.4% attending in the Aberdeenshire council area.[7]

While there are regional differences in churchgoing and affiliation, apart from Eilean Siar, the 2011 Census and 2016 Church Census demonstrate that this variation is not significant enough to give us second thoughts regarding the secularisation of Scottish culture. Protestants may be stronger in one area and Roman Catholics in another, but the overall picture is much the same.

This is confirmed when we turn to the results of the Scottish Social Attitudes Survey for 2011 and 2016. While 36.7% in the 2011 government Census identified with 'non-religion', when the Social Attitudes Survey asked: 'Do you consider yourself as belonging to any particular religion?' 53% of Scots in 2011 answered 'No', rising to 58% in 2016.[8] The suggestion is that, when asked to be more specific, Scots display higher rates of non-religion than census questions based on affiliation alone. If these national statistics are worrying, we gain an even more frightening picture when we turn to differences between age groups. In 2011, 67% of 18–34 year olds said they did not consider themselves to belong to any particular religion. By 2016, however, this figure had risen to 74%. This stands in marked contrast to those aged 65+. Only 30% of this age group did not identify with a religion in 2011, and only 34% in 2016.[9]

The Scottish Social Attitudes Survey reveals that religious decline has not yet plateaued and, if anything, has speeded up in recent years. This is also shown by statistics concerning another aspect of religiosity: life events. In 2011, 19.1% of weddings were conducted by the Church of Scotland and 5.9% by the Roman Catholic Church, with the Humanist Society of Scotland conducting 8.5%. By 2016, however, the situation had changed, with the Humanist Society of Scotland conducting 13.6% of weddings, the Kirk conducting 12.6% and the Roman Catholic Church 4.6%. Once again, the statistics seem to suggest that it is the Kirk that is losing out most in the turn towards non-religion, a fact perhaps explained by its historically high levels of nominalism.[10]

While these figures seem unambiguous, a prominent line of critique from Grace Davie argues that while these statistics do display a decline in Christianity, they primarily reflect disaffiliation from organised religion and religious institutions. In this line of thinking, the people of Scotland 'believe without belonging' and still have a moderate level of Christian belief.[11] This is not borne out by the statistics, however, which in addition to declining rates of affiliation and life events also reveal a corresponding decline in belief. In a survey from 2018, for example, 49.2% of Scottish respondents said that they do not have any belief in God, with only 31% suggesting that they do.[12] This certainly reveals that more people believe in God than attend Church – something that is not in doubt – but it is still significantly below the affiliation rates recorded in the census. In the absence of evidence to the contrary, there is no reason to think that belief in God will not continue to decline.

Christianity and Culture

These trends are not only reflected in statistics, however, but in contemporary Scottish music and culture. We see the changing fortunes of the nation's relationship with Christianity in the lyrics of that most quintessential of Scottish bands, The Proclaimers. There are references to prayer and eternal life scattered across the Reid brothers' first album *This is the Story* (1987). These references increase dramatically on their second album *Sunshine on Leith* (1988), whose title track – sung at many a Hibernian match – is essentially a hymn of thanksgiving to God for the life of the singer and his partner. The faith of The Proclaimers reaches its climax in 1994 with 'The More I Believe' from *Hit the Highway*, which by invoking the omniscience of God, final judgement and justification by faith alone represents some of the most evangelical lyrics in contemporary pop.

When we come to 2012, however, the faith of the Reid brothers sounds increasingly shaky. In 'What I Believe' from *Like Comedy*, they wonder aloud about the compatibility of science and faith in a twenty-first-century European nation like Scotland, and by 2015's 'Through Him' from *Let's Hear It for the Dogs* they sing of their disdain for street evangelists, and of the Gospel message presented by them.

If there is a trajectory of spiritual change in the work of The Proclaimers, there is more ambiguity in the work of other contemporary Scottish musicians. In Arab Strap's 'The Night Before the Funeral' from *Philophobia* (1998), Aidan Moffat displays a critical attitude towards faith, expressing his disbelief and disengagement when attending the funeral of a family member. Yet by 2009, Moffat – though an unbeliever – can express in 'Atheist's Lament' from *How to Get to Heaven from Scotland* a wistful desire for the comfort and certainties of faith.

This mixed bag of reactions towards faith can also be seen in former Aberdeen divinity student and lead singer of Franz Ferdinand, Alex Kapranos. In 'The Fallen' from *You Could Have It So Much Better* (2005), Kapranos deploys a wide range of biblical imagery, showing respect for the person of Christ while rejecting religious hypocrisy and violence. Later in his career, Kapranos displayed a similar nostalgia for faith in 'Fresh Strawberries' from *Right Thoughts, Right Words, Right Actions* (2013), singing repeatedly of his desire – yet inability – to believe.

In contrast to this ambiguity, the band CHVRCHES criticise the hypocrisy and dogmatism of faith in 'Deliverance' from *Love is Dead* (2018). In a recent interview, vocalist Lauren Mayberry said:

Growing up in Scotland and living in Glasgow, you see the heritage that religion has had and how something that in theory is about kindness and community and caring for each other is used to persecute people.[13]

In the same interview, another band member – raised Roman Catholic – describes the disgust he felt when his younger sister came home from school one day in tears, having been shown a video imagining a conversation between an aborted child and its mother.

That a younger, socially conscious band such as CHVRCHES would hold such views in twenty-first-century Scotland is not surprising, if still disheartening. In contrast to such critical themes, the lyrics of Stuart Murdoch from Belle and Sebastian are noteworthy for their positive references to faith. Christian and biblical themes are found throughout their work, with songs such as 'If You Find Yourself Caught in Love' from *Dear Catastrophe Waitress* (2003) seeing Murdoch appeal to his listeners to thank God for their lives and ask him for the new hope that comes with faith.

These works – whether critical, supportive or ambivalent – pale in comparison, however, to the simple *absence* of Christian references in contemporary Scottish culture. Even accounting for differences of scale, there are few – if any – mentions of clergy, churches or faith in Scottish broadcasting, as compared with English programming such as *Rev*, *The Vicar of Dibley*, *Grantchester*, *Emmerdale* and *Coronation Street*, which all feature clergy characters. While these programmes often feature storylines in which clergy must come to terms with contemporary morals and sexuality through their own – sometimes spectacular – falls from grace, their presence speaks of a continuing interest in the Church, and Christian themes of sin, grace and vocation.

The reason for this absence is that the prevailing attitude towards faith in contemporary Scotland is one of sheer *indifference*. This is sometimes hidden to Church leaders and members, whose faith is the centre of their lives. Yet the massive indifference of Britons and Scots towards religion is well attested through a range of studies. At the heart of religious indifference is a reality identified by a report of the Church of Scotland: 'One of the main barriers to belief is simply the fact that many people feel no need of it.'[14] That report – much like our analysis in Chapters 3 and 4 – identities the self-sufficiency achieved through welfare and affluence as an important part of this indifference.[15] All of one's needs and desires – so it is thought – can be met through material and social means alone, and there is therefore no need to turn to religion. If I have mental health issues I can receive counselling or psychiatric treatment. If I want to be a better person I can buy a book on popular ethics, or join a local volunteering project. This self-sufficiency and self-satisfaction means that the majority of questions asked by Christians such as 'How am I saved?', or 'What does God want me to do?' are of little relevance to the overwhelming major-ity of Scots. As Bruce puts it, 'The arguments that excited the Victorians and Edwardians now fall on deaf ears.'[16] In addition to this simple lack of interest is a general sense that Christianity has been tried and found wanting. Like communism or other ideologies of yesteryear, it is now simply passé, redundant, 'naff'.[17] The result is that the Church 'occupies only a little shelf space in the supermarket of ideas in a pluralist and multi-faith society'.[18] The Gospel may be the greatest of all treasures, yet few Scots want what the Church is selling.

From this, it may be thought that those indifferent to reli-gion have adopted a strong anti-religious identity. Yet this is not the case. As Lee puts it, the majority of the population are so indifferent to religion that they are equally indifferent to being anti-religious.[19] When pushed to define their position, the more articulate or intellectual of Scots may disclose a position such as agnosticism. Yet this is only a result of direct question-ing, and may play little or no role in their personal identities or everyday lives. Where this can change, however, is when their rights, or the rights of others, are threatened, as in the case of LGBT+ issues. In these situations, indifference towards religion can give way to anger and activism, but will return to relative indifference when the perceived threat is overcome.[20]

The exception to this general rule is atheism and organised

anti-religious scepticism. Atheism has achieved a greater public profile in recent years due to the activities of the so-called New Atheists. This loosely affiliated group of authors took their impetus from the Islamist attacks of September 11. Yet given their personal religious backgrounds, and the Anglophone culture they were raised in, they have focused an inordinate amount of time not on Islam but on Christianity.

There is little new in the intellectual position of recent high-profile atheists. Their arguments are drawn from a rich British and American tradition of scepticism and anti-clericalism that stretches back to the early modern period.[21] The arguments they deploy do not refute the Christianity held by the majority of Christians, but a form of Christian theology that is now held by very few people in Scotland apart from young earth six-day creationists.[22] The result is that mainstream atheists and unbelievers have increasingly distanced themselves from their more polemical peers.[23]

What *is* new with New Atheists, however, is the level of publicity afforded to their views, along with the high degree of public acceptance these views have found. In previous ages, 'atheist' was a slur that one hurled at one's opponents, and something to be vigorously refuted. Yet it is now acceptable – and even 'cool' – to describe oneself as an atheist. While a relatively small number of Scots defined themselves as 'atheist' in the last census,[24] this does not mean that the sceptical attitudes and beliefs of New Atheism do not have wide currency. They do, and they inform a wide range of non-religious and irreligious identities stretching from indifference to outright rejection of the Christian faith.

Although atheist and rationalist ideas may have wide currency in Scottish society, the main objection to the Church is not that it is against reason, but that it is against the moral values of contemporary society, most commonly in relation to abortion and LGBT+ rights. When organisations such as the Humanist Society of Scotland tap into this moral and political animus against faith, they can achieve some level of political success, such as banning certain forms of religious instruction in schools or removing church groups from the grounds of reproductive health clinics. Yet the base strength of organised atheism in Scottish society is minimal. While the Scottish Secular Society has achieved notoriety for its angry letters to newspapers up and down the land, it is run by a handful of individuals. As both myself and Steve Bruce have argued, the strength of organised unbelief is directly related to the strength of religious conviction in society, one reason why the high-water mark of organised atheism was the Victorian Age.[25]

While atheism garners headlines, and is in some respects the 'face' of contemporary unbelief, the small number of determined atheists makes it a loud but largely ineffectual opponent. Indeed, by keeping questions of religion in public consciousness, vocal atheism is generally *beneficial* to the Christian faith, helping to maintain the public profile and importance of religion, and providing opportunities for Christians to present an account of the hope that is in them.[26] In short, organised atheism helps to keep the Church in business. The same cannot be said, however, for religious indifference. Indifference is the most serious obstacle to the advancement of the Gospel in contemporary Scotland. As the outcome of a consumerist and materialist culture, indifference robs the Gospel of relevance, and presents the Church with an opponent whose position is so self-satisfied and secure that it does not even deign to defend itself. Unlike apologetics, which can be used to successfully refute atheist arguments, fighting indifference is like boxing with jelly, and – as we shall explore in later chapters – requires a specific set of tools and strategies.

Scottish Spiritualities

While the predominant spiritual attitude of contemporary Scots towards Christianity is indifference mixed with scepticism, this does not mean that Scots have completely abandoned the spiritual aspects of life. The spirituality in question is heavily individual and materialistic, however, and is more closed to transcendent or supernatural realities than is sometimes supposed.

The most defining aspect of Scottish spirituality from the perspective of the Church is *idolatry*: the worship of material and worldly things as if they were God. This approach to culture has a long history within Israel and the Church, and was central to the development of monotheism, the worship of the transcendent and all-powerful Creator God. Israel's polemic against the pagan cultures that surrounded it was twofold: first, that the gods they worshipped were not real, being projections of their own desires and fears, and second, that their faith in idols would ultimately destroy them. Psalm 135:15–18 illustrates this well:

> The idols of the nations are silver and gold,
>   the work of human hands.
> They have mouths, but they do not speak;
>   they have eyes, but they do not see;
> they have ears, but they do not hear,
>   and there is no breath in their mouths.
> Those who make them
>   and all who trust them
>   shall become like them.

Israel's polemic against idolatry was given new impetus at the Reformation. In an influential account of idolatry, Martin Luther argued that:

> A 'god' is the term for that to which we are to look for all good and in which we are to find refuge in all need ... For these two belong together, faith and God. Anything on which your heart relies and depends, I say, that is really your God.[27]

Overdependence on any created object, idea or person amounts to *worship*, and whatever we worship we treat as our God.

While the issue of idolatry divided Scottish Christians for centuries, such differences are minor when viewed in relation to a contemporary culture that venerates *almost anything* other than God. Scottish society is full of references to the religious and spiritual significance of objects or services. Beauty

products called *Pure* invite us to purge ourselves of the physical sins of ugliness or laziness, while bath products named
Ritual offer a practice that can remove our stress and anxiety.
Faith shoes allow us to meet our daily chores and schedules
with confidence, while *Sky* television invites us to believe in
better. Even spas and bottled water call to mind earlier habits
of visiting holy wells and springs to find vitality and healing.
One of the most interesting examples of consumer idolatry
comes in a recent publicity drive for 3 Phones. In these adverts,
a flickering text first reads '#PhonesAreGood' before changing
to '#PhonesAre*God*'. The message is not hard to grasp.

The same flirtation with idolatry can be seen in the corporate
identities of businesses and other organisations. In the past, it
was the Church – and perhaps God – who had a *mission*. Now
it is businesses that have 'Mission Statements', along with
'Values', 'Ethics' and 'Philosophies', phrases which all have
their origin in the Church and Christian NGOs.

None of this borrowing is intentional or conscious, of course.
It is not as if those who enjoy Sky Sports or Pure moisturiser
are consciously worshipping these things as divine. Yet in the
context of the consumerist world surveyed in Chapter 4, and
in light of the secularisation of Scottish society and the pluralisation of religion, it is hard to escape the conclusion that in
Western consumerism we see a blurring between the material
and the divine, one which, in a post-Christian world, serves
a spiritual purpose. The destiny of Scotland is no longer to
become a godly commonwealth, but an affluent consumer
market. As Leonard Cohen put it:

As he died to make men holy, let us die to make things cheap[28]

It is possible, of course, to dismiss this line of interpretation as
misanthropic and overly gloomy. They are the fulminations,
some might say, of a formerly privileged majority, now grown
bitter and resentful due to their new status as a minority. Yet
pastoral experience suggests otherwise. Anyone with ears to
hear and eyes to see will soon recognise that according ultimate value to things that are not God – whether it be people,

success, beauty, popularity, a world view or anything else – contributes to the anxiety, despair and unhappiness that typify a growing number of Scots, particularly the young. Simply because a position is overstated does not mean that it is wrong.

While idolatry represents a particular lens with which to interpret contemporary culture, one with a stronger basis in the social sciences is the phenomenon of personal spiritualty. The popularity of notions such as 'spiritual but not religious' allow Church leaders and members to take comfort in the idea that there is a hidden wellspring of spirituality waiting to be tapped, and that, if the correct approach can be found, Scotland can be won back for the faith.

The word 'spirituality' has its roots in Roman Catholic tradition, being particularly associated with the spiritual disciplines of St Ignatius Loyola.[29] Yet the use of the term to describe a form of personal religion unconnected to the Church is of very recent origin, achieving popularity only from the 1960s onward. That is because it is a direct result of the changes in Scottish culture described in Chapters 3 and 4. These changes gave Scots the financial independence to break away from community ties and deference to wealthy elites, and choose a spiritual outlook that appealed to them personally. While these changes are sometimes typified as leading to the *privatisation* of religion, this is not quite accurate. After all, these alternative spiritualities often garner a high public profile. A better way of understanding the changes that took place is to see them as the *individualisation* of religion: the granting of authority on religious questions to the individual, who is as much an invention of prosperity as the spiritual questions she is now asked to adjudicate on.

Before entering into further analysis of spirituality, one thing must be made clear: there is no agreed academic or popular definition of spirituality.[30] It is a 'vague and indistinct category',[31] which might be classified, at best, as 'following intuitions that can lead to fullness of life'.[32] Given its foundation in the particular experiences, beliefs and desires of disparate people, this lack of definition should not surprise us. Despite how vague the concept is, however, it still enjoys popular appeal, and has led commentators to hold wildly differing views on its nature and significance. On the one hand, a number of writers follow a 'social narcissism' critique of spirituality. For these commentators, 'spiritualities offer succour and relief to an alienated and dehumanised congregation of individualised consumers'.[33] Spirituality is not only an aspect of materialist consumerism, but is also one of the means by which Western, capitalist democracies insulate themselves from reform and rebellion. According to Bauman, spirituality creates 'perfect consumers', who rather than challenging the existing social and political system retreat into themselves, and the quietist darkness of mystery.[34] On the other hand, writers such as MacKian have cautioned that we should not seek to explain spirituality away by seeing it only as a symptom of diseased capitalism, and that to ignore the supernatural or transcendent elements in popular spirituality is to misinterpret them.[35] Similarly, Drane has argued that despite some of its aberrations, the Church ignores popular spirituality at its peril, for it is now part of the lived reality of many of our neighbours.[36]

There is truth in all of these viewpoints. It is certainly the case that individualised religion and spirituality are direct results of welfare security, personal affluence and consumer society. Yet the Church undermines its ministry and mission if it ignores the lived experience of ordinary men and women. We can take social realities seriously, and understand them accurately, without agreeing with them. Where those with a more positive attitude towards spirituality go wrong, however, is thinking that popular spirituality is either the same thing as Christianity, or necessarily leads to it. When sociologist Linda Woodhead presented her findings on contemporary spirituality to a group of Church of England bishops, they were incredulous that the spirituality she discovered did not lead directly to Christian faith.[37] Yet the bishops were wrong. There are materialist spiritualities, pagan spiritualities, atheist spiritualties, agnostic spiritualities and Humanist spiritualities. There are countless rivers of spirituality and they do not flow inexorably to the sea of Christianity. They follow their own course and have their own unique ends. As Inglehart notes, this is one of the ironies of our contemporary move towards postmodernity. More people may be interested in spirituality and the 'big questions', but would never for a moment consider going to church.[38] While we must listen to the spiritual experiences of non-Christians and seek to understand them, we must also be careful not to equate Christianity with spiritualty so closely that the Church ceases to exercise the ministry of the Gospel, and becomes instead a midwife to the private religiosities of confused and hurting people.

Whatever stance we take towards spirituality, it is important to assess its scale and social importance properly. Despite its salient public profile, there are indications that spirituality is of limited relevance to the majority of Scots. The first indication concerns gender. In a recent study, it was found that the overwhelming majority of those interested in non-Christian spiritual practices were women, who in many situations accounted for 100% of participants.[39] While part of this high female representation is due to negative experiences women have had with the Church,[40] it also arises from the connections between spirituality and physical health. Studies have shown that women are more concerned with health and fitness than men, and alternative spiritualities often use the same language of 'wellbeing' and 'mind, body and spirit' that feature in practices such as Pilates and Yoga. As Trzebiatowska puts it, 'The key question then becomes, not why are women more spiritual than men, but why are women apparently much more interested than men in a certain type of health and exercise.'[41]

A related issue concerns the connection between spirituality and counselling. Counselling, psychology and psychiatry have important roots in Christianity and philosophical theology. Yet the opposite is also true, for therapy has directly and indirectly influenced the language and very notion of spirituality. As Bregman describes, much of the basic language of spirituality – self, wellbeing, self-knowledge, self-transformation, acceptance and so on – come from counselling and therapy. This is not surprising, as spirituality and counselling serve very similar therapeutic functions. They are both related to the self, and seek the liberty and salvation of the self not in inherited traditions, but in whatever 'works' for the individual. Spirituality, then, can be understood as a non-specialist and holistic form of counselling, seeking coherence not only in one's life narrative, but in everything.[42] Indeed, in a Scottish study by Kasselstrand, when those interviewed were asked to describe their spirituality, they typically responded in terms of their own personal peace, strength, power and potential. The 'spirituality' in question was so mundane and 'this worldly' that Kasselstrand questions whether spirituality is a religious category at all.[43]

While gender and exposure to therapeutic culture are important indicators of interest in spirituality, this cannot be separated from the further factor of *age*. In the 2001 Scottish Social Attitudes study, those who said that they were spiritual were largely from the baby-boomer generation who came of age in the 1960s and 1970s, the period that – as we have seen – was the first to disassociate itself from institutional Christianity. Apart from this group, interest in spirituality was limited. When the survey asked respondents if they were religious or spiritual, only 16.4% of those asked said they were spiritual, while 35.5% said they were religious and – crucially – 48.1% said they were neither.[44] While more research is needed in this area, it is not unreasonable to conclude that 'spiritual but not religious' is a placeholder term for the transition period between Christian and post-Christian Scotland, from a form of communal religion dependent on the Church to one dependent on consumerism and individualism.

Humanism: the New Normal

That conclusion is supported by what is perhaps the most notable change in the spiritual and religious complexion of Scotland: the rise of Humanist weddings, funerals and other life events.

The first reason for the growth in Humanist life events is, somewhat paradoxically, a preference for ceremonies that incorporate elements of ritual. In Kasselstrand's study, Scots who had chosen Humanist weddings were shown to be dissatisfied with the bureaucratic feel of civil weddings, and preferred instead the opportunities for symbolic acts and traditional motifs that Humanist weddings afforded.[45] The lesson from this appears to be that Scots still prefer a quasi-religious element to their life events, but don't see Christianity or any other organised religion as being connected with this preference.

The second and third reasons for the growth of Humanist ceremonies, however, flow directly from Humanist philosophy itself. In a break from Scotland's Calvinist and Roman Catholic past, Humanism affirms the basic goodness of all people, and denies the need for a Saviour. What, after all, do we need to be saved from if we are all inherently good? This affirmation of human goodness gives rise, in turn, to an affirmation of the personal choices and life-narratives of individuals and couples, and the location of these choices and narratives within the universal experience of our common humanity.

This is another way in which Humanist ceremonies are quasi-religious in nature, for they enable Scots to experience a limited form of transcendence. Humanism provides two interrelated kinds of transcendence: transcendence through *close relationships* and universal transcendence through the idea of *humanity*. We saw in Chapter 4 that one of the most important forms of transcendence in contemporary life is through close relationships with others. From Disney cartoons to *Cosmopolitan* and Hollywood blockbusters, the personal fulfilment that comes through romantic and family ties is consistently held up as being the most important for human beings. If Luckmann is right that the participation of individuals in realities greater than themselves is the essence of religion,[46] in offering rituals at birth, marriage and death, Humanism provides Scots with opportunities to express and enact this transcendence. Naming Ceremonies – the equivalent of christenings – express the child's transition from 'bare birth' into a family in which they are named, honoured and given a place, along with the transcendence of existing identities that adults experience when they become parents. Humanist *marriages* express and enact the truth that individuals can only achieve fulfilment by transcending their narrow self-interest and living with and for others, a reality brought about by the power of love. Importantly, the ability of Humanist celebrants to solemnise same-sex marriages brings them in line with the public affirmation of LGBT+ communities outlined in Chapter 5. Finally, at the end of life, Humanist *funerals* express the unconditional worth of all people through the celebration of life, and the dignity and significance of the narratives and meanings they forge for themselves. In all of these life events, however, the skill of the Humanist celebrant comes not only in expressing the personal meanings of individuals and families, but in their weaving of these personal forms of self-transcendence into the universal experience of humanity. For just as Christians – as members of Christ's Body and the communion of saints – are never truly alone, so too is no man or woman an island, but part of the great family of humanity. The individual may blossom and flourish, wither and perish, yet humanity lives for ever.[47] As such, by fully living our own *particular* lives, we participate in a spiritual reality that is greater than all of us.

Because of these features, Humanism is the ideal spiritual philosophy for contemporary Scots, and it is no surprise that its popularity is growing. Many Christians will feel threatened by this rising popularity, and the rejection of Christianity it implicitly – and sometimes explicitly – implies. Yet the Church must also recognise the skill and creativity of many Humanist celebrants in the conduct of meaningful life events, and the great joy and comfort they provide for a growing number of Scots. In the wake of mass secularisation and the disenchantment of the world, Humanist ceremonies are oases of meaning that express our deepest personal loves, and connect us to our fellow human beings through the pathos of shared joys and common sorrows. Humanist celebrants offer an important public service, and the Church must be charitable enough to acknowledge this.

While there is much to appreciate in Humanist life events, no account of Humanism would be complete without an examination of its *shadow-side*. For a focus upon idiosyncratic meanings, and the importance of a small number of family and friends for self-fulfilment, mean that the form of transcendence offered by Humanism is limited, and can easily lapse into self-indulgence and narcissism. While it is good that individuals seek self-fulfilment through spouses, children, family and friends, this is *not* true transcendence. If the only people who are significant to us are those we like and identity with, we are no better than the sinner who loves those who love him and hates those who hate him (Luke 6:32–4; Matthew 5:46–7). We 'transcend' ourselves only to find ourselves with people who are just like us. The same lack of transcendence is seen in the conception of universal humanity that provides the ballast to the personal narratives that drive Humanist ceremonies. As was recognised as long ago as the 1930s, Humanism *does not* encompass all of humanity, for it is dependent on challenging and excluding people, ideas and traditions deemed *in*human.[48] The evil of the twentieth century furnishes much evidence for this. The only true form of universal humanity is of a *redeemed* humanity, a humanity whose faults are named, forgiven and transcended by Christ. *True* transcendence is participation in the one who is fully transcendent, the Holy Trinity of Father, Son and Spirit, and membership of a Church created from every cultural, religious and psychological background, including – crucially – people who are *not* like us, and who we *do not like*. In short, Christianity is true Humanism.

The Broken Body of Christ

While many Scots have abandoned their faith, or taken up other forms of alternative spirituality, this does not mean that the Scottish Church is finished. We must therefore conclude our survey of Scottish spirituality with an examination of the dechurched, and the different Christian traditions that together comprise the Scottish Church.

The process of secularisation we have been examining has focused primarily on those who have lost their faith, or never had faith to begin with. Between these groups and churchgoers, however, are a wide variety of Scots. Some are those who believe in God or a higher power, but who would rarely if ever go to Church. Others are those who combine pagan or alternative spirituality with a belief in the power of prayer in Jesus' name. Others still are those whose theology and practice are still largely Christian, but who – often for personal reasons – no longer feel able to be part of a congregation.

As we saw above, there are surprising levels of Christian belief and practice in Scotland outwith the Church. In the work of Francis and Richter, it was shown that many of these people have suffered traumas that should have been picked up by more proactive pastoral care, or have fallen foul of British – and Scottish – reserve, when friends and neighbours did not want to pry into why they stopped attending church.[49] In Scotland, Aisthorpe's *Invisible Church* recorded the experiences of a range of Christian and semi-Christian Scots who are currently not being reached by traditional forms of Church. The problem – so Aisthorpe's hypothesis goes – is not with the Church per se, but with the communities and styles of worship it currently offers. Change these and the dechurched may return.

Yet how many are open? Aisthorpe's own study revealed some ambiguity here. Of those who claimed that faith was 'central' to their lives, only 41% said that they would ever consider rejoining the Church. While analogous research has not been carried out in Scotland, a Church of England report found that only around 20% of those currently not attending church would consider doing so.[50] On one level, this is a depressing statistic, as 80% of those not attending church have no interest in doing so. Yet it does suggest that among the broken Body of Christ in Scotland, there are still a minority who, on some level, wish to be united with their brothers and sisters, and would – in the right circumstances – join or rejoin them.

This brings us to the Scottish Church itself. In the wake of schism, welfare security, personal affluence and consumer culture, Scotland has undergone mass secularisation. The result is that, on average, only 7.2% of Scots attend church each Sunday, which means 92.8% do not.[51] This has not only given rise to the closure of many churches, but a reduction in energy, morale and finance among those that remain. Of churchgoers in Scotland, 56.7% are over 55, with this proportion being higher in traditional denominations such as the Church of Scotland and Roman Catholic Church.[52] In the absence of younger people to take their place, churchgoers are having to bear more burdens into old age, a reality that privileges maintenance over mission.

While the Church can now only rely on approximately 7.2% of the Scottish population, the situation is actually worse than this sobering statistic conveys. For it is compounded by a further factor that directly and indirectly effects the success of mission in contemporary Scotland: Christian disunity. In Chapter 1, we saw that Christ's Church is one. Yet as we discovered in Chapters 2 and 3, the Christians of Scotland have failed to maintain this unity. This failure led to religious violence and schism culminating in the Disruption, an event that directly contributed to the secularisation of Scotland. Christ commanded, the Church failed to act, and now we and the people of Scotland are facing the consequences

We are heirs to the fratricidal disputes of earlier times. The 2011 Census revealed that there are over 80 different Christian denominations and communions in Scotland.[53] While this plurality brings some advantages – which we shall examine in Chapter 8 – the fragmented, uncoordinated and sometimes hostile state of the Scottish Church greatly reduces its power to resist the social, political and spiritual pressures that animate contemporary society. Very often we are competing against each other, rather than cooperating for the blessing of Scotland.

In previous centuries, the major division in Scottish Christianity was between Protestants on the one hand and Roman Catholics on the other. Now, however, another division has arisen in the Lord's field of wheat and tares: that between conservative Christians and liberal or moderate ones. This has given rise to what might be termed a *new sectarianism*, one which hinders the ability of the Church to coordinate its activities and pool its resources to meet the challenges of the age.

This othering had been present many times in Scottish history, yet it took on a new form when Scotland experienced the social and economic revolution explored in Chapter 3.

Scottish Christians were then faced with a number of choices: do we hold firm to our history and traditions, or do we move with the times? If we do move with the times, what is dispensable and what should be retained?

In the Church of Scotland – and to a lesser extent the Scottish Episcopal Church – growing tensions arose over moves to ordain gay and lesbian ministers, and to celebrate same-sex marriages.[54] Whereas evangelicals in the mid-nineteenth century seceded from the Kirk in an organised and coordinated manner, today's evangelicals have – following the pluralisation and individualisation of society – simply voted with their feet and left.[55] The secession of thousands of evangelicals from the Church of Scotland and other traditional denominations represents a *silent disruption*.[56] Importantly, this is the case even for the children of members and clergy from traditional denominations, who feel little or no loyalty towards the churches in which they were raised. While less pronounced, a similar situation exists within the Roman Catholic Church, where traditionalists – sometimes identifying with Benedict XVI – grow frustrated with the apparently liberalising tendencies of Pope Francis.

In the Scottish Church Census of 2016, Brierley determined that 40% of Scottish congregations could be classified as 'evangelical'. Among independent churches – understood as being self-financing and unrelated to a wider denomination – 90% defined themselves as evangelical. Despite 40% of Scottish congregations classifying themselves as evangelical, only 20% of Church of Scotland congregations classified themselves as such, even if the number of evangelical ministers and members is higher.[57] While Brierley's categorisation showed that 'mainstream' evangelicalism is growing in the Church of Scotland, he determined that the proportion of 'Reformed Evangelicals' – understood as conservative evangelicals of a broadly Calvinist theology who reject charismatic Christianity – has more than halved between 1994 and 2016, a decline due, in part, to the silent disruption just described.[58]

The Church Census of 2016 also provided information regarding the relative strength of 'liberal' or 'broad' churchmanship in Scotland. Brierley found that this category of churchmanship was in heavy decline across the Scottish Church, more than halving between 1994 and 2016.[59] If one discounts his rather vague 'Reformed' category – which could apply to a wide range of theological positions – one finds that the proportion of evangelical and liberal Christians in the Scottish Church is roughly equal, encompassing a third each.[60] Nevertheless, Roman Catholics already outnumber liberal Protestants in most categories, while at the same time showing less sign of numerical decline.[61] Moreover, the current equanimity of liberals and evangelicals in the Scottish Church belies the heavy age concentration of Scottish liberals. Evangelicals match or outmatch liberals in every age category apart from that of 65+, suggesting that the liberal constituency in Scotland dates from the mid-twentieth century, and that, in future, it will become a minority.[62]

Before we turn to the practice of mission in Part 3 of this work, we must spend some time investigating in greater detail the relative strengths and weaknesses of liberal and conservative Christianity. This is important, as we need to have a clearer picture of what form of churchmanship is best placed to reach the unchurched, and survive and grow in twenty-first-century Scotland.

Liberal Christianity has its origins in the thought of the German theologian Friedrich Schleiermacher. Under the influence of both pietism – a cousin of evangelicalism – and the Enlightenment, Schleiermacher believed that experiencing Christ in community was the means by which Christians discern and formulate true doctrine. While Scripture *could* be true, it was true because it contained accounts of real experiences of God, and not because of inspiration as traditionally understood.[63] This means that liberal Christians balance the witness of Scripture against their current experience of the world, an experience that is also shaped by reason.[64]

Because of its experiential focus and moderately sceptical attitude towards Scripture, doctrine and traditional ethics, liberalism should *logically* lead to more Scots attending church. In practice, however, it is conservative churches – and not liberal ones – that generally stand a better chance of surviving and growing in the difficult context of contemporary Scotland. In his study of the contrasting fortunes of UCCF (The Christian Unions) and SCM (Student Christian Movement), Bruce identified the following features of liberalism that render it ineffective at sustaining and transmitting faith:

- A lack of specificity in doctrine
- A lack of social and religious boundaries
- Difficulty expressing the Gospel in clear terms
- A lack of seriousness in bringing children up in the faith
- Difficulty in maintaining commitment to nebulous beliefs.[65]

These features make liberal Christianity difficult to learn, teach and transmit to future generations. Bruce's findings are also supported by McLeod, even though McLeod himself is sympathetic towards theological liberalism. Interiorising the contemporary message that faith was not socially useful, many liberals of the 1960s and 1970s charged the Church with failing in its duties to society, and abandoned Christian mission for social work or other secular enterprises.[66] We can see why this happened by considering the views of a liberal Scottish clergyman such as Johnston McKay, who once held the post of Head of Religious Broadcasting at BBC Scotland. According to McKay, Jesus:

> refused to be dogmatic, clear, definite, about who he was – he left the rumour hanging in the air that he might be the Messiah, God's Son. But it might not be any more than a rumour.[67]

Whether we agree with McKay or not, the implications for mission are clear. What sense is there in seeking to bring people to faith in something that may, after all, just be a rumour? Why would one risk embarrassment or social stigma by telling friends or family about Jesus when one can't be certain who he even was? A lack of certainty about Jesus and the teaching of the apostles has direct implications for one's *motivation* to engage in mission, the *kind* of mission that one engages in and the *efficacy* of this mission, more of which shall be explored in Chapter 7.

McLeod also notes the strongly intellectual aspect of liberalism. This has two aspects. First, the deconstructive and revisionist approach of liberal preaching is generally only attractive to those who have been raised in orthodox Christian faith, for without traditional faith it has no material to deconstruct or differentiate itself from. In this way, liberalism is parasitic or symbiotically dependent upon the traditional Christianity it rejects.[68] Second, this deconstructive and revisionist approach to faith not only requires existing knowledge of Christian tradition, but a great deal of intellectual ability, as one must first be able to understand scriptural passages literally before interpreting them in a non-literal way. What sense does it make, after all, to preach a sermon saying that the Gospels are allegories, creative expressions of internal spiritual states, unless you and your audience already know the stories in question, and possess the intellectual agility to extract their spiritual core while believing that, in fact, they did not actually happen?[69]

Compared to this, traditional forms of Christianity possess many missional advantages. By being more 'literal' – in the sense of taking the Bible at its word – traditional forms of Christianity are easier to learn, teach and transmit to future generations. By believing wholeheartedly in the teaching of Scripture, rather than being sceptical of its contents or reinterpreting to the point of denuding them, orthodox Christianity stands a better chance of producing committed, passionate and missional Christians. Moreover, in a society that is in a constant state of change and flux, and in a postmodern context that tends to downplay the possibility of objective moral truth, traditional Christianity offers intellectual certainty and existential security. The world may be dark, confusing and fallen, but God is our strength, and the Gospel floods our hearts with its light.

These observations concerning the missional fitness of liberalism are confirmed by a number of recent studies from North America. Using the same data sets as other commentators predicting a collapse of *all* Christianity in the United States,

Schnabel and Bock showed that while the data supported a decline in moderate or liberal Christianity, 'intense religion' – defined by regular attendance, high commitment and high levels of belief – is actually *growing* in America.[70] In another study from Canada analysing the respective fortunes of congregations within the same mainstream denomination, Haskell, Flatt and Burgoyne found that:

> The clergy and congregants of growing churches are more theologically conservative and exhibit higher rates of Bible reading and prayer. Growing church congregants are more likely to agree that their congregation has a clear mission and purpose, and to identify evangelism as that purpose. Growing churches are more likely to emphasize youth programs and to use contemporary worship styles. They also tend to be younger, and to have younger congregants and slightly younger clergy.[71]

While a number of causes were found to lead to church growth, almost all of them were directly related to the conservative theological basis on which the churches in question stood.[72] Put simply, if a person strongly believes in the revelation of God in Christ, and the record of that revelation in Scripture, then one will be far more likely to be confident and evangelistic in one's faith. Yet if one is uncertain about what has been revealed then one will lack confidence, and be less willing to share one's faith with others.

In addition to the findings of these studies, we should also note the organisational basis of much evangelicalism. As we will see in more detail in Chapters 7 and 8, evangelicals in independent congregations, or those belonging to loose denominations, are able to employ greater entrepreneurship and innovation in relation to ministry and mission. This increases their ability to contextualise the Gospel in new ways, thus aiding their success in reaching and recruiting new members.

There seems to be evidence on both sides of the Atlantic, then, that the numerical health of churches – at least Protestant ones – is in some way related to a more conservative theological position. This was also the conclusion of Scottish priest and sociologist of religion Duncan MacLaren. At the end of his analysis of how different forms of Christianity might fare in our contemporary context, MacLaren argued that the type of Christianity most likely to survive is what he calls 'benign sectarianism'.[73] Benign sectarianism refers to churches that have strong beliefs, committed and motivated members and robust bulwarks against the social forces that lead to secularisation. Such churches cannot be *too* sectarian, however, as this – much like the case of Exclusive Brethren – hinders evangelism and growth. For that reason, evangelical Protestants and certain kinds of traditional Roman Catholic are the most likely to resist the forces of secularisation, and perhaps enjoy modest growth.

While liberal and moderate churches appear to be at a serious disadvantage when compared with their conservative cousins, this does not mean that they serve no missional purpose. Positively, liberal theology allows Christians who have been hurt or demoralised by traditional faith to remain within the Church. It can, to quote Erasmus Darwin, be a 'feather bed to catch the falling Christian'.[74] While some conservative Christians may sneer at this, it is not obvious that losing one's faith and leaving the Church for ever is better than joining a liberal church. It may not win many new converts to the faith, but liberalism can save Christians from falling out of it altogether.

Conclusion

In this chapter, we have examined the spiritual context of contemporary Scotland. We have seen that, due to secularisation, there has been a massive decline in churchgoing, with a resulting decline in Christian belief and practice. In place of faith has arisen massive indifference to religious questions of any kind, with the majority of Scots finding it easy to live their lives without God. Occasionally, more vocal forms of non-religion manifest themselves in movements such as New Atheism. Yet because it keeps religious questions in public consciousness and discourse, militant unbelief can be beneficial to the Church. In the midst of indifference and scepticism, however, comes individualised religion. This 'spirituality' is an outcome of the secularisation of public life, the granting of authority on matters of meaning to the individual, and the growth of consumerism. Spirituality takes as many forms as there are people, and while sometimes leading to an interest in Christianity, it generally does not. In the midst of indifference, scepticism and alternative spiritualities stands the Body of Christ: divided, declining and unsure of the way ahead.

Despite this mixed religious and spiritual picture, there are important trends in contemporary spirituality that the Church should appreciate and empathise with. While they may be far from orthodox Christianity, the Church ignores the spiritual experiences of Scots at its peril, for these may be the first inroads of God into our neighbours' lives, and be important starting points for evangelism. As we have seen throughout Part 2, the Church is not faced with a stark choice between celebrating contemporary culture or condemning it, but can affirm what is good in Scottish culture while telling a better story about it, one that points our neighbours to the God who alone can meet their deepest needs and aspirations.

PART 3

Practice

7

Service

In Part 1, we examined the background to mission in contemporary Scotland, charting the development of the parish state and its disintegration through schism, welfare security and personal affluence. Part 2 then examined the contemporary context created by these social, political and economic changes. We saw how welfare security and disposable income allow Scots to abandon history, tradition and community and forge non-religious identities through consumerism. The result is that most Scots are largely contented, a contentment that means that they are not opposed to Christianity but simply indifferent to it.

In Part 3, we turn to examine the missional response of the Scottish Church to its context. This chapter begins that examination by describing two forms of Church that have developed since the Scottish Reformation, and which shape the mission of the denominations in decisive ways: one that is inherited, communal and institutional and one that is voluntarist, associational and congregational. These two forms of Church produce different mental pictures of the congregation, the community and the activity of God, giving rise, in turn, to different missional emphases. We will then describe the forms of mission that are most prevalent in contemporary Scotland, forms of service centred on emotional support, practical aid and community development. The chapter ends with an exploration of the theological assumptions that ground models of mission centred on care and service, and a critique of churches that privilege service to the exclusion of evangelism and discipleship.

Patterns of Belonging

As we saw in Chapter 3, there has been an increasing tendency in some missional thinking to relegate the Church to the periphery of God's purposes. This is an understandable reaction to centuries of denominational baggage, and a desire to focus on the mission of God rather than the preservation of the institutional Church. Yet even if Scottish Christians may wish to leave their institutional and denominational baggage behind, this does not mean that they do not have an ecclesiology, or that their ecclesiologies do not influence – sometimes decisively – what they do or do not do. Indeed, to say that one does not have an ecclesiology *is itself* an ecclesiology, and perhaps the greatest danger is not holding a strong account of the nature and purpose of the Church but being unaware of how one's implicit ecclesiology shapes and guides one's mission.

In order to understand why Scottish churches engage in the forms of mission they do, and why they sometimes *do not* engage in mission, we must understand the forms of Church that have arisen since the Reformation, and the implicit ecclesiologies that shape them.

The form of Church that has been most successful in Scotland since the Reformation can largely be characterised as *inherited, communal and institutional*. *Inherited* relates to the way in which Christian identity comes to the individual. In previous centuries, religious identities were far more likely to be a 'given', something that was part of our objective identity as much as our family origin, our class and the region of the country we were born in. While people sometimes did 'choose' a new religious identity, they did so far less frequently than today, and in a different way. *Communal* is related to this. Just as faith was largely inherited from one's family and immediate context, so was there a much closer alignment between the practice of one's religion and other social, political and economic activities. In an agricultural community in the early eighteenth century, for example, where everyone – at least nominally – belonged to the Established Church, Sunday worship *really was* the community at prayer. Worship was, of course, a distinct kind of activity. Yet it was only one aspect of a unified social, political and economic system centred on the parish church. One did not choose to freely associate with other people around a particular religious identity. Rather, worship was simply one thread in the rich tapestry of community life. The third aspect of this form of Church is its *institutional* form. This relates to the way in which inherited and communal patterns of worship were regulated and shaped. Whether through the church courts of Presbyterianism or the hierarchy of Roman Catholicism and Episcopacy, the identity or 'DNA' of the churches was preserved through carefully defined authorities, which ruled church members through canon and church law. Charismatic leadership – in the original, not contemporary usage – was eschewed in favour of objective and enduring mechanisms of control that transcended particular leaders or congregational cultures.

The second form of Church has its origins in various schisms that affected the Scottish Church from the eighteenth century onward, schisms that were related to industrialisation, patronage and the growth of evangelicalism. This form of Church may be characterised as *voluntarist, associational and congregational.* It is *voluntarist* insofar as it is a *chosen* identity, one that Scots do not maintain purely to please family, superiors or members of the community, but that meets their individual spiritual needs. It is *associational* because individuals with particular theological or liturgical views enter into free association to participate in and promote these theological and liturgical preferences. As it is chosen by each individual, and because individuals only associate on account of their theological or liturgical views, Christianity forms an integral part of their personal and corporate identity and, in many situations, will be the most important thing about them. This is in contrast to situations where individuals congregate out of habit or routine. Lastly, this form of Church is *congregational* rather than institutional. It is governed less by church law, or systems of authority that have been in existence for centuries, and more by a web of relationships that exist to maintain the community, and further its interests through mission.

Inherited, communal and institutional forms of Church originated in, and were best suited to, a society that was hierarchical, relatively fixed and at a low level of social complexity. Voluntarist, associational and congregational forms of Church originated in a period of increasing social mobility, affluence and social complexity, and are best suited to contexts of that kind. While the former form of Church most closely maps on to the traditional denominations and the latter on to the growing evangelical and charismatic sector, these forms of Church are involved in a complex theological and social dialogue with each other, and are not as distinct as they may appear. Rather than being mutually exclusive, each of these contrasting approaches to Church might be thought of as poles on a scale, with each denomination – and even each congregation – exhibiting a unique combination of both. Indeed, part of the story that will unfold in the coming chapters is of inherited, communal and institutional forms of Church adapting to twenty-first-century Scotland by becoming more voluntarist, associational and congregational, while smaller denominations – buoyed by growing numbers and finance – are beginning to exhibit an institutional character not dissimilar from traditional models of Church.

At this point, readers may wonder what the relevance of these categories is. Is this not a book about mission rather than ecclesiology? Yet these factors play an important role in determining what forms of mission a congregation or denomination will, or will not, participate in, and are therefore crucial for understanding the practice of the churches in contemporary Scotland.

Without wishing to pre-empt the following discussion, we may say that inherited and communal forms of Church will be less focused on conversion and evangelism than voluntarist and associational churches. This is for the simple reason that a smaller proportion of the congregation will be converts, or those who have chosen Christianity as the core part of their identity. Seeing less distinction between Church and world, the missional focus of these Christians will be upon *service*, engaging in acts of mission that are considered beneficial by wider secular society. The institutional aspect of this form of

Church is also significant. As authority is concentrated in episcopal hierarchies, church courts or church law, there is less scope for personal or local initiative in mission, with a sometimes complex series of hoops to jump through before securing denominational support or funding. This does not mean that this form of Church is not Christian. Rather, it means that many of its assumptions and practices took shape in a different historical context, and now face serious challenges.

In distinction from inherited and communal forms of Church, voluntarist and associational Christians will typically hold to a different set of priorities. As they are a group of Christians who have actively chosen their faith, and have made it the core part of their identity, they will typically hold conversion to be of greater importance, and will actively seek to bring this about through evangelism. Recognising more distinction between Church and world, they will also be more alert to the importance of stressing the *Christian* character of their acts of service, and the importance of integrating service and evangelism. As authority is largely exercised at congregational level rather than being concentrated in the hands of hierarchies, courts or church law, there is also more scope for personal initiative and local leadership in mission. The downside of this, however, is that coordination and partnership between churches is sometimes hindered.

These differing emphases should be kept in mind throughout Part 3, as they inform not only what churches do or do not do, but have implications for the unity of the Church, and its capacity to pool resources and personnel for mission in the difficult social context of twenty-first-century Scotland.

Caring and Sharing

We begin our survey of the practice of the Scottish Church by considering the most common forms of mission undertaken by churches: those concerned with the material needs of others, and meeting these needs through the provision of food, goods, advice and shelter.

These activities should be seen in the context of two major developments that we surveyed in previous chapters. The first is the growth of the state. Christian disunity led to the state gaining control over vast areas of Scottish life that were previously the domain of the Church. This greatly curtailed the types of service the Church could legally offer its neighbours. This external change, however, was matched by the adoption of Kingdom theologies influenced by men like Robert Flint. These not only authorised state control over areas such as healthcare, social welfare and education, but taught that God worked through the state as much as – or more than – the Church, and that it was not evangelism that mattered most to God, but service and advocacy towards the poor.

We begin our survey of Christian missional service by considering that ubiquitous feature of the Scottish Church: pastoral care. Due to its ubiquity, however, the nature and purpose of pastoral care is not always considered by Church leaders and members. In one academic work, pastoral care is defined as:

> The healing acts, done by representative Christian persons, directed towards the healing, sustaining, guiding and reconciling of troubled persons whose troubles arise in the context of ultimate meaning and concerns.

Definitions such as this are suitably vague, and correspond to the diffuse and multi-faceted ways in which pastoral care is exercised. Two features of this definition are nevertheless relevant to the mission of God in Scotland. The first is the *representative* nature of pastoral care. This is reflective of the fact that, for better or worse, there is a connection in many churches between pastoral care and the person of the minister, priest or pastor. They represent the congregation and Christ to the troubled person, and it is therefore thought that the responsibility for care should largely lie with them. Whether it is clergy or other representative persons, such as elders, who undertake pastoral care, the fact that few of these representative persons are trained in counselling or other therapeutic practices recognised by wider society means that, second, pastoral care is typically accessed only by existing Christians. Those who have a connection with these 'representative Christian persons' might look to them for help, yet those without a connection will not. They will be far more likely to approach a paid professional with accredited qualifications.

As pastoral care is the primary activity of the Scottish Church outwith Sunday worship, this means that almost all the activity of the churches is taken up with activities that do not reach non-Christians in any way at all. For this reason, a growing number of Scottish congregations and Christians are attempting to turn pastoral care inside out, reimagining this ubiquitous Christian practice, and directing it outward towards the non-religious.

These forms of therapeutic service can be based both in churches and outwith, with a variety of emphases and specialities. CrossReach, the Church of Scotland's social care charity, operates a number of counselling centres throughout Scotland. These are typically based in standalone premises, and offer services based on therapeutic models also used by secular counsellors. Another example is the counselling service of St John's Church, Linlithgow. Counsellors at St John's are trained in secular counselling practices too, but have a particular expertise in Christian Counselling, which offers counselling within a biblical framework. While many forms of emotional care are connected with churches directly, others are not. Hope Counselling, for example, was established by a group of Christians in Aberdeen who wanted to live out their faith by helping those facing emotional distress. While the management team are all members of local churches, they run their practice independent of direct congregational or denominational control.

This turn towards counselling and listening is indicative of the therapeutic complexion of much contemporary Christianity. Yet its direction towards non-Christians is an expression and sign of the new creation, and the divine injunction laid upon God's people to *heal*. In Scripture, the restoration of Jerusalem is accompanied with the healing of the brokenhearted and the binding up of their wounds (Psalm 147:3), a time of new creation in which every tear will be wiped from every eye (Revelation 21:4). Listening, comforting and simply being with our neighbours in their time of distress witnesses to the God who is with us in all things (Psalm 139). It is not by chance that the greatest summary of Christian ethics, the parable of the Good Samaritan, is framed around a story of healing (Luke 10:25–37).

The meaning of this healing is sometimes overlooked or misunderstood, however. On the one hand, Christians are often content with their actions simply being a 'good thing' without any further reference to their faith. This minimises the theological significance of care as an expression of God's character, and a sign of the coming Kingdom. On the other hand, emotional care that is undertaken with an evangelistic and proselytising objective, yet without genuine interest and care for the one who is suffering, can be a *denial* of God's Kingdom. While it is God's desire that all should come to faith, his interest in us is not ultimately dependent on whether we have faith or not. God is infinitely interested in each one of us, and the way we witness to this with our neighbours is by being interested *in them*. Being interested in a person and their story is one of the most important forms that love takes.

If Scottish churches are reimagining pastoral care to offer support for the emotional needs of their neighbours, they are also reimagining their provision of practical aid. At the most basic level, churches are among the largest providers of food banks, offering free food to those in need. Given that demand for foodbanks has increased by a shameful 80% in only five years, Christians are often the only people standing between their neighbours and starvation, a situation that increased during the coronavirus pandemic.[1] Many foodbanks in Scotland are affiliated with the Trussell Trust, while others are connected with local congregations. Local governance encourages experimentation, with Love Falkirk, for example, operating an enhanced pantry service that is integrated with a number of other church initiatives.

While food is a basic need, it is only one among many. The Salvation Army operates Lifehouses across Scotland, providing emergency shelter and supported living for hundreds of men and women. In hostels like Wallace of Campsie in Glasgow and the Pleasance in Edinburgh, the Army expresses its faith in Christ by offering sanctuary to some of the most vulnerable Scots. While the Salvation Army is the largest Church provider of housing in Scotland, local congregations are also engaged in supporting the homeless and vulnerable. After a union with a neighbouring parish, Gorgie Dalry Stenhouse Church in Edinburgh, in association with Bethany Christian Trust, converted the former sanctuary of Stenhouse St Aidan's into a *literal* sanctuary for dozens of homeless men. The Scottish Church is not only engaged in the provision of emergency and supported accommodation, however, but also in supporting its neighbours in their new homes. Fresh Start, for example, assists those moving on from homeless hostels and council-subsidised B&Bs with white goods, utensils and other household goods, helping our neighbours live dignified, independent lives.

While the Scottish Church offers material aid to Scots, it also offers practical advice and support. The Living Room in Largs partners with Care for the Family to provide a range of resources, talks and courses to help parents navigate the complexities of contemporary life, and do the best for their children. Recent years have also seen the expansion of Christians Against Poverty (CAP). CAP operates debt centres, job clubs and life-skills centres across Scotland, and in 2018 helped over 24,000 people across the UK.[2] Part of CAP's success has been its balance between national organisation and local partnerships with congregations. Despite its unashamedly Christian identity CAP has won wide praise, with television money expert Martin Lewis being a leading advocate of its work.

While many – perhaps the majority – of Scottish Christians offer practical aid simply because it is 'the right thing', or because of a deep and largely unreflective desire to care for others, in doing so, they fulfil the command of Christ, his prophets and his apostles. In Deuteronomy, the people of Israel are ordered to open their hands to the poor, and not to have any bad thought in their hearts when they do so (Deuteronomy 15:7–11). The Proverbs of Israel declare that whoever is kind to the poor gives not only to them but to God (Proverbs

19:17) and that whoever oppresses the poor shows contempt not only for them but for the majesty of God (Proverbs 14:31). The prophet Isaiah declares that we should offer the homeless shelter and cover their nakedness (Isaiah 58:7), while Christ says we should give to anyone who asks, not withholding the clothes from our own back (Luke 6:30–36).

In its provision of practical aid to the poor, the Church not only encounters its neighbours, but encounters *Christ* himself. The presence of God in the world is sometimes difficult to detect. Yet Jesus makes it clear that he is present among the poor and because the poor are always with us, so too is he (cf. Matthew 25:31–46 and 26:11). God's presence among the poor is not only an indication of his bias towards them, however, but of their importance in God's plans for the realisation of his Kingdom, and the coming of the new creation.[3]

The healing of our neighbours, and the provision of practical aid is not simply a way of worshipping or encountering Christ, however. When Christians offer practical aid to those in need, they extend the Kingdom of God to the lives of more Scots. It is *God's will* that the despairing should find hope and the homeless be fed and sheltered, just as much as it is his will that all should come to faith in his Son. Yet as we saw in Chapter 1, God's reign is not a selfish reign – as if God *needed* praise – but a restoring and creative reign. If indifference and cruelty mar the image of God in both giver and receiver, then care restores it. In the one who cares, the image of God is revealed more clearly than in other everyday situations. In the one who is cared for, the image of God is healed and restored, so that they, in turn, might manifest the image of God to *others*. As such, emotional support and practical aid have an eschatological significance, and point to the new creation when God will be all in all, and the humanity perfectly realised in Christ will be realised in all people (1 Corinthians 15:20–28). Some Christians may see outward-facing counselling, listening and practical aid as mere 'social care', or 'chaplaincy to a sinful, consumerist society'. Yet if done for the love of Christ, in obedience to his commands and integrated with the wider life of the Church, they are indispensable forms of mission.

All of these forms of mission were expressed during the coronavirus pandemic. Churches were often at the forefront of delivering food, medical supplies and emotional support to their neighbours during lockdown. Our study at Brendan Research showed that while 47% of congregations were offering fewer community initiatives than before, 27% were offering *more* initiatives, and a slim majority (51%) reported that – irrespective of the number of services offered – *more beneficiaries* were being served during lockdown than before.[4]

Community and Enterprise

The forms of service we have examined so far are primarily directed towards meeting the material and emotional needs of individuals. Yet human beings are social creatures, created to manifest the perfect society of the Holy Trinity. As such, the Church does not only care for individuals, but for communities. Service that is directed towards communities is known as *community development*.

The definition of community development given by the United Nations is 'a process where community members come together to take collective action and generate solutions to common problems'.[5] The growing importance of community development for Scotland is demonstrated by the presence of the headquarters of the International Association for Community Development in Glasgow, and its financial support by the Scottish Government.

Before we look at the churches and community development in more detail, we must ask a basic, but important question: why is community development needed in Scotland?

In previous chapters, we saw how, despite being good in themselves, affluence and the welfare state removed much of the need for close, interdependent relationships of mutual aid and care. Put simply, the more 'stuff' Scots have the less they need others, and the more community will decline. But while affluence and welfare *both* break down community, they do so in different ways. Affluence breaks down community by decreasing dependence on neighbours and the state.[6] Yet the loss of community does not mean that we no longer need. Rather, it means that goods and services that were previously provided for free, or were set within long-established relationships of mutual aid, are now *commodified*; that is, they are bought and sold at a cost.

The middle classes are the most affected by this form of community decline and its resulting commodification. Yet because the poorest in Scotland are still materially better off than their forebears, even poor communities suffer from this kind of atomisation. Added to this form of atomisation, however, are the particular effects of welfare security. When families are trapped in cycles of joblessness that span generations, and when they are incapable of securing or holding on to employment due to chaotic lifestyles, poor educational attainment, morbidity or drug and alcohol misuse, they come to look to *the state* for support. This has two effects. On the one hand, they are disempowered, and do not exercise their God-given agency. On the other hand, because their support comes from the state, they do not look to their neighbours for support and strength.

Affluence and welfare security, then, are both corrosive of community, albeit in different ways. For these reasons, an increasing number of Scottish churches are re-envisioning their provision of emotional and practical support in terms of community development. As they are sometimes one of the few organisations remaining in poor areas, churches can occupy an important position in community transformation. As communities of locals who meet together for mutual aid and support, churches, in important ways, model community development *in embryo*. If they are part of larger denominations, they also possess financial and human resources that can help support or grow other forms of community.

There are a number of different forms of community development that churches engage in, but the most common are needs-based, asset-based and activism-based.

Needs-based community development seeks to create community projects to meet real or perceived need. An example would be the food banks that are now found throughout

Scotland. While needs-based approaches can address needs overlooked by the state, they risk strengthening the disempowerment that those living in poverty already experience. They can, in addition, contribute to a 'Messiah complex' among Church volunteers. The result is one-sided relationships in which the good Christians give and the poor people receive, yet without the mutual gain that arises from authentic relationships and friendship.

For these reasons, *asset-based* community development has grown in prominence over recent decades. This seeks to build community not around *lack*, but around the skills, passions and strengths of the community. An example from Edinburgh would be Granton Community Gardeners, which was started by a team linked to local churches. By reclaiming waste ground in Wardieburn council estate with local residents, the team not only realised the potential of neglected land, but harnessed the skills of residents from many nationalities and cultural backgrounds. The produce they grow has now given rise to community meals and a community bakery, where everyone – no matter their ability or educational attainment – is able to help each other.

Because many of the causes of poverty are systemic rather than local or personal, however, *activism-based* community development is also sometimes necessary. This involves encouraging local people to take action to rectify a particular problem, and build confidence and agency in the community. An example from Glasgow is the work of the Revd Brian Casey at Springburn Parish Church. After a large number of overdoses, Brian placed hundreds of crosses outside the parish church, and led a candlelit procession through the streets to demand better government support for users and the communities they live in.

In cases such as Springburn, local clergy who have lived in a place for some time will already have intimate knowledge of the problems and potential of their communities. In many other cases, however, a community audit will be undertaken. This first involves analysing data from sources such as the Scottish Index of Multiple Deprivation (SIMD), the Church of Scotland's Statistics for Mission and the Scottish Government's

Statistics Service. Once a broad overview of the community is established, survey questions can be compiled. These surveys not only provide more localised information on relevant topics, but also – importantly – provide a way to meet neighbours and build relationships. This is essential not only for community development but, as we will see in Chapter 8, for evangelism and fresh expressions.

The professional practice and study of community development only began in the twentieth century, but has important echoes in Scripture. It mirrors the prophecies of Isaiah 61:4 and 58:12 that the people of God will rebuild the ruined cities and restore their inhabitants to life. It also echoes biblical teaching on the *imago Dei* that we encountered earlier. By focusing not only on need, but on the potential and agency of communities, community development enables the Church to restore the image of God in its neighbours and make them independent, skilled and flourishing people who mirror something of God's new creation.

It is at this point that creation care should be discussed. Creation care has three potential beneficiaries: individuals, communities and creation itself. A good example comes from Possilpark in Glasgow. Clay Community Church, led by Paul Ede, was responsible for reclaiming a number of brownfield sites, as well as creating a local nature reserve. These improvements raised the aspirations of local people, provided new facilities for families and brought together a community of people to care for the new areas. While, for Ede, these acts were good in themselves, they also held a greater significance. They were not only acts of urban regeneration, but tangible signs of the new creation, when nature and humanity will be at one through their reconciliation with God.[7] As we saw in Chapter 1, God's salvation is not only focused on individuals or the Church community, but is cosmic in scope. Creation has inherent value independent of its utility to human beings, and creation care participates with God to restore and renew his creation.

When community development projects develop around goods or services, they can also take the form of social enterprises. Social enterprises are businesses, yet use their profits not for the private gain of their shareholders, but for the benefit of society or the environment. Social Enterprise UK define social enterprises as businesses that, among other things:

- Have a clear social or environmental mission that is set out in their governing documents;
- Are independent businesses that earn more than half of their income through trading;
- Are controlled or owned in the interests of their social mission;
- Reinvest or give away at least half of their profits or surpluses towards their social purpose.[8]

Social enterprises have many of the same aims as other community development projects, seeking to empower marginalised groups through job opportunities, or release the potential of impoverished communities. In a Church context, however, social enterprises carry specific benefits. As businesses with directors, social enterprises permit churches to partner with entrepreneurs and business people. This allows the Church to benefit from a wider range of expertise than is sometimes present within congregations, enabling it to respond to social need in more creative or specialised ways. It also opens up alternative funding streams to finance the Church's charitable activities. There are specific funds set aside for social enterprises, and these enterprises – as secular undertakings – will not be hindered by funding criteria that sometimes disadvantage religious organisations.[9]

Social enterprises have many benefits, but they, like other community development projects, also present potential pitfalls for the Church. While strategic partnerships with local organisations or entrepreneurs are often useful, they can also cause the Church to have less control over the values and direction of projects. 'Control' or 'influence' are dirty words among some Christians, and it is certainly true that, in and of themselves, they are ambivalent and can tend towards sin. Yet control and influence, when directed towards Kingdom ends, are not only good but essential. Jesus came, after all, to extend the Father's Kingdom (*basileia*), a Kingdom whose true translation is closer to *reign*. Jesus came to extend the Father's *reign* or *power* over everything, and this reign is essential for the establishment of the new creation. If non-Christians come to predominate in the leadership of a project it will quickly lose its Christian ethos, and there is then no guarantee that the project will further the Father's reign.

This problem is related to two other features of community development and social enterprise projects. The first is 'mission-creep' of the unhealthy kind. Because one of the reasons for creating community development projects and social enterprises is to access alternative sources of funding, this can lead to funding criteria determining the aims and objectives of Christian projects, rather than aims and objectives determining which funding streams to access. This can result in the adoption of secular aims that are parallel, yet not convergent, with the Gospel, and the Church's mission slipping into philanthropic Humanism without anyone even noticing. Second, even if the Church is successful in insulating the aims and objectives of God from secular influence, the setting up of separate financial procedures, different employment structures and places of operation can lead to a 'professionalisation' of Christian mission, one that separates the Church's service from the actions of its members. On the one hand, this might be thought to be a good thing. How can it be bad if specialised personnel are funded and set apart to provide exemplary care, community development or goods? Yet if the Church's mission ceases to be undertaken or managed by Christians it very quickly ceases to be Christian, and leads to a divorce between worship and mission, Church and world, service and evangelism.

The Limits of Service

This brings us to the most important and controversial aspect of the Church's mission in contemporary Scotland: whether the Church's service to the world should be separate from its worship and evangelism.

This issue concerns three common and related beliefs:

- That Christian mission refers only, or primarily, to service.
- That service, worship and evangelism should not be mixed.
- That even if it means the Church dies, it is imperative that Christians focus their resources on serving their neighbours, challenging unjust social structures and caring for creation.

The idea that mission should only, or primarily, be concerned with service is a legacy of Christendom. In centuries past, most Scots were – or were *assumed* to be – Christians, and there was therefore little reason to share one's faith with one's neighbours.[10] Added to this, as we saw, was the belief that only those trained and educated should speak about God. In our day, when many in the Church assume that the 'spirituality' of their neighbours is the same thing as Christianity, another analogous excuse is available. Yet if Christian mission *only* meant service, then Jesus' ministry would have consisted solely of healings. Indeed, if Jesus were following the models of ministry argued by some, he would have set up a worker's cooperative, or employed lobbyists to harass Pilate to improve the bread dole for the homeless. Yet this he did not do. Jesus spoke frequently and passionately of his unique relationship with the Father, and of the need for people to repent of their sins and turn to him in faith.

This brings us to the second assumption present within some missiologies of service: that service should be kept firmly apart from worship and evangelism. Before critiquing this belief, let us concede what is true in it. First, Christian service *should* be unconditional, and should not be done solely that people come to faith. To fail in this would be to risk treating people as means rather than ends, and could encourage manipulative practices that dishonour God and distort personal relationships. Second, the power disparity that sometimes exists between Christians and those who live with poverty, mental illness or loneliness should not be overlooked. It is wrong to use these advantages to coerce people into attending church or an enquirers' event.

Yet as Murray argues, these concerns are often misplaced. When the Church had the social power surveyed in Chapter 2, the risk of coercion and manipulation was high, but in a context where the Church has been pushed to the margins of relevance and respect, it may be *our neighbours* who are in positions of power rather than us, and they are often far more robust than our fears would suggest. As D.T. Niles put it, evangelism is 'one hungry person telling another where to get bread', and not a Machiavellian ploy to amass status and wealth for ourselves.[11] The problem now is not a 'holier-than-thou' Church lording it over frightened parishioners, but a culture that is blind to its own faults, and convinced – despite great evidence to the contrary – that it is building a secular utopia with no need for God.[12] Service and love are the foundations of the Church's approach towards the world, yet sometimes the most courageous act of love is asking the beloved whether their error is leading them into unhappiness and self-destruction.

The belief that mission should only ever be service also, somewhat ironically, misunderstands the nature of service and the nature of love. We noted in Chapter 3 that the Scottish Church *itself* has been secularised in a number of ways. Part of this secularisation is the secularisation of Christian understandings of service and love. In Philippians 2, we read that Jesus came from heaven and 'emptied himself', taking the form of a slave. Following from this, it is sometimes thought that we too should 'empty ourselves' of our faith assumptions and just 'be there' for others, giving them whatever they need without anything else on our part. This belief is also supported by practices from the realm of therapy and counselling that stress the importance of listening over judging, and of the role of the listener in providing 'space' for the other to discover their own form of flourishing.

Yet Christian service is not secular counselling. Christian service is self-sacrificial, which means that we not only give our attention, or our material goods, or our professional expertise to our neighbours, but *ourselves*. There are two aspects to this. The more generic aspect is that, if we refrain from revealing our faith commitments with the one served, then we are not giving them all we have. We are holding back, and refusing to share all that we could. On a deeper level, however, is the issue of *authenticity*. If we, as Christians, do not share our faith with those we love and serve, then we are showing them *part* of ourselves but not all. Crucially, we are not showing them the most important part. This arises due to fear of being socially inappropriate and 'weird', or from misplaced concern about appearing 'unprofessional'. Yet perfect love casts out fear. When we fully love we fully give ourselves, and when we fully give ourselves to another we reveal ourselves. If we are a Christian, this will reveal that our service is motivated by the faith and love of the Living God. Through giving ourselves fully to our neighbours, we become witnesses to Christ. Through our self-giving witness, God is revealed and glorified.

We see this in the life of Christ. In emptying himself and giving himself for the world, he witnessed to and glorified his Father. In loving others, he revealed God. In this, Christ followed the divine logic of the Trinity, in which the giving of each Person to the other not only honours the identity of the beloved, but reveals the identity of the one who loves. In giving himself for the world, Jesus showed love to the loveless that their worth might be revealed, and in so doing, revealed his identity as the Son and the identity of his Father in heaven. True love, then, reveals the goodness not only of the giver but of God, and witnesses to the power of him who alone is able to save. This does not, of course, mean that the relationship between service and evangelism is straightforward, or that it does not require thought in each context. As Ecclesiastes 3 puts it, there is a time to speak and a time to keep silent. Yet as Ballard argues, there is – and will be till Kingdom come – a genuine tension between Church and world, service and evangelism. This, however, is a *creative* tension, and one that should not be collapsed into unthinking affirmation of the chains that bind our neighbours.[13]

Having considered the first two of our assumptions regarding Christian service, we are better placed to consider the most serious one: that God's Kingdom is independent of the Church, and it does not matter if the Church survives in Scotland.

The idea that the Church may have 'done its work' in relation to the improvement of society extends back at least as far as the German philosopher Hegel. Hegel saw the Church as invaluable to the development of freedom and reason in Western societies. Yet during his early to middle period, he came to believe that it had been superseded by the state. By recognising the worth of each person, and providing aid and protection to its citizens, the state had realised the aspirations of the Church, yet – crucially – without recourse to faith or transcendent realities.[14] Given what we saw in Chapters 3 and 5, Hegel's thesis regarding the development of the state is supported by the experience of secularisation in Scotland.

Hegel's argument has also been picked up by a number of theologians. According to Jüngel:

> The Church can be grateful that its spiritual assets now also exist in secular form ... [They are] secularised treasures of the Church, not least of the Protestant Church – treasures of which the full significance was often recognised even only as the result of secularisation.[15]

Jüngel's argument can be seen as a development of the principle at work in the thought of Flint that we examined in Chapter 3. As we saw, Flint believed that the Kingdom of God could be extended through the state and civil society, and that, in important ways, they could discern God's will independently of the Church. Indeed, insofar as they had their own access to God, they might discern and enact God's will better than the Church. For this reason, ministers like John Harvey can write: 'I am not unhappy about the secular vision of the world which we now hold, and I do not feel any need to fight against it.'[16]

This belief is attractive because it removes an important part of the Church's responsibility for the world. If the state and civil society can further God's will as much as – or even more than – the Church, then we can relax about decline. There may not be a Church in Scotland after our deaths, but if this is God's will then so be it. It is also attractive insofar as, while the Church *is* here, we can focus our attention on things that are of relevance to people. In an influential line of thought emanating from Hoekendijk and certain World Council of Churches publications, the Church is only a minor part of God's work. His main priorities lie elsewhere. As Hoekendijk writes:

> When one desires to speak about God's dealings with the world, the Church can be mentioned only in passing and without strong emphasis.[17]

For Hoekendijk, God works far more *outwith* the Church than within it, and it is the world – and not the Church – that sets the agenda for the Church's mission. If the world says that it requires help with tackling poverty, or violence against women or nuclear weapons, then we should divert our attention and resources from evangelism and other non-relevant forms of activity to what our neighbours want.[18]

Unfortunately, there is little evidence in Scripture for this view of the Church. If it was the Father's intention to advance his mission primarily through the state, it seems unlikely that his Son would have taken flesh, and suffered, and died and risen again in the way he did. He would have taken flesh as a Roman Senator, and – working his way through the *cursus honorum* and into the Imperial Household – would either have influenced Augustus and Tiberius or, alternatively, have taken the purple for himself. Yet this he did not do. Likewise, if it was God's intention that civil society should be the primary agent of his Kingdom, he would have taken flesh as a sculptor, philosopher or even a gladiator. Yet this he did not do. On the contrary, God's response to the pain and sin of the world was to take flesh as an ordinary Israelite, and suffer, and die and rise again. His response to the pain and sin of the world was to give his Spirit to a part of humanity, to found *a Church*, that he commissioned to serve and make disciples of all nations, and which even the gates of hell would not prevail against.

While, as we shall see in Chapter 9, there is much work to be done in persuading the state and civil society to do what God wills them to do, as we discovered in Chapter 1, the Church is the sign, foretaste and instrument of God's Kingdom. It is the primary instrument by which he wills to extend his reign and bring about his new creation, and far from being an appendage to the Kingdom, it is of vital importance to it. In Revelation, the new creation does not consist of citizens animated by Humanist philosophy and ordering the Holy City by means of human rights, but of redeemed sinners worshipping the slain Lamb upon the throne. One day, the Church as we know it *really will* be no more. Yet that will not be because its role has been supplanted by the state, but because all humanity will witness to the glory of the Living God when they see him face to face, and he becomes the light of all.

Until that day, however and as long as we live in this vale of tears, service is indispensable. First and foremost, it is Christ's command, one of the great commissions he gives his Church. Yet in addition to this, service piques the indifference that is the greatest enemy of Christ in contemporary Scotland, and raises the plausibility of the faith. If the decline of Christianity in Scotland arose from the Church's loss of social significance and the removal of its core functions by the state, service *restores* the Church's significance. It makes the Church relevant to the lives of average Scots, a relevance that provides a foundation for hearing the claims of Christ. By creating and sustaining communities of care and hospitality, the Church expands the imaginations of Scots, making them see that, rather than a pipe-dream, mere 'pie in the sky when you die', Jesus is making all things new *today*. The indifferent may struggle to connect with an apologetic tract, or an expository sermon, but they will pay attention if the Church meets one of their needs, or the needs of their family or friends.

This service will only have its full effect, however, when it is wedded to Christian witness. Evangelism completes other forms of mission and points to their ultimate meaning.[19] Just as baptism and the Lord's Supper point to the new creation through the use of Word and Sacrament, so service, love and sacrifice, when wedded to explicit witness, can be signs and foretastes of the world to come, where death itself will be ended and every tear wiped from every eye.

Conclusion

In this chapter, we have seen how changes in Scottish society gave rise to two forms of Church, and how their different assumptions impact mission. We then examined the types of care and service undertaken by the Scottish Church, spanning the full gamut of human need and potential. Yet we also examined how the Church has often failed to understand the nature of its service, confusing secular for theological ends, and wrongly neglecting its own role in God's mission. Because service alone does not exhaust God's will for the Church, we now turn to its other great commission: to make disciples of all nations.

8

Evangelism

The last chapter concluded with the argument that missional service is incomplete without the sharing of faith. Without this sharing, Christians fail to give themselves fully to their neighbours, maintaining artificial barriers whose origin is not theological but secular. Yet what form should this sharing take? Which forms of evangelism are appropriate and which are not? Which methods are 'successful', and which less so?

These are some of the questions that we will now seek to answer, as we examine the attempts of the Church to evangelise Scotland. We shall see that while most forms of evangelism have their merits, it is those which operate from – and invite Scots into – *worshipping communities* that have the best chance of successfully communicating the Gospel and making disciples. When wedded to loving service and contextually relevant forms of worship, worshipping communities offer the best opportunity for communicating the Gospel, piquing the interest of the religiously indifferent, and creating local cultures of plausibility that can resist the toxic effects of secularity.

Evangelism and Pre-Evangelism

Before we can properly analyse the efforts of the Church to evangelise Scotland, we must first clarify what evangelism is.

The word 'evangelism' – and its related terms – comes from the Greek *euangelion*, meaning 'good news'. The English word 'Gospel' has the same basic meaning. Evangelism, then, is sharing the Good News of Jesus. 'Evangelisation' is a related word most commonly found in the Roman Catholic Church, and is generally used to refer to evangelism in cultures that were formerly Christian.[1] Pre-evangelism denotes a range of practices that attempt to remove obstacles to the successful sharing of faith that are typically intellectual in nature but not exclusively so.

We have already seen that the concept of evangelism, as opposed to ministry, has played a relatively limited role within the post-Reformation Scottish Church. It was commonly believed that recalcitrant Scots were bad or deficient Christians rather than non-Christians. Where the concept of evangelism *was* used, it was generally in relation to overseas mission, or the conversion of Christians from one tradition to another. With the changes recounted in Chapter 3 and the spiritual context explored in Chapter 6, however, the existence of non-Christian Scots has become all too evident, and the importance of evangelism much clearer.

In this section we will examine forms of evangelism and pre-evangelism in Scotland that generally take place *outwith* regular worship, focusing on street evangelism, apologetic ministries, Alpha courses and similar undertakings.

Before we turn to these and other forms of evangelism, however, and by way of contrast, it is useful to consider Scottish Roman Catholic approaches towards evangelism. While the Roman Catholic Church in Scotland operates a similar – though more sacramentally focused – online presence to Protestant churches through the work of individual parishes or Roman Catholic media agencies like Sancta Familia in Mossend, it generally has a distinct understanding of evangelism. The Second Vatican Council was insistent that mission is of the *being* of the Church, and that congregations are called to engage in mission within their particular contexts.[2] Nevertheless, it is also true that this missional focus – following Western Christianity more generally – has been more directed to overseas mission than domestic mission, as seen in Scottish Roman Catholic mission agencies such as Missio and Scottish Catholic International Aid Fund (SCIAF).

Roman Catholic approaches to evangelism – or the more Roman Catholic phrase evangelisation – tend to focus on two strands: personal witness and institutional learning. The Catechism of the Roman Catholic Church recognises the desirability of the laity communicating the Good News in their day-to-day lives.[3] This is encouraged through weekly homilies, and through occasional parish missions led by bishops, priests or one of the preaching orders. The emphasis in these missions, however, is on the personal awakening of church members, and not on the direct evangelisation of non-Christians.

The more widespread and obvious example of Roman Catholic evangelisation is, of course, Roman Catholic schools. As the Scottish Catholic Education Service explains, the Roman Catholic School sector in Scotland stands in continuity with the Catholic education offered when Scotland was first evangelised.[4] Through its religious education, school ethos and interactions with parish priests, religious orders and the diocese, the Roman Catholic Church attempts to raise the young of Scotland in the faith, and shape them into the Scottish Catholic leaders of tomorrow.

While an emphasis on personal holiness and discipleship has parallels with the Protestant models of discipleship that we shall explore below, the Roman Catholic understanding of evangelisation through education is quite distinct. Non-denominational schooling – except in non-urban areas – has largely ceased to be Christian in Scotland, and public institutions do not play much of a role in the missional thinking of most Protestants. This is unfortunate, as the Roman Catholic emphasis on education displays a great deal of common sense and pragmatism. As the product of immigration and a historically high birth rate, the Roman Catholic Church in Scotland realised long ago that it is easier to make and educate Christians than to convert them.

In contrast to the Roman Catholic education sector comes that most quintessential of Protestant practices: street preaching. Street preaching is found in most Scottish cities – and occasionally towns – and is generally undertaken by single preachers, who preach sermons in busy areas with or without amplification. Sometimes, however, it can take the form of small groups such as Street Church in Edinburgh, who, in addition to street preaching, also pray and share the Gospel with passers-by on a one-to-one basis.[5] In Scotland, such practices have a historical origin in the mendicant orders, as well as the covenanters and Haldane preachers surveyed in Chapter 2. This historical backdrop means that street preaching is largely associated with conservative evangelicalism. On one level, the aim of these activities is simple: to convert non-Christians and win them for Christ. Yet they are also *political* acts, transgressing widely held views regarding the personal and private nature of spirituality, and – increasingly – those regarding sexuality and gender. As such, freedom of speech for street preachers is being increasingly challenged, something we will examine further in Chapter 9. By transgressing the implicit and explicit norms of Scottish society, street preaching also stresses the *offence* of the Gospel, the way in which salvation in Christ requires a rejection of many of the beliefs and lifestyle choices held by contemporary Scots.[6] Because of this intentionally confrontational emphasis, street preaching can be viewed with deep mistrust by some Christians, who question its non-relational format and polarising effect.

A related, though distinct, form of street evangelism is seen in The Turning. The Turning is an ecumenical venture led by Yinka Oyekan. Oyekan has spent most of his ministry in England, but was born, educated and converted in Edinburgh. The Turning sees Christians from different denominations venturing out on to the streets in pairs to give strangers the opportunity to hear the Gospel and respond in faith. Using a pre-written script, those they encounter are told that God loves them, that he has a plan for their lives and that by accepting Jesus they can be saved. If they accept, they are then prayed for and asked for their contact details, so that a follow-up meeting can be arranged. Starting in Reading, The Turning moved across England and as far as France and Belgium, before coming to Scotland. In Scotland, it is supported by the Baptist Union of Scotland, the Redeemed Christian Church of God, Destiny and Scottish Network Churches among others. In its first two years of operation, The Turning claims to have trained over 4,000 evangelists and seen 13,000 positive responses to the Gospel.[7]

The Turning replicates elements of the 'Gospel of offence' seen in street preaching, breaking social norms by approaching strangers in the street to talk about Jesus. Yet it differs from most street preaching through its intention to form lasting discipleship relationships with those reached. In its early iterations, The Turning sometimes struggled to realise the intention of translating these street encounters into lasting discipleship.[8] Efforts at follow-up improved, however, with more detailed procedures, and an app that those who have made a commitment are encouraged to download prior to their next face-to-face meeting with an evangelist. While many readers will be repelled by unsolicited conversations with strangers, the use of a script and the request for contact information, The Turning nevertheless stands as a testament to the courage of ordinary Scottish Christians, and their desire for unity in mission. It also reminds the Church that radical – and controversial – methods may be necessary to reach those Scots other methods do not reach.

If street evangelism breaks social norms by 'invading' public space with the Gospel, other evangelistic ministries seek to break intellectual norms for the sake of Christ. SOLAS Centre for Contemporary Christianity is an evangelistic ministry based in Dundee. While originally connected with St Peter's Free Church Dundee led by David Robertson, its Trustees and Council of Reference now include representatives from different sections of the Scottish evangelical world. SOLAS offers resources and events to equip the Church to be confident in sharing its faith. Its Short/Answers series offers responses to a wide range of questions about Christianity, and its Confident Christianity conference seeks to teach church members the basics of apologetics and evangelism. In addition to these resources and conferences, SOLAS also works with local congregations to organise evangelistic events aimed at mixed Christian and non-Christian audiences in venues such as cafés and bars.

An analogous ministry is Grasping the Nettle (GTN). GTN is an ecumenical ministry involving representatives from the Church of Scotland, the Roman Catholic Church and the

Free Church, among many others.[9] GTN developed from Exploring the God Question (ETGQ), a resource created by Scottish-based Kharis Productions and Search for Truth Charitable Trust. ETGQ – along with its variations – presents the scientific and philosophical evidence both for and against the existence of a Creator, featuring interviews with leading theists and sceptics. After successfully broadcasting ETGQ on television networks throughout the world, the BBC's refusal to air the series led Kharis' Co-Founder Iain Morris to start a new grass-roots movement to enable people across Scotland to view ETGQ and the evidence for a Creator. The majority of GTN events take the form of local viewings with discussion of the ETGQ material, yet also include annual conferences and What a Wonder-Full World events, featuring live music, drama and interviews. Through partnerships with schools – particularly within the Roman Catholic sector – GTN has enabled hundreds if not thousands of school children to hear the evidence for the existence of God. In addition to these activities, GTN has brought high-profile figures such as the Vatican Astronomer Guy Consolmagno to Scotland, a visit that resulted in wide coverage on television, radio and newspapers and an opportunity to present the evidence for a Creator to a national audience.

Ministries such as SOLAS and GTN represent important Scottish-based responses to the intellectual context of the contemporary West. They equip church members with the confidence to initiate conversations about faith, and the knowledge to answer common objections against Christianity. Through their online and in-person activities, they also seek to go into the 'lion's den' and engage in debate with non-Christian Scots, including those vehemently opposed to faith.

We have already identified some of the limits of intellectual debate in relation to faith. In short, because the primary causes of secularisation and non-religion are social, economic and political, intellectual approaches can fail to address the root causes of unbelief.[10] Yet the evidence for a Creator is robust, and in some situations persuasive. High-profile accounts exist of apologetics playing a role in the conversions of writers such as C.S. Lewis and Alister McGrath, as well as many ordinary Christians recorded on the websites of apologists such as William Lane Craig.[11] It must also be remembered that intellectual and social forms of evangelism are not competing but complementary. Debates, film screenings and other evangelistic events provide an opportunity to build relationships with the non-religious, which – as the present author's experience testifies – can play an important role in bringing non-Christians to faith. Truth alone can be cold. Yet truth, wedded to love and friendship, can bear fruit.

Before we conclude our survey of forms of evangelistic activity that happen outwith regular worship in Scotland, we must turn to what is perhaps the most ubiquitous evangelistic initiative of all: the Alpha Course. If we place the evangelistic activity surveyed so far on a scale of relational interaction, street preaching stands at one end and Alpha at the other. Alpha began life in 1990 at Holy Trinity Brompton in London under the leadership of Nicky Gumbel, before becoming ecumenical and international. As Alpha puts it, the course provides 'a space, online or in person, where people are excited to bring their friends for a conversation about faith, life and God'.[12] It is based around the three practices of hospitality over a meal or tea and coffee, listening to a talk and discussing a series of questions based on that talk. All of these elements are important. Hospitality allows relationships to form. These begin with the friendships that already exist between church members and their non-Christians friends, but develop – ideally – into the non-Christian participants becoming part of the wider Church community. It is in this context of supportive friendship and community that the apologetic talks can be heard with greater openness. They can also be contextualised within the life of a concrete, local congregation, engaged – ideally – in making their community better. As such, the friendship and community afforded by Alpha become key parts of the plausibility structure within which the Gospel is heard and received.

Alpha has been adopted by almost all Scottish denominations, including the Roman Catholic Church. In addition, it has given rise to a wide range of analogous courses, such as Christianity Explored, Emmaus and others, each offering differing theological and methodological emphases. Unfortunately, no robust and accessible research exists that quantifies the number of conversions associated with Alpha. Despite the absence of such research, anecdotally, Alpha appears to encourage at least some non-Christians to come to faith. Despite its widespread popularity, Alpha has nevertheless been criticised from a number of angles. Male has questioned whether the 'converts' are not actually dechurched Christians, rather than the truly unchurched.[13] Some have written Alpha off as being prohibitively bourgeois and middle class, a course written by the middle classes for the middle classes.[14] Others have noted the difficulty of integrating those converted through Alpha into regular worship, with some participants dropping away after coming to faith or insisting on continuing meeting together in their group.[15] A final criticism concerns the apologetic emphasis of Alpha. If Scottish society is as indifferent to religious and metaphysical questions as Chapter 6 suggested, who really cares what 'the' meaning of life is? Don't we all make meaning for ourselves now?[16]

While there is some truth to these criticisms, they nevertheless highlight two important missiological principles. As we shall see, homogeneity is an important – if controversial – element in evangelism, as is the establishment of small groups in church life. Through its basis in hospitality, friendship and discipleship-centred community, in important ways, Alpha represents both the culmination of evangelistic activity, and the moment at which evangelism outwith regular worship spills over into the establishment of new worshipping communities.

New Worshipping Communities

While evangelism and pre-evangelism play an important role in the life of the Scottish Church, as the success of Alpha shows, evangelism is not sufficient, in itself, to hold and develop Scots in the faith. *Community is necessary.* Community and social life are the foundation upon which all belief is built.[17] Truth is not 'free-floating', existing on a detached intellectual plain, but arises from, and is grounded in, concrete social interaction and living communities. Community provides the plausibility structure in which the truth of the Gospel can be successfully communicated. It provides face-to-face, daily corroboration of the power, truth and 'common sense' nature of faith. Without it, the seeds of faith scattered by evangelism and apologetics struggle to find fertile soil. Given that God's mission has a Church, none of this should surprise us. Christ does not reveal himself in an abstract, or 'naked' way to Scots. He is seen in, through and with the Church, the family and household of God. It is therefore the nature and activities of the Church, as the community of the people of God, on which the plausibility of the Gospel largely stands or falls.

Yet what kind of community? Are there not Church communities all over Scotland? If so, why are we failing to reach our neighbours?

As we saw in Chapter 3, despite popular assumptions to the contrary, the Scottish Church tried – and often succeeded – at keeping pace with population growth and new housing projects. The missiological assumption behind these activities was simple: if we build churches and provide them with clergy then Scots will come and worship. This assumption was summed up in a memorable slogan from one of the post-war church building campaigns: 'Every New Steeple Means More Christian People'.[18]

Yet because the churches planted in new housing areas were largely traditional in outlook, many of the post-war congregations struggled to keep pace with frantic social change. They became oases of the old Scotland in the midst of the new, with the children and grandchildren of their founders spurning a Church that was – from a social and cultural perspective – living in a different age. Because of the jarring of cultures between Church and Scottish society, the situation of these congregations became analogous to that of the Scottish missionaries who evangelised Africa and Asia in centuries past. The crucial difference, however, was that these domestic congregations did not realise that they were in a similar missionary context, with analogous cultural barriers to overcome. While some Scottish denominations – particularly the Church of Scotland – believed that with the correct central, regional or local structures the tide could be turned, as Harvey argued, the problem was not with the Church's structures, but with its *people*. While good and faithful, they had little knowledge or training to engage with the changed culture around them, and many found themselves isolated from the communities that they purported to represent and serve.[19]

This situation would not have been a problem if, as was traditionally thought, the existence of a 'good church' in a particular area could be fully equated with the presence of a minister preaching the Word and celebrating the sacraments. Yet as Van der Borght argues, if we view ministry from the perspective of mission, a minister who only serves a diminishing group of Christians is problematic for a God who desires a saving relationship with *all* people.[20] Within this older, 'Christendom' model, evangelistic activities are sometimes undertaken, of course. Yet they take the form of 'outreach': holding one-off events designed to attract non-Christians to Church.[21] As Tom Allan recognised over sixty years ago in *The Face of My Parish*, however, even if this outreach is successful in leading non-Christians to attend church for a time, it is, in the long term, largely futile. That is because the culture of Church is so alien to non-Christians that it forces them to choose between it and 'normal' culture. When posed in that way, most non-Christians open to Christianity will try Church culture for a time before returning to the culture in which they were raised, and in which they feel most comfortable.[22] Unless the culture and worship of the congregation changes, outreach – no matter how creative – will bear little lasting fruit.

A growing awareness that the inherited culture and worship of the Church was unable to meet the missional and evangelistic challenges of contemporary Scotland led to a call from the General Assembly of 1999 to appoint a Special Commission to examine the primary purpose of the Church for the twenty-first century. The Commission's report, *Church Without Walls*, was largely authored by Peter Neilson, with important

contributions from other figures such as Albert Bogle. It recognised that the primary crisis facing the Church of Scotland
– along with many other traditional denominations – was its
culture, which was dominated by clericalism, traditionalism
and a distorted view of its place within Scottish society. The
report argued for the equipping and deployment of church
members and elders through new training structures, the
creation of evangelists and greater experimentation with worship.[23] Despite its forward thinking, and an impressive variety
of follow-up conferences that reached 44% of Church of Scotland congregations, its more radical proposals were quashed
by powerful vested interests, organisational confusion and the
failure of the Church of Scotland to develop and invest in new
training structures.[24]

Shortly after *Church Without Walls* was presented to the
General Assembly, the Church of England's General Synod
received a report that would revolutionise the Church in Britain:
Mission-Shaped Church (MSC). MSC built on the *Breaking
New Ground* report of the early 1990s, as well as the Church
Army's booklet series, Encounters on the Edge. MSC argued
that the changing culture of British society required a change in
Church culture. Whereas, in centuries past, society was organised geographically, often around the parish church, now it was
organised nationally, institutionally and culturally. In order to
adapt to this reality, the Church could no longer offer a 'one
size fits all' approach to worship, but one that recognised the
plurality of cultures in Britain, and the corresponding need for
a plurality of worship forms.[25]

These new forms of worship for a pluralist, post-Christian
society were termed 'fresh expressions of Church', a phrase
drawn from the Declaration of Assent at Anglican ordinations,
where ordinands affirm the need to proclaim the Gospel
'afresh' in every generation.[26] While MSC did not offer one
particular definition of the phrase 'fresh expressions',[27] in its
more missionally focused forms, it is generally taken to mean
'a form of Church for our changing culture established primarily for the benefit of people who are not yet members of any
church'.[28]

In its attempt to provide a theological and missiological rationale for new forms of worship within the Church, MSC grouped together a wide variety of worshiping communities under the single term of 'fresh expressions'. The main types of fresh expression identified in the report were:

- Alternative worship communities
- Base Ecclesial Communities
- Café church
- Cell church
- Churches arising out of community initiatives
- Multiple and midweek congregations
- Network-focused churches
- School-based and school-linked congregations and churches
- Seeker church
- Traditional church plants
- Traditional forms of Church inspiring new interest (including new monastic communities)
- Youth congregations.[29]

While the supporters of *Church Without Walls* struggled to promote fresh expressions with the Church of Scotland, the Church of England now boasts thousands of fresh expression communities. They currently account for 15% of Church of England congregations, and engage more than 50,000 people.[30] While fresh expressions share a common title, these forms of worship are, in fact, very different from each other.[31] The main dividing line concerns the difference between church plants – and related communities such as multi-site, midweek – and the others. Church plants and related forms of Church are not new. Churches have been planted in Scotland for centuries, and – as we have seen – formed an important part of the Church's mission in the post-war period. We must also bear in mind the differing motivations for engaging in fresh expressions or church planting. Paas suggests that there are three broad motivations for planting churches: confessional motives, growth motives and innovation motives.[32] Murray goes further, and lists over fifteen motivations for church planting.[33] Further, individual projects often combine all of these motivations, as particular team members will engage in fresh expressions for different reasons. As such, while they may all fall under the one name of 'fresh expressions', the motivation and purpose of these new forms of Church can be very varied.

We shall return to the categorisation and effectiveness of each type of fresh expression later in this chapter. For now, however, we will examine in more detail how the different elements of fresh expressions of Church work to make the Gospel more plausible than some forms of inherited Church. In doing so, we will necessarily focus on the *evangelistic* importance of fresh expressions, recognising that this is not always the primary motivation of their leaders, and that evangelism does not exhaust the purpose of fresh expressions.

The first aspect of fresh expressions that makes them potentially successful vehicles for evangelism is *worship*. As we saw in Chapter 1, the worship, adoration and contemplation of God is the end of mission. The Church is not called to grow for its own sake, but so that all people might worship the Father, in the Son, through the power of the Spirit. As Piper puts it: 'Mission exists because worship doesn't.'[34]

Worship performs a number of roles within mission. It is an act of mission in its own right, a resource for mission and the very life of mission.[35] Worship can be an act of mission in its own right because worship is fundamentally about re-narrating and reimagining the world. In the world, God may be forgotten, and injustice, and cruelty and sin run rampant. Yet in worship, we bring to mind the God who is the same yesterday, today and for ever, who came once in Jesus of Nazareth and will come again to judge the nations with righteousness. As Brueggemann argues, worship is about articulating, communing with and actualising – however imperfectly – a different world, a world in which God is glorified, men and women flourish and the earth is renewed. Worship is 'speaking from the future', the means by which God speaks into our context to transform it into the new creation.[36]

In this way, worship is one of – and perhaps the key – principle that informs Newbiggin's understanding of the local congregation as the 'hermeneutic of the Gospel'.[37] Hermeneutic of the Gospel means that the world sees and understands the Good News of Jesus *through the Church*. If worship is dowdy, and passionless and irrelevant, then non-Christians will think the Gospel is too. Yet if it is vibrant, Spirit-led and directed towards real-life issues, then the Gospel will be provocative, engaging and compelling.

If worship is the goal of mission, and a vital part of the 'hermeneutic of the Gospel', it is also a crucial resource and motivation for mission. Intellectually, good worship prepares us for mission by helping us understand what is going on in our communities, and re-narrating secular narratives in a Christian way.[38] Yet spiritually, as we give glory to God, he glorifies himself by transforming us. He forgives our sin, weans us from idolatry and prepares our hearts to serve, that we might glorify him in the transformation of others.[39]

Worship, then, is central to the mission of the Church. Yet dangers lie everywhere, dangers that are related to *inculturation*. Inculturation is the process by which the Gospel takes root in, and is clothed by, secular culture. When inculturation goes wrong, however, it can subvert another key aspect of Christian life, the *pilgrim principle*. This is the principle that the Church is called to be a distinct, holy community, that while being sent to the world, does not ultimately belong to it.

The first danger of inculturation in relation to worship – and that seen most commonly in Scotland – is the danger of believing that only one cultural form of worship is *truly* worship. This leads to uniformity and a disapproval of experimentation, with the result that, as society changes, 'true worship' becomes meaningless and irrelevant. As Kernohan says of his Church of Scotland tradition, 'In theory we should be the most flexible of all churches in our worship. In practice we are not.'[40] This is because some traditions have an 'over-realised eschatology' when it comes to worship. They believe that their church – unique among others – has found *the* way to worship, and that anything else is less than true worship. Yet this is to make an idol of a particular form of worship, seeing worship as a closed system rather than a Spirit-led practice orientated towards

God's *future* reign. That reign overthrows the universal pre-tensions of *every* culture, that God might be all in all.[41]

If there is a danger that inculturation can make a particular form of worship absolute, there is also the opposite danger of making worship so malleable that it loses some or all of its Christian character. In the push to be 'relevant' to cul-ture through the creation of new forms of Church that are attractive to the unchurched, we can jettison important ele-ments of our theology and liturgy, to the point that we forget who we are. By believing that mission is an end in itself, and that anything that keeps the unchurched from coming to Jesus must go, Christians can empty the Church of structure, ordination, communion, religious symbols, liturgy and almost all theology.[42] This phenomenon is not helped by notions such as Hirsch's famous – yet frequently misunderstood – dictum that Christology precedes missiology and ecclesiology.[43] While all Christian mission must be Christocentric, this maxim overlooks the fact that the Church is Christ's *Body*. For that reason, ecclesiology and Christology cannot be fully separated. Further, in commissioning and empowering the apostles, Jesus set important boundaries for what the Church can and cannot do. As Moynagh says: 'Worship must be true to God before it can be true to the God-seeker',[44] a lesson that over-zealous inculturation can sometimes miss.

How, then, are these potential dangers to be avoided? By pay-ing careful attention to how Jesus himself undertook mission.

This brings us to the so-called 'Incarnational principle'. As we saw in Chapter 1, when God assumed human flesh in Jesus Christ he did not only assume human flesh 'in general' but became an *Israelite*. Jesus entered into the culture of the people of God to transform that culture from within. Yet by going deep into the culture of his own particular people, Christ revealed a Gospel for *every* culture. As such, the Incarnation is 'the first divine act of translation into humanity that gives rise to a constant succession of new translations'.[45]

This process of cultural redemption developed further in the ministry of Paul and the apostles. Paul did two things. On the one hand, he refused to make *any* culture absolute, for every culture was under divine judgement. Yet on the other hand, he taught that, because of the righteousness of Jesus, *any* culture could be redeemed.[46] To put it another way, there is no universal cultural expression of the Gospel but, rather, a Gospel that must be universalised to every distinct culture.[47] If we take the Incarnation seriously, the Word has to 'become flesh' in every new cultural context.[48] We must *go out* to every culture in Scottish society, and then *go deep* into it, that Christ might be all in all.[49]

So how is this to be done? It means, first, engaging seriously, yet critically, with Scottish culture, as we have tried to do throughout this book. As Gay notes, Christians often make the mistake of believing that they are unaffected by secular culture, or, as we have seen, that only one cultural form of Church is true.[50] But secular culture is so pervasive and changing that neither of these attitudes will allow us to do mission as Jesus did.

While many definitions of culture might be given, at its heart, culture is about the meaning that we attach to practices and objects. These meanings are generated socially by ordinary people in day-to-day interactions. Because practices, objects and people change over time, so too does meaning and culture.[51] Because meaning is constantly changing – especially in contemporary Scotland – Ward argues, 'The Church needs to be made and continually re-made if it is to be a meaningful way of believing in the present.'[52] This process is not only human, however, but involves the activity of God, who re-shapes and re-forms his Church in every age. The Trinitarian God advances his mission by using his Church to 'sift' cultural practices and objects to see which can be used for his purposes.[53] This process of sifting is called *contextualisation*. On the level of teaching, this takes the form of re-narrating elements of Scottish culture to show their Christian meaning.[54] On the level of things, contextualisation means re-purposing music, technology and phenomena like the internet for Kingdom purposes. As Cardinal Newman noted, this power of assimilation is a key indicator of the health of the Church.[55] If the Church has the skill and vigour to gather, sift, re-narrate and re-purpose cultural forms then it retrieves what is good in secular culture while discarding what is sinful. In doing so, it creates forms of worship, ministry and mission that do not reject Scottish culture, but redeem it. It can then create forms of Christian culture that are intuitive and relevant to Scots, yet which also challenge them to be conformed to Christ. It is this process of cultural assimilation that makes fresh expressions of Church 'fresh' rather than stale.

This process of contextualisation cannot take place, of course, without a sound understanding of context. Those wishing to develop a fresh expression of Church need to research their national culture – as we have done in this work – before learning about their local cultures. This can be done partly through local histories, but should also include questionnaires and interviews with neighbours. The aim of this listening is to do what we examined in Chapter 7: determining the needs, potential and aspirations of the community. Yet for evangelistic purposes, it must also include research into what the community thinks about faith, spirituality and the Church. By gathering this material together, new missional communities can then create forms of worship and service that are relevant and attractive to their neighbours.

Nevertheless, there are limits to contextualisation. Some elements of Scottish society – such as the idea that individuals are the highest spiritual authority, or that human sexuality should not be policed – are simply wrong, and should be named and rejected. For this reason, in his comprehensive study of models of mission, Bevans identifies a 'counter-cultural' model as the most suitable for Western societies. As he says, 'some contexts are simply antithetical to the gospel, and need to be challenged by the gospel's liberating and healing power.'[56] This will stick in the throat of some Christians, who would like to believe that Scottish morals and values largely conform to God's will. They will see such a view as being 'backward', 'bigoted' and potentially harmful to mission. Yet as Bevans goes on to say, the counter-cultural model is *counter* and not *anti*-cultural.[57] It sees the Church as the 'critical friend' of culture, helping society to be happier and better. While there is no doubt that criticism can sometimes harden into contempt and hatred – attitudes that certainly *are* harmful to mission – being a critical friend is a *good*, and not a bad, thing. As Scripture says, the wounds of a friend are sweeter than the kisses of an enemy.

Engaging with culture, then, is one reason why fresh expressions are more likely to reach the unchurched than traditional forms of Church outreach. Yet culture affects not only the *form* of Church but Christians themselves. This brings us to the topic of missional discipleship. As we saw in Chapters 2 and 3, the Scottish Church has traditionally suffered from nominalism and a disempowered laity. Churchgoing and moral conformity were seen as sufficient indicators of faith and members were trained to aid the ministry of the clergy by undertaking practical tasks rather than preaching, planting or evangelising. Yet the massive numerical and financial decline of the Scottish Church means that the Church can no longer rely upon a small number of highly educated and paid professionals to fulfil the fullness of God's mission. *All* church members need to be mobilised, equipped and deployed.

While fresh expressions of Church are sometimes thought to avoid the dangers of nominalism, similar problems can be present, albeit for different reasons. As McCarthy notes, because many fresh expressions take listening to their communities so seriously, they sometimes fail to *tell them* the Gospel, and transform their neighbours into disciples.[58] While community development is good, without discipleship, it simply replicates nominal Christendom in a new form, and the Church's investment in fresh expressions will not bear fruit.[59] A further problem relates to leadership style. Fresh expressions are generally more relational and egalitarian than older forms of Church, and this can mean that their leaders can be uncomfortable with directing the spiritual journeys of others.[60]

For this reason, missional discipleship is essential if contextualisation and community-building is going to result in a worshipping Christian community. As Breen says, 'We don't have a missional problem in the Western Church. We have a discipleship problem.'[61] Yet what is discipleship? Discipleship is the process by which people draw nearer to Christ and become more like him.[62] In the past, faith was either taken as a given (as in the parish state) or was a once and for all decision (in some forms of classic evangelicalism). Discipleship recognises that faith formation is a process, something that involves development and change over time. This is sometimes visualised in the Engel scale and its derivatives, where all people – Christians included – are closer or further away from Jesus, and conversion is only one point on the scale rather than its summit.[63]

Discipleship does two things that are essential for mission. First, it shapes the *identity* of individual Christians and the worshipping community as a whole. As Paul says, we should not be conformed to this world – the world of Chapters 4 to 6 – but be transformed in the renewing of our minds. An example of *not* being transformed in the renewing of our minds comes from Dowie's ethnographic study of a prominent Church of Scotland congregation in the West. Despite its beautiful building and worship, its members were riven with disputes, animosities and grudges. Of the anonymous comments made to Dowie, the church's members admitted:

'It's not a religious place.'
'There's no evangelism, no faith, no glow of Christian
  fellowship.'
'It's all based on surface values.'[64]

Dowie's observation on the congregation's predicament is telling: in a worshipping community where the boundaries between Church and world are too porous, secular forces – and not Christ – will shape the identity and values of the congregation.[65]

Discipleship in a missional context, however, allows the Church to *reset* its culture and begin anew. It can abandon centuries of cultural baggage and toxic practices, and start again in an intentional way. This is possible for two reasons. First, the leaders of fresh expressions will tend to have unusually high levels of faith and commitment. Why else, after all, would they give up their time and resources and risk the possibility of failure? This high level of faith means that their relationship to each other and to those attending is not primarily social but *Christian*. They assume leadership primarily for missional purposes rather than custom, pride or a desire to dominate others. For those attending, the 'cultural reset' of fresh expressions also brings benefits. As the community is new, leaders, existing Christians and non-Christians are all 'in this together'. In and out group dynamics will also be less entrenched, blurring the boundaries between established and new members. Moreover, as an intentional Christian community, their core identity and values will be shaped less by the world and more by Christ.

In addition to safeguarding the identity of the Church, missional discipleship also allows individuals to discover their giftings, and play their part as members of Christ's Body. Fresh expressions are generally marked with smaller numbers and greater egalitarianism, and this means there is both more opportunity and more need for all members to contribute. Fresh expressions understand that the distribution of spiritual gifts is not a substitute for Christ's presence, but the very mode of that presence.[66] When the giftings of Christians are identified, developed and released, the missional health of the Church improves, and the Body of Christ is revealed in the world. An increasing number of Scottish Protestant churches look to Ephesians 4 for guidance in this regard, recognising not only the pastoral ministry identified by Calvin, but the offices of apostle, prophet and evangelist.

Spiritual giftings – as is made clear by Paul – work together for the good of the whole Body.[67] Nevertheless, fresh expressions increase the importance of *all* disciples exercising elements of leadership and entrepreneurship. Discipleship, as Hirsch says, is primary, and leadership is always secondary.[68] It is what happens when people grow more confident in their identity and giftings, and begin to use them to impact others. As we have seen, this missional leadership has been curtailed in a number of ways throughout Scottish history. The Church largely trained lay managers to fulfil certain circumscribed tasks, yet denied them entrepreneurial initiative.[69] It is widely recognised, however, that the future success of mission and evangelism will depend on developing entrepreneurial and experimental attitudes in as many Scottish Christians as possible.[70] As Stark has argued, the growth of Christianity in the Roman Empire was only possible because of individual Christians taking the initiative to witness to their Lord in everyday life. Every time someone came to faith, a host of new social connections were opened up to evangelism and the 'surface' of the Church increased, allowing it to reach and transform more areas of social, political and economic life.[71] The reach of the Church in contemporary Scotland is directly proportional to the extent that ordinary Christians feel empowered to exercise initiative and leadership in their respective walks of life.[72] There is no realistic future for the Scottish Church apart from this spontaneous form of lay ministry.

The evangelisation of Scotland and the proliferation of new forms of Church are therefore heavily dependent on discipleship and missional leadership. So how are these to be realised? As we have seen, catechesis – a form of discipleship – had largely died out by the turn of the twentieth century. Scottish Christians were therefore left with sermons and Bible studies, but, as we have seen, this was not particularly effective. One option would be to increase access to higher education for Christians, offering courses in missiology and missional discipleship at institutions of higher learning. Something like this happened after the Second World War in Scotland, with figures like Ian Fraser arguing for the democratisation of theology. This led to the creation of entities like Scottish Churches Open College.[73] Yet while these approaches represented serious investment in the development of church members, they were still largely academic and institution-based. As Hirsch argues, however, one cannot *think* oneself into a new form of missional practice. Rather, one must begin with practice and then witness how one's ideas change.[74] That is why the future of missional training in Scotland will look something like Forge Pioneer Training Course. In Forge, students still learn missiology and write essays. Yet the majority of the course is spent on location at missional projects, with students assessed on plans for concrete missional projects.

The Scottish Church, then, cannot *think* itself into renewal, nor determine in advance exactly *how* it will come about. Yet it can create the *conditions* for renewal,[75] which will involve community listening, discipleship, entrepreneurship and innovation, virtues inculcated by training structures that are highly contextual, practice-based and which integrate spiritual formation with education.

The promise of fresh expressions, therefore, is of intentional, passionate, contextual communities, witnessing to the Gospel through relevant worship and service. It is the possibility of communities in which worship, evangelism, service and discipleship are all closely integrated, and which better witness to the new creation than many traditional forms of Church. In so doing, they can act as a contextually relevant 'hermeneutic of the Gospel', increasing the social significance of the Church, and the plausibility of the Christian faith.

Assessing Fresh Expressions

Despite the appeal of fresh expressions of Church, they have been subject to sustained criticism from a wide variety of sources, including those sympathetic to their intentions.

The first, and perhaps most common, form of objection is that they ignore existing forms of Church. Rather than planting more churches, we should be working harder to revitalise existing churches. Programmes like the Church of Scotland's Path of Renewal, for example, work with ministers, elders and church members to adopt elements of discipleship and mission into church life in an attempt to increase congregational health and possibly boost numbers.[76] While it is no doubt a good thing to try and revitalise congregations, we must also remember Jesus' warning that new wine cannot always be poured into old wineskins. There are sometimes severe limitations to transforming existing Church cultures. As such, writers such as Guder argue that the attempted resuscitation of dying congregations can sometimes be 'a tragic diversion, and not to be confused with the resurrection of the Church'.[77]

While this form of criticism is found most commonly among churchgoers themselves, the majority of criticisms of fresh expressions come from theologians. The most common argument is that fresh expressions of Church represent a diluted and corrupted understanding of Church. In what is probably the most trenchant criticism of fresh expressions in print, Milbank and Davison accuse fresh expressions of Church of succumbing to secular assumptions and methods. Rather than challenging individualism and consumerism, fresh expressions canonise them, and make them a fundamental part of their ecclesiology.[78]

This criticism is related to a further one regarding the *purpose* of mission. If the purpose of fresh expressions is to bring the unchurched to faith, then what is the point of bringing the unchurched to faith? By making the conversion of the unchurched their ultimate goal, fresh expressions risk making the Church and its worship into mere means, when, as we saw in Chapter 1, the purpose and end of mission is worship. In this, fresh expressions are in danger of making the sole mark of the 'true church' its ability to bring people to faith,[79] which not only leads to dismissive attitudes towards congregations that struggle to grow, but also impoverishes the life of the Church. Mission is of uncontested importance, but we are ultimately missionary 'for ends that lie beyond mission'.[80]

This is seen in the importance of the *form* that worshipping community takes. Milbank and Davison argue that while it is commonly thought that the content of the Gospel can be neatly separated from its cultural forms, this is not the case. Some forms *corrupt* the Gospel, while others strengthen it.[81] A good example of this is what is called the 'homogeneous unit principle'. This is the idea that worshiping communities grow better when they mainly consist of the same age, or race, or culture, or interest group. In a Scottish study, Akomiah-Conteh found that this has been the 'reigning dogma' of church plants in Glasgow in the past twenty years, especially among ethnic minorities.[82] While there is some evidence that the principle works,[83] it is not the picture that we see in the New Testament. On the contrary, the explicit purpose of the mission of Jesus and the apostles was to make a church of *all* nations, *all* cultures and *all* types of person. Heterogeneity in the future or the eschaton is not good enough. Rather, difference must be part of the intrinsic DNA of any worshipping community.[84]

This issue is also related to the level of cooperation that is possible among fresh expressions of Church. As we saw in Chapters 2 and 3, Christian disunity was a key factor in the secularisation of Scotland. While fresh expressions often think of themselves as being post-denominational, this sometimes masks implicit ecclesiologies and biases that increase disunity and distort the Gospel. Dozens of studies have shown that human beings instinctively mistrust and think badly of those who do not belong to their real or perceived group. While this is more intelligible – if still sad – when deep theological differences divide groups, it has been found that mistrust and dislike persist even when the *only* difference between groups is that they are not the same group.[85] The proliferation of fresh expressions of Church and church plants, regardless of good intentions, therefore risks *increasing* disunity and fragmentation in the Body of Christ.

In addition to these criticisms come methodological ones. Some church planters believe that starting a new worshipping community will automatically lead to growth, or that growing the number of plants is an end in itself. For such people, gathering in new communities and doing evangelism are one and the same thing.[86] This misplaced enthusiasm arises, so critics claim, because church planters and pioneers tend to work with the assumption that everyone has a felt need for Christ and that they are all just waiting for the right form of Church to come along.[87] As we saw in Chapter 6, however, this is unlikely to be the case. Moreover, even if fresh expressions and church planting *could* be shown to work, their advocates overlook the fact that the majority of Scottish churchgoers are elderly, lacking in confidence and more business-orientated than evangelism-orientated.[88] As such, while fresh expressions may provide a plausible template for growth, we may lack the resources to realise them.

A final line of critique concerns *who* is reached by fresh expressions of Church. The explicit hope is that the unchurched will be reached, yet anecdotal evidence suggests otherwise. Male muses whether the main demographic reached is not the unchurched but the *de*churched, that broad range of disaffected Christians we examined in Chapter 6. Hirsch argues that fresh expressions can sometimes resemble 'soul spaces' for the burned-out middle classes, or adrenaline-fests for immature consumers rather than places of formation for earnest disciples.[89] The myth of reaching genuinely unchurched people is maintained, however, due to a paucity of good data. For writers such as Paas, much 'research' into church planting is simply 'magic with numbers' and bears little relation to reality.[90]

What, then, are we to make of all of this? Are fresh expressions the salvation of the Church and of Scotland, or little more than a distraction from the serious work of ministry?

We will begin with what is true in the foregoing critiques. First of all, no matter their potential, fresh expressions of Church alone will not reverse the secularisation of Scotland. When Moynagh says, for example, that fresh expressions of Church are based on the assumption that the secularisation thesis is incorrect, we must state – sadly – that he is wrong.[91] Reverting to Christendom, or establishing a future where all Scots are Christian, is not going to happen without calamitous social change, which the Church has no means of realising.

This is related to another critique of fresh expressions: that many of them are naïve in what they think can be achieved. As church planting theorists now admit, Wagner's dictum that church planting was 'the single most effective evangelistic method under heaven' is overstated at best and, at worst, delusional.[92] That is because – as we have shown – religious demand in Scotland has fallen significantly due to the adoption of non-religious identities and the individualisation of spirituality. As such, at least in Scotland, the 'rational choice theory' – that a diversification of worship styles will meet unmet religious need – is incorrect. Greater choice will never be effective if there is no demand to begin with.

Before we turn to assess the most common forms of fresh expression in more detail, it is important – particularly in light of the coronavirus pandemic – to consider the experience of online Church as a form of fresh expression. The *Everybody Welcome* report from England demonstrated a large upturn in views and participation in online worship during the early stages of the national lockdown.[93] Likewise, a study of the Scottish experience by myself and my colleagues at Brendan Research has shown that online worship increased from 18% before the pandemic to an astonishing 95.5% during lockdown. Moreover, 82% of respondents reported their desire to continue some form of online worship after the pandemic ended.[94]

Because of the growing significance of online worship, however, issues of categorisation are particularly important. Who is online Church primarily for? Is it primarily for Christians or non-Christians? If both, should it be characterised as mission or alternative worship?

We can illustrate this issue with two Scottish examples. The first is Destiny Church Edinburgh's online ministry. This is intentionally described as a *location*, being directly analogous to Destiny's physical locations. It is also explicitly directed towards the unchurched, helping people 'who don't come to church explore the Christian faith and find out about a God who loves them'.[95] It has its own leaders, who host a special session before livestreamed worship. They also chat to those attending, and answer any questions they have about faith. As with all of Destiny's worship and mission, there are also many moments in this online activity when attenders are invited to make a response to the Gospel. Another example is Sanctuary First, an online worshipping community of Falkirk Presbytery. Sanctuary First's aim is to be 'a resource for the wider church and a fresh way to engage with Christianity for those who are unfamiliar or unused to church'.[96] It began life as a daily devotional, but has now evolved into a multi-media community encompassing live music, discussion, book groups and physical Connect Groups.

These two forms of online Church demonstrate differences of intention and method. Destiny is single-mindedly evangelistic, while Sanctuary First is primarily concerned with discipleship, but with the hope that the dechurched or unchurched will find their community more engaging and attractive than traditional forms of Church.[97] Whatever the intention behind online Church, however, it is difficult to see how discipleship can develop and grow without the service and sacrifice that go with physical congregational life. Moreover, it is not clear if online Church is ultimately compatible with the new creation witnessed in the Sacraments. God's will for creation is of an *embodied* salvation, and not of disembodied spirits in remote communion. Online Church is a legitimate expression of Christian community, yet it may be incomplete without physical and spatial community.

Unfortunately, there is little to no data from Scotland to illuminate the question of how effective *physical* forms of fresh expression are. The existing material is largely qualitative, which – while useful – does not directly address the question of the numbers of people who are impacted by these forms of Church.[98] What we do know, however, is that new congregations are being planted in Scotland all the time. Brierley found that two hundred congregations had been planted in Scotland between 2002 and 2016,[99] while Akomiah-Conteh – perhaps due to her more focused local study – found that 110 new churches had been planted in Glasgow *alone* during the same period.[100]

Nevertheless – and while bearing in mind cultural differences – English data provides a picture of the relative effectiveness of different kinds of fresh expression. Among the least effective at recruiting the unchurched would appear to be alternative forms of worship, such as art installations, drama and similar events. These – somewhat unsurprisingly – presuppose that people are interested in worship, prayer and biblical themes, which most Scots are not. Of middling success are multi-site churches and – slightly less effective – church plants.[101] These forms of evangelism benefit from the apparent ability of smaller churches to grow more quickly than larger ones, a phenomenon that seems to be connected to the better quality of relationships in smaller gatherings.[102] Of the historic denominations, the Free Church has invested most in traditional church plants, with dozens appearing in recent years. Multi-site churches such as The

Tron in Glasgow or Catalyst Vineyard (formerly City Church) in Aberdeen, also have a tried and tested formula which – in the case of the old City Church – saw the church packing equipment and a team into a van and moving from location to location. Likewise, small denominations like Destiny, having found a model that leads to conversions, largely replicate this in each new location. While the English data suggests that church plants and multi-site churches are resource-intensive and do not yield as many converts as some other methods, done well, they are still a helpful addition to evangelism in Scotland.

In addition to the data from England, we can also reach some further conclusions from our own explorations of why fresh expressions are potentially effective. Given that – theologically and sociologically – it is worshipping *communities* that are most likely to attract non-Christians, we can say with some confidence that single pioneers or church planters are unlikely to be effective. Such 'parachute pioneers' are only typically used in international mission, when the cost of sending a larger team is too prohibitive.[103] If cost is less of an issue, however, then there is no reason not to send a team. The only hope for single pioneers is to recruit and train a team as quickly as possible. Yet given that many pioneer contracts in Scotland are only for three to five years, this is not always an easy task.

From the data available, the most effective form of fresh expression would appear to be those aimed at young families, exemplified by Messy Church and similar initiatives. This was the clear outcome of the *Day of Small Things* report and the Church Army's later research on Messy Church,[104] along with research by Walker, which showed that Messy Church was the *only* form of fresh expression to attract significant numbers of unchurched families.[105] Crucially, however, these forms of fresh expression only experienced significant growth when the leaders thought and acted as if they were standalone churches, and not alternative forms of worship or feeders for 'real Church' on a Sunday morning. When leaders thought of these fresh expressions as standalone, they invested in discipleship, teaching and the sacraments, and at that point growth became more likely.

How, then, should we summarise the place of fresh expressions in the life of the Scottish Church? We can say with some confidence that fresh expressions – if shaped by the principles surveyed in this chapter and properly supported – *can* work. In particular, those focused on families have been empirically proven to reach the unchurched in our near neighbour England, and there is good reason to think Scotland would be similar. Nevertheless, there are outstanding theological questions concerning some types of fresh expression, and there is little doubt that new forms of worship, in and of themselves, will fail if not accompanied by a renewed culture of entrepreneurial discipleship.

The Scottish Church, then, must invest a good deal more of its resources into creating the conditions for fresh expressions to grow. These conditions include training for church members, intentional discipleship and the releasing of funds to support new initiatives. The future, then, will be a 'mixed economy' – or better yet, a 'mixed ecology' – of traditional and fresh expressions of Church.[106] This will not be a regimented ecology, however, but a 'wild' one, with traditional churches adopting elements of fresh expressions into their congregational life and fresh expressions – particularly as they mature – taking on some of the characteristics of inherited Church. This mixed ecology will necessarily move resources away from inherited forms of Church. Yet Church leaders in the traditional denominations know that it is not a question of *if* inherited forms of Church will one day cease to be but only *when*. As such, the creation of fresh expressions is analogous to the Church sending out lifeboats from the sinking *Titanic*, allowing the people of God to survive their impending disaster.[107] Another – more positive – analogy is that of the dandelion. When the height of summer is over, the dandelion changes. It sheds its bright flowers and reveals the seeds that will ensure its genus survives the coming winter. The wind blows and disperses the seeds far and wide, creating a new generation of flowers. That is what God is doing with his Church. He is changing us for the coming winter, creating *many* forms of Church where there were previously only a few. The challenge, of course, is to ensure that, in this dispersal, the DNA of the Church remains intact, and that these new forms of Church resemble both each other and their Creator.

Conclusion

In this chapter, we have examined the Church's efforts to evangelise Scotland after the collapse of the parish state and the coming of secularisation. We have explored direct forms of evangelism as well as pre-evangelism, and the relative effectiveness of fresh expressions of Church. This analysis confirmed many of the lessons of Chapters 2 and 7, that the most successful ways of creating and developing faith are those that are based in Church communities, and which integrate discipleship, service and evangelism. Rather than simply focusing on worship, or keeping service and evangelism apart, the churches that are growing in faith and numbers are those that integrate all of these, and contextualise them in ways appropriate to their communities. Encouragingly, the most effective of these new forms of Christian community appear to be those focused on young families, which are not as resource-intensive as other forms of fresh expression such as church plants. Turning back the tide of secularisation may be impossible, yet fresh expressions of Church can help create local cultures of plausibility and provoke and nurture faith in those of our neighbours who are still open to hearing the voice of Christ.

9

Public Witness

Service, evangelism and the creation of new Christian communities are the most important forms of Christian mission. They are the forms that most impact the day-to-day lives of ordinary Scots, and those that are most important in creating the local micro-cultures on which the plausibility of the Christian faith is founded. Yet, as we have seen, the local and personal are only two aspects of life in contemporary Scotland. Of great importance is the *public life* of Scotland, found in its Parliament, state institutions, media and civic organisations. These are the embodiment of Scotland's national consciousness, and are the organs of society most responsible for the shaping of public opinion. As such, the Church cannot be indifferent to them, for they have the potential to be great allies – and great opponents – of God's mission to Scotland.

In this chapter, we will examine the public mission field of contemporary Scotland. We will look at the role of the state in God's providential order and the relation between its authority and Christ's. We will then examine how the Scottish Church relates to the state and civil society, noting important divergences within the aims and methods of denominations. We then turn to consider what the aims of the Scottish Church should be in relation to the state and civil society, and conclude with an overview of a distinctly Christian public ethic, which has significant policy implications for the state and public institutions.

Powers and Principalities

Given the dominance that the Church would eventually attain in Scotland, it is easy to forget that Christian political theology formed in a context of public hostility and sometimes violent state persecution. While a natural response to this context would have been an aggressive anti-state world view that legitimised rebellion, that is not what happened. Instead, following Jesus' lead in Matthew 5:38–48, Matthew 22:15–22, Mark 12:13–17 and Luke 20:20–26, the Church did the exact opposite. In Romans 13:1–7, Paul writes:

> Let every person be subject to the governing authorities; for there is no authority except from God, and those authorities that exist have been instituted by God. Therefore whoever resists authority resists what God has appointed, and those who resist will incur judgement. For rulers are not a terror to good conduct, but to bad. Do you wish to have no fear of the authority? Then do what is good, and you will receive its approval; for it is God's servant for your good ... Pay to all what is due to them – taxes to whom taxes are due, revenue to whom revenue is due, respect to whom respect is due, honour to whom honour is due.

In this passage, Paul makes it clear that those in authority are appointed by God, and that it is the duty of Christians to obey them. If they do not, they will be liable to both worldly and divine judgement. In this, Paul displays his belief that rulers play an important role in God's providence as punishers of wrongdoing and upholders of justice.

We see a similar message in 1 Peter 2:12–17:

> Conduct yourselves honourably among the Gentiles, so that, though they malign you as evildoers, they may see your honourable deeds and glorify God when he comes to judge ... For the Lord's sake accept the authority of every human institution ... Honour everyone. Love the family of believers. Fear God. Honour the emperor.

Once again, we see the same injunction for Christians to submit themselves to worldly authority, as rulers have a God-given authority to punish wrongdoing. The writer of 1 Peter also deploys an important apologetic argument, that the obedience and good conduct of the Church would silence those who think that Christians are bad or criminal people.

From these passages, it might be thought that the apostles had a quietest political outlook, in which the one political duty of the Christian was to obey the powers that be, in the hope that the world would not think too badly of the Church. Yet that is only part of the political theology of the early Church. For the other part is far more dramatic and surprising. In Colossians 2:15, Paul writes of Jesus' Cross:

> He [Jesus] disarmed the rulers and authorities and made a public example of them, triumphing over them in it.

The early Church could teach obedience only because they thought that the power of the state and its rulers had been completely destroyed on the Cross, in which the power and authority of the world had been shown to be incapable of killing God. The crucifixion *should* have been the climax of the world's struggle with God, where earthly power finally killed God and destroyed his people. Yet the opposite was true. The crucifixion of Jesus *confirmed* God's authority, and became the source of salvation for the Church. The overthrow of earthly rulers is not limited to those who reigned at the time of the crucifixion, however, but extends to *all* rulers, along with the non-Christian world views they hold and promote. That is why the earliest Christian proclamation 'Jesus is Lord' is a *political* proclamation. 'Lord' (*kyrios*) is the same word used for those in secular authority, and means that it is Christ – and not the powers that be – who holds ultimate authority. In 1 Corinthians 2:6–7, Paul writes:

> Yet among the mature we do speak wisdom, though it is not a wisdom of this age or of the rulers of this age, who are doomed to perish. But we speak God's wisdom, secret and hidden, which God decreed before the ages for our glory.

Paul makes an important connection here between the 'wisdom of this age' and the 'rulers of this age'. What the ruling class believe to be true in any age is what is taken as 'wisdom', because they use their power to shape and form popular opinion. Paul therefore accepts some of the arguments of critical theory – and Marx – in seeing 'truth' as being closely linked to political power. Yet power has its limits, for if rulers do not recognise Jesus Christ as Lord and Saviour then they are doomed to perish, for the only wisdom that enables institutions and governments to survive across time is the wisdom of Christ. Importantly, this is the case for *any* government, whether they be liberal, conservative or progressive.

The New Testament, then, teaches that rulers have been appointed by God to punish wrongdoing and injustice. They have a legitimate role within the divine providence, one that deserves the support and respect of Christians. Yet the authority of the state is not intrinsic but extrinsic: it belongs to God alone. For this reason, if rulers consistently disobey God's decreed will for creation, then he will overthrow them.

If the political theology of the early Church did not advance very far beyond 'love the Church and honour the emperor', this changed with the elevation of Constantine to the Imperial throne.[1] In the Edict of Milan, Constantine introduced a form of religious freedom that ended the persecution of Christians. He then began to favour the Church with gifts, and take an interest in its affairs. This meant that the Church had to develop a political theology for a wholly unforeseen situation: *Christian* rulers.[2] While it would be frequently contested by earthly powers, the Catholic Church adopted the belief that because the authority of rulers came from God, and because the Church was his representative, earthly power was mediated from God through the Church. In effect, the Church was the true ruler of the world.[3]

After the Reformation, Scottish theology re-purposed these principles in the doctrine of the Two Kingdoms. In the account of that doctrine given in the Westminster Confession, God does not give power to the magistrate through the Church, but *directly*. Church and magistrate hold different jurisdictions which should not be confused. Nevertheless, Christians are permitted to hold public office, especially to maintain the good order and social position of the Church.[4] In addition, *all* of society should be subject to the Word of God.

With the advent of industrialisation, and the need for increasing state intervention to moderate the crushing effects of poverty, Scottish Christians, as we have seen, adopted Kingdom-centred theologies that stressed not only the judicial and punitive role of the state, but its positive, interventionist role in improving society. This theological belief directly influenced the creation of the welfare state in Britain, with Archbishop William Temple and the Christian Socialist tradition providing important theological rationales for the state as the embodiment of Christian principle.[5]

These traditional understandings have become increasingly strained in the wake of the secularisation recounted in Chapters 3 and 5. If the Scottish and UK Governments no longer acknowledge that their authority is dependent on God, what is God's view of them? If they no longer look to the Church as an equal partner with its own jurisdiction and immutable social role, how should the Church relate to them?

Two approaches have presented themselves in recent years. The first is derived from the anabaptist tradition, and is represented by missional writers like Murray. According to this line of thinking, the Church's primary political objective should be to safeguard religious freedom, and model an alternative form of community to demonstrate God's intentions for society.[6] This view animates many Baptist churches in Scotland, but is now increasingly found in conservative Reformed circles. This is due, in part, to their common experience of marginalisation, sometimes related to their opposition to same-sex relationships. Yet it also stems from the growing influence of American and Dutch Reformed theology in Scotland. American Reformed theologians come from a context that never had a parish state like Scotland, and the Dutch Reformed experience was of a nation that secularised earlier and in a different way from Scotland. The Dutch neo-Calvinist concept of *pillarisation* has thus gained some traction, a position that argues that Christians should create their own institutions and sub-culture – including schools and media – to maintain their faith, and balance out the power of the state and other groups.[7]

The second approach also comes from the Reformed tradition, but represents a more moderate, Scottish strain of Reformed thought, building on the thought of John Baillie's 'middle axioms'.[8] For Fergusson, secularisation means that the days of elaborate political theologies conjecturing the ideal relationship between Church and state are gone. In their place, the Church should seek to build partnerships in civil society, an area in which it can have greater influence. This is elaborated further by writers like Storrar, who argue that the Church should seek to foster a new form of popular civic democracy, in which the Church and other partners serve as a counterweight to the Scottish Parliament.[9]

While one of these perspectives is more outward facing and confident about civil society than the other, *all* are a response to the secularisation of the state. In a context where we cannot expect the state to give preferential treatment to the Church, we must look for alternatives, either within our own church life or with partners in civil society. Both options have merit. Religious freedom is the basis of liberal democracy, and the Church should jealously guard its own and other's freedoms. It is also true that, with the growing complexity of Scottish society and the proliferation of groups within it, the Church no longer has one major partner but potentially thousands. Yet neither approach fully reflects the New Testament position. The apostles are clear that, because of what was accomplished in Jesus, earthly rulers are subject to the authority of God, and in order to maintain their authority they must do his will. As such, despite their failure to recognise the reign of God, they still play an important – if largely unconscious – role in his mission to the world. It is also the case that the churches – as we shall see – still *expect* the state to do certain things, and sometimes exert considerable resource to make these things happen. For these reasons, the Scottish Church must still think through what it is trying to achieve in its relationship with government and state institutions.

Faith in Politics

Before we can know what this relationship is, however, we must first survey the activity of the churches in relation to the state and public life in Scotland. There are a number of levels of complexity to this. First, denominations make public statements in their own right on a range of topical issues. Second, individual leaders and congregations within these denominations also make statements on issues of public interest, which are sometimes in alignment with their denominational position and sometimes not. Third, in addition to these denominational and congregational pronouncements, congregations and denominations can also be part of para-church groupings that purport to speak for their members. Due to this complexity, it is very difficult – with the possible exception of the Roman Catholic Church – to say definitively what a denomination believes about issues of public importance. With that caveat aside, however, it is still possible to discern broad approaches to public life across different Scottish denominations and networks. These reveal divergences within the Scottish Church's thinking on the purpose of public engagement, and the relationship between Church, state and civil society.

Until recently, the public largely identified the Church's engagement in Scottish society and politics with the Church and Society Council of the Church of Scotland.[10] The remit of the Church and Society Council is 'to engage on behalf of the Church in the national, political and social issues affecting Scotland and the world today'. It does this through 'the development of theological, ethical and spiritual perspectives when formulating policy and by effectively representing the Church by offering appropriate and informed comments'.[11] In recent decades, the Council has been associated with a broadly left-wing agenda – in part due to the influence of the Iona Community – which has sometimes sat uneasily within a Church that was traditionally Conservative in orientation.[12] This has included support for nuclear disarmament, wealth redistribution and care for creation, long before environmental issues were popular. As such, public mission for the Church and

Society Council primarily means persuading politicians and others in power to advance a social justice agenda. Despite the Church of Scotland's Christian character and historic role in education and public life, it is interesting to note the absence of sustained interest in gender and sexuality, religious freedom or preserving Christian influence in schools. Indeed, the Church and Society Council worked with the Humanist Society of Scotland to rebrand religious observance in schools as 'time for reflection', mirroring the pluralist and inter-faith approach to religion followed in the Scottish Parliament.

In years past, there was much interest in the work of the Council and its predecessors. Copies of its – often lengthy – reports would be sent to Cabinet Ministers and every Scottish MP, and during the presentation of its report, Scottish politicians and civic figures would take up seats in the public gallery of the General Assembly hall to hear what the Church would decide. Yet with secularisation, and the diminishing social significance of all the churches, interest began to wane, with cabinet ministers – even in the late 1980s – admitting the Church's views now counted for little.[13] Commentators such as Wickham-Jones began to wonder aloud whether the Church's investment of significant time, personnel and finance was being well spent, with the fear that the mark of success for Conveners was getting deliverances passed in the General Assembly rather than influencing society and the state.[14] Despite its commitment to developing theological perspectives on topical issues, the Council's predecessor Committee has also come in for criticism from Duncan Forrester for not providing theological justifications for its views, with its reports sometimes being little more than a summary of the year's events along with a list of political demands.[15]

The Church of Scotland's public mission is not only carried out through the Church and Society Council, however, but two other bodies. One of these is the Joint Public Issues Team (JPIT), a partnership with the Baptist Union of Great Britain, the Methodist Church and the United Reformed Church. While JPIT's areas of interest are also focused on social justice and creation care, it is interesting to note that it defines its mission as 'to work for God's kingdom on earth as it is in heaven' and uses explicit theological language to describe and justify its work.[16]

In its relationship with the Scottish Parliament, the Church and Society Council is also represented by the Scottish Churches Parliamentary Office (SCPO). SCPO is a collaboration between a number of Scottish denominations, including the Scottish Episcopal Church, the United Reformed Church and the Baptist Union of Scotland. It defines its mission as enabling Scottish churches to:

- Engage effectively in the political process
- Translate their commitment to the welfare of Scotland into parliamentary debate
- Contribute the range and depth of their experience to the decision-making process.[17]

It does this through the production of briefing papers on upcoming legislation, highlighting government consultations and running the Meet Your MSP programme for congregations. It sums up its agenda under 'Doing politics differently', encouraging participatory budgeting, local democracy and creating opportunities for MSPs to hear the voices of poor and marginalised people. SCPO, then, primarily sees its public mission as one of facilitation and advocacy: conveying information to churches, creating opportunities for congregations to meet politicians and encouraging politicians to listen to those they would not normally hear.

This approach to public mission stands in contrast to that of the Evangelical Alliance in Scotland (EA). The EA represents a wide range of congregations, organisations and businesses in Scotland, and has as its motto 'Together making Jesus known'. Like other Scottish Church organisations, the EA is also interested in social justice issues and recently established SERVE Scotland to represent the views of members engaged in care and community development to the Scottish Government. Yet social justice issues are not the principal focus of the EA. Instead, its primary role is communicating evangelical concerns to government, and seeking to influence its policy. In addition to replying to consultations and sending correspondence to Scottish Government ministers, it also lays great stress on public leadership. There are two parts to this. The first is its Speak Up initiative. This aims to educate Christians as to their legal rights, and use their freedom of speech to share their faith in their personal and professional lives. The second is the training of Christian leaders. The SENT resource is intended for congregational use, and encourages Christians in business and the public sector to think through what it means to be a Christian leader. The EA also offers the more in-depth Public Leader's Course for those in their 20s and 30s. This offers teaching, mentoring and support to young Christian leaders, equipping them to be public witnesses for Christ in a variety of fields. This is part of the EA's intention to enable Christians to be a 'creative minority', to be salt and light in every section of society so that Christ may be known and his Kingdom come.

While the Roman Catholic Church in Scotland works with the SCPO, it also maintains its own Catholic Parliamentary Office (CPO) in Edinburgh. The mission of the CPO is to ensure that 'the values of the Gospel are prominent in public life and that the Social Teaching of the Church is made known to those active in politics and more widely known in society'.[18] Interestingly, it has the same core values as those of the Evangelical Alliance, seeking a society that is rooted in love, truth, justice and freedom.[19] The social teaching of the Roman Catholic Church includes social justice issues such as poverty and care for creation that are of interest to the major Scottish Protestant denominations. Yet it also campaigns on a number of issues that are absent from the public mission of the Church of Scotland, the SCPO and the majority of its constituent members, namely opposition to abortion, same-sex marriages and assisted suicide. Indeed, the Roman Catholic Church in Scotland has often become the public face of Christian resistance to these social phenomena, with Cardinal O'Brien taking the lead against same-sex marriage prior his downfall following allegations of inappropriate conduct with young men. The Roman Catholic Church's political activities – including 'leaning on'

Roman Catholic MSPs – is generally thought to be more effective than that of the Church of Scotland.[20] This may be due, in part, to the consistency of Roman Catholic theology, and the ability of the church's leaders to make binding pronouncements for its members. Yet it also breeds resentment, as politicians feel they have to take the Roman Catholic Church's views into consideration despite fundamentally disagreeing with them.[21]

Despite differences in their policy objectives, Scotland's churches and Christian organisations generally relate to the government in similar ways. They answer government consultations, try to build relationships with politicians and lobby the government in an attempt to influence its thinking.

This is in contrast to two other forms of Christian political activity: Christian pressure groups and Christian political parties. Christian pressure and advocacy groups such as Christian Concern and the Christian Institute seek to do two things: first, to defend the rights of the Church, particularly in relation to free speech; second, to lobby for Christian values in schools and public institutions. These interests converge in the cases they support, often concerning Christians who have been arrested for street preaching, sharing their faith at work or articulating traditional views regarding gender and sexuality. While interdenominational groups, both largely represent – and are led – by evangelical Protestants who feel under attack by secular society. For this reason, while of a very different religious and political outlook from groups such as Stonewall or the Scottish Trans Alliance, such groups may be taken as examples of Christian identity politics, examples of what happens when conservative Christians feel under threat from wider society.

The second – and related – phenomenon that diverges from the approach of the denominations is Christian political parties. The intention behind these political parties is not simply to influence legislators, but to *become* legislators, thereby providing a distinct Christian voice in Parliament. One of the conditions for the possibility of socially conservative political parties was provided by the Roman Catholic Church in Scotland. The Scottish Bishops lobbied for abortion to be devolved under the Scotland Act before the Parliament was created, believing that Scotland was more likely than the rest of the UK to favour curbs on terminations (a view also shared, albeit on opposing lines, by politicians such as Robin Cook).[22] In the 1999 Scottish parliamentary elections, Scottish Roman Catholics were involved in canvassing for the ProLife Alliance, which put up a number of candidates in the greater Glasgow area. The Alliance only secured 2% of the vote, however, and eventually disbanded in the mid-2000s. Then came the pan-UK Christian People's Alliance – which drew approval from Cardinal O'Brien and Bishop Tartaglia – and later the Scottish Christian Party. While the leader of the Scottish Christian Party, George Hargreaves, managed to pull 7.2% in the Western Isles constituency at the 2005 General Election, none of its other results have matched or bettered this.[23] More recently, the Scottish Family Party – led by teacher Richard Lucas – has sought to challenge the consensus at Holyrood concerning LGBT+ rights, especially in relation to Time for Inclusive Education (TIE) in schools. Lucas ran in the 2019 General Election in the Ross, Skye and Lochaber constituency, but garnered only 0.7% of the vote.[24]

Having described the broad contours of the political activity of the Scottish churches, we turn now to analysis.

Following Scripture and the Western theological tradition, it is clear that the Scottish churches accept the authority of the Scottish and UK Governments. This was true even during the unprecedented events of the coronavirus pandemic, and the regulations governing public worship that accompanied it. Moreover, whether they be conservative, moderate or liberal, Scotland's denominations largely accept the principle that the state should intervene, at least in certain situations, to improve society through the exercise of legal and political force. For these reasons, Scotland's denominations seek to work with the state, and within the political framework recognised by other social groups.

Christian political parties also operate within Scotland's existing political framework, but are likely to be less successful than churches at effecting social change. The first – contextual – reason for this is that, unlike in continental Europe, where political parties have frequently formed around religion (e.g. Angela Merkel's Christian Democratic Union), this has not happened in Scotland. While Roman Catholics traditionally voted Labour, this was primarily due to their *class* rather than their *religion* and, as we saw earlier, the SNP has not cultivated an affiliation with Presbyterianism. Given the social context outlined in Chapter 4, and the growth of nationalism seen in Chapter 5, it is highly unlikely that socially conservative Christian parties will have any success contesting elections. The second difficulty relates to the social base of political parties. Political parties generally represent a distinct constituency within society, a group of people related by ethnicity, class or belief. Due to the declining number of Scottish Christians, taken with the division of the Scottish Church, Christian political parties in Scotland will struggle to find a constituency to support them. Third, even if a conservative Christian party were to be elected to the Scottish Parliament, given that they would be a tiny minority with unpopular views, they would be rounded on by the other parties, making it hard for them to normalise their socially conservative beliefs. In such a situation, their only strategy would be to hope for a hung Parliament and leverage policy compromises. Yet given their small size, such policy gains would be extremely limited, and they would also risk being frozen out of negotiations due to their beliefs. While the creation of distinct Christian political parties is unlikely to bear much fruit, this does not mean that individual Christians in government cannot effect change, a possibility that we will examine later.

If Christian political parties suffer from the unpopularity of their views, moderate and liberal churches suffer, paradoxically, from their views being *too* socially acceptable. In many ways, this is a positive situation. As we have seen, the state is also called to further God's mission, and unanimity between Church and state leads to a mutually beneficial relationship between the two. Yet there are problems with this convergence of political outlooks. In the rhetoric of mainstream Protestant churches, much is made of 'speaking prophetically' and 'speaking truth to power'. Yet the social policy positions of many churches are almost indistinguishable from those of centre-left political parties such as the SNP. Reduction of poverty, elimination of homelessness and participatory democracy are all part of the mainstream of Scottish political culture, and there is nothing distinctively Christian about these policies save that they are held by Christians. This is not entirely irrelevant, of course. At least one of the purposes of Christian political engagement is to present the views of *the Church* on these matters. If the government is already minded to do something then the added imprimatur of Scotland's churches may be enough to occasionally push them over the line. Yet what does it mean to speak truth to power when the powers that be already hold those truths? What does it mean to do politics differently when the politicians are already 'different' in the way that we would like them to be?

Because of the large degree of overlap between the political views of the mainstream denominations and those of the Scottish Government, Sutherland has spoken of the creation of an 'informal religious establishment' in Scotland. In previous centuries the Church of Scotland was fully established, receiving financial and political support from wealthy elites and the government. In today's post-Christian Scotland, this kind of public support is impossible. Yet by advancing social policy positions in line with those of the government, Scottish churches *do* receive benefits. They obtain greater access to cabinet ministers, and preferential treatment with regard to funding support for their projects. This is particularly so when they work ecumenically and inter-faith. That is because, as we have seen, the Scottish Government has used the ending of sectarianism as one reason for the Parliament's existence, and with Islamist terrorism and prejudice against Muslims in the public spotlight, the government has an interest in stressing Scotland's religious harmony. The contrary is also true, however. Churches that are not so comfortable with ecumenical or inter-faith working will find themselves with less political access, and less access to public funds.

Having politically respectable views, then, can bring some benefit to the Church. Yet it is legitimate to ask whether the

Church's witness to Christ can be done without stressing the distinctiveness of the Gospel. Is it possible to translate Christianity into public speech without speaking of Jesus? Can Christians do politics without being explicitly Christian?

When mainstream denominations interact with government and civil society, they are in danger of falling into two errors. The first is to believe that the *primary* role of Christian political engagement is to represent 'the mind of the Church'. Nowhere in Scripture does it say that it is the role of the Church to communicate the political views of its members or leaders. We are not called to communicate the 'mind of the Church' but to have the mind of Christ and to witness to him. We are ambassadors *of Christ*, and to be that faithfully means to use language, concepts and methods that are similar to his, and those of the apostles he appointed. The second danger is being thought of as 'just good people', rather than Christians who represent their Lord. Humanism – the dominant spiritual philosophy of our time – interprets the good actions of Christians not as an example of the power of Christ, but of the goodness of humanity. By not being explicitly Christian in the motivation, rationale and expression of our political views, the world may think well of us, but we will not be effective witnesses to the glory of the God who inspires and directs us.

For that reason, there is good sense to the political approach of the Roman Catholic Church and the Evangelical Alliance. While not rejecting the importance of social justice issues, these are balanced with more distinctive Christian positions on gender, sexuality and religious and political freedom. These are clearly 'religious' in a way that poverty reduction is not, and therefore immediately point towards the distinctive claims of the Gospel. By holding a range of distinctive political positions, conservative Christians have more opportunities to point others to God in a clear and direct way. Many of the positions adopted by conservative Christians are, of course, deeply unpopular, and liberal and moderate Christians will reject them as being inauthentic expressions of the Gospel. There is also the risk, as we examined earlier, of conservative – and in particular evangelical – Christian action becoming yet another form of identity politics. Just as ethnic, gender and sexual minorities have been radicalised, so now have evangelicals. Like these other groups, focusing only on the rights of *our* group leads to resentment among other groups. Christians are not set apart from the world to receive special rights from the state, but set apart to seek the welfare of others and to make Christ known.

Doing Politics Christianly

Now that we have described and analysed the broad contours of Scottish Christian politics, we are in a position to make some suggestions as to how the mission of God might be advanced through the political action of the Scottish Church.

First and foremost – and following the Trinitarian logic of service and witness explored in Chapter 1 – Christian political action must be both genuinely altruistic and explicitly Christian. Christians should be deeply concerned about poverty, inequality and the environment, and it is legitimate to use the Church's resources to seek the good of the city and the welfare of our neighbours. This is part of the core business of the Church, and cannot be excluded. Yet without theological motivations and rationales these actions will be thought of as the actions of good people rather than good Christians. In this way, God will not get the glory, and little connection will be made between the good that Christians do and the truth of what they proclaim. For that reason, we must justify our public interventions by reference to Christ and not only to the 'mind of the Church', as if our leaders were representing a trade union or a business association.

Genuine political altruism is not only limited to improving the material wellbeing of Scots, but to improving their *spiritual* wellbeing. Our society makes people ill. Unbounded freedom robs our neighbours of their intrinsic worth, purpose and community support networks, and capitalism exploits them by producing artificial wants and insecurities that they seek to satisfy through the fruitless accumulation of property and designer lifestyles.

Christian leaders must therefore be more forthright in doing two things: first, in naming the power structures that enslave our neighbours; second, in proclaiming the life-giving power of Christ. Following Walter Wink, we must unmask the 'lordless powers' of sociology, capitalism, social media and other harmful forces.[25] This will involve Church leaders and members educating themselves about the society in which they live, something that we have tried to do throughout this work. Yet second, having seen these powers at work, they must redouble their faith, and find the confidence to speak. This speech must not only be negative, however, but positive. It is only because we know of a higher Lord and his perfect will that we are able to present Scotland with an alternative vision of reality. A reality where, in worshipping communities, the good life is named and lived, and Scots learn of their unconditional worth and role in God's mission to Scotland.

Yet witnessing to the Kingdom of God is *costly*, and if Scots do this they will quickly find themselves under attack. That is why Scottish Christians must live and proclaim an alternative political ethic founded on three foundations: the image of God (*imago Dei*) in all people, the fallenness of all humanity (including Christians) and the status of all human beings as the objects of God's saving love.

As we noted earlier, the image of God has been interpreted many ways in the history of the Church. Yet, fundamentally, it describes the role of humanity within creation. Human beings are the creatures that God has chosen to most clearly manifest his nature and glory, and to represent the rest of creation before him. They bear his image both individually and socially. Each person is made in his image in a unique way, but this image is only completed in the community of the Church as the Body of Christ. Human beings, however, have refused to be fully conformed to the image of God revealed in Jesus Christ and, for that reason, all have sinned and fallen short of his glory. Crucially, this includes the Church, which though united with Christ as his Body is conformed to his likeness only imperfectly. Yet God despises nothing he has created, and in Jesus Christ, the coming of the Spirit and the activity of the

Church, he has reached out in love to redeem our divine likeness, and restore us to life.

This may seem very abstract, but it has five concrete ethical outcomes. First, because of our fallenness, we must not be surprised when our neighbours say or do the wrong thing, and should – within limits – exercise mercy in all our dealings with them. Second, because we bear the image of our Creator, anyone who slanders and dishonours another person slanders and dishonours God. For this reason, we must, third, listen carefully to everyone, no matter who they are. Part of this is related to the dignity of human beings, a dignity we only fully recognise when we listen to them. Yet because human beings were created to manifest the goodness and wisdom of God through their speech, they may – intentionally or unintentionally – reveal something of God's truth, and should therefore be listened to. Because *we ourselves* are called to reveal the wisdom and goodness and glory of God, however, we must, fourth, speak the truth. Listening is not enough. Fifth and finally, because our neighbours are the objects of God's saving love, our speech and actions must be directed towards restoring the divine image in them. We must make it easier for them to become who they were created to be, and exercise *their* gifts for the mission and glory of God.

These values, founded on the image of God and the fallenness of each person, give the Church a vital contribution to make to Scottish politics: *a politics of grace*. In a context marked with disunity over Brexit, Scottish Independence, race and issues of gender and sexuality, public discourse – particularly online and in social media – is frequently poisonous, dehumanising and threatening. Some dishonour others randomly for kicks, feeling empowered by their 'trolling' of strangers. Others, convinced of the stupidity or evil of their political opponents, send them death threats, insulting messages, or seek to have them sacked from their jobs. At the heart of these attitudes is the belief that 'all is politics', that in a world without God the ends justify the means, and that as long as we are winning, or at least humiliating our opponents, then abuse, lies and deceit are justified. Christians must mark themselves out from their neighbours not only by their loving actions or truthful speech, but by their ability to do what our society seems increasingly incapable of doing: *speaking the truth in love.* Speaking the truth in love witnesses to the fact that there is *something more than politics,* that there is a transcendent reality in which the values we bring to political discourse and action are just as – and perhaps more – important than the ends that we struggle for. This gifting is particularly important when we consider others to be wrong, unjust or immoral, for it is in those situations that we will be most likely to dehumanise them, and dishonour God.

Through a commitment to mercy, respectful dialogue and listening to all people, the public mission of the Church must steer a middle course between two contemporary extremes. On the one hand, there is much in so-called 'identity politics' that the Church should affirm. In Christ, God displayed a 'preferential option' for the poor, marginalised and oppressed, recognising and ennobling those who were rejected by society. They bear the likeness of God, and historically marginalised groups must be respected, listened to and their demands for justice taken seriously. Those demands for justice will – as has been seen in the Black Lives Matter movement – extend to the Church, and we must be humble enough to acknowledge any hurt we have caused, ask for forgiveness and – if relevant – make reparations. Yet this respect and solidarity cannot extend to silencing or marginalising others, even if they are deemed privileged or oppressive. As we saw in Chapter 5, some Church leaders actively campaigned for Franklin Graham and Destiny church to be de-platformed, despite their views and theologies being common within the Scottish Church. No matter how much we dislike another person's views, and no matter how privileged or oppressive we consider them to be, they are made in God's image also, and silencing them, campaigning for their ruin and rejoicing in their downfall are examples of cruelty rather than justice.

For this reason, the Church must agree with libertarians and liberals who are committed to free speech. Allowing others to speak, and responding to them with civility, is central to human dignity and a flourishing society. Scottish society has much to learn from J.S. Mill's views in *On Liberty*. In that work, Mill argued that it is vital to allow all people to speak because their views may be fully or partly true, and therefore necessary for correcting our own views. Yet even if their views are totally incorrect, they remind us of *why* our views are true, and prevent the truth we hold from slipping into self-righteous dogmatism.[26]

Robust discussion, untempered by fear, is necessary to arrive at truth. For that reason, the Church should defend the freedom of speech and freedom of association of all Scots against the government and other civic groups, even when we do not agree with the views represented. Yet against certain types of libertarian, the Church must side with Paul and say that, while we are free to speak as we wish, we should not use this as a licence to sin. Speech has its limits, both in terms of what is said and also who has the prerogative to say it. For this reason, the Church must ensure that the voices of the marginalised are given equal airing over and against those who have the privilege of dominant speech.

These are fine distinctions, of course, and it is for Christians in each context to decide where the line falls. That is why one of the most important ways in which the Church can advance the mission of God in Scotland is discipling Christian leaders in every walk of life. This is not about preserving Christian dominance in society. As the preceding chapters should have made clear, even if this were desirable, it is now impossible given the small proportion of committed Christians in Scotland. Yet because of the election of the Church in Jesus Christ, it is *Christians* who have been given the primary responsibly for advancing Christ's Kingdom, and that requires influencing government and society. In this, the Evangelical Alliance's leadership programmes are to be commended, and should be extended to all denominations. Lay Christians in government, business and civil society require specialised support and mentoring to witness to their colleagues and shape their organisations along Christian lines. Sadly, their huge potential is largely untapped by the traditional denominations, often due to the misguided belief that ministry and mission is the preserve of ordained clergy, or that discipleship is exhausted by Word and Sacrament on a Sunday morning. Jesus makes it clear that *all* Christians are to be salt and light in the world, something small, invisible, barely there, yet something that makes all the difference. As Scripture shows, if the people of God ascend to positions of importance, and through their skill, humanity and virtue win friends and influence, they can do extraordinary things. In the case of Nehemiah, that even extended to rebuilding Jerusalem. If Nehemiah can rebuild the Holy City, whose walls had been torn down, and its gates burned with fire, then Christian politicians can further the new creation in the peaceful and affluent Scotland of today!

One's willingness to engage in the political process, however, will be determined by one's attitude to politics and the secular world. On one extreme are those who – adopting a Kingdom theology in which God works through secular society as much as the Church – see culture as fundamentally good, and the world as the domain of God's progressive revelation and activity. At the other extreme are those who view society as fallen and almost totally sinful, a dark world where God is not, and where the Church must fight for survival and a voice, while keeping its righteousness and identity intact by distancing itself from the gutter-world of the political.

Most Christians, however, will occupy a place in-between these extremes. On the one hand, they will acknowledge the sin of contemporary society, and the brokenness of political leaders who not only do not know how to reform society but, even if they did, lack the virtue to accomplish it. Yet, on the other hand, they will also believe that there is not a single inch of reality over which Christ is not sovereign. Drawing upon the old doctrines of common and special grace, they will see in society the fruits of the common grace by which God preserves society from the full – natural – effects of the Fall, and will discern in political events the work of his providence.

The common grace of God not only preserves society and politics from dissolution, however, but provides the motivation and goal of Christian political participation. If Scottish public life really did lack the presence and activity of God, then Christians might be justified in fleeing from it. Yet because God's common grace is present within it, Christians can enter into politics and the world with confidence. They are not fighting against the tide alone, but with the Lord of Hosts himself. Further, the very structure and nature of society is conditioned by God's will. In creating the world and human societies, God has structured them in such a way that certain things will aid their flourishing, while others will mar it. While it may take time for society to understand what is harmful and what is beneficial, this will eventually come to light, and gain at least some acceptance. In addition, God's Spirit has gone ahead of us to bestow virtue, understanding and civility to our non-Christian political opponents. This should give us hope that the arguments of Christians can be both intelligible and attractive to those without faith.

So much for common grace. Yet what of the special grace given to Christ's Church through his Spirit? In Chapter 1, we saw that God has elected the Church to be an instrument of the new creation. It achieves this by being salt, yeast and light, something small that sanctifies, uplifts and illuminates the whole. The Church, in short, is a *catalyst*. It encourages, speeds up and facilitates the activity of the Spirit in society. As a catalyst, it fertilises the seeds of common grace scattered by the Father, and enables them to reach maturity. In relation to the state, therefore, the Church is called to encourage the coming of the new creation by influencing the levers of secular power to be used for divine purposes. Power, in and of itself, may tend towards evil, yet power can – as the power of the Father shows – be used for good.

The political activity of individual Christians is not enough, however, to further the mission of the Church in the public square. Given the decreasing Christian constituency in Scotland, the Scottish Church must create a single inter-church body that is able to speak for the overwhelming majority of Scotland's Christians. While this was part of the intention for Action of Churches Together in Scotland (ACTS), structural issues thwarted its efficacy, and the Scottish Church Leaders Forum

(SCLF) and the nascent Scottish Christian Forum (SCF) are in the process of taking over its functions. If these new bodies are to extend God's mission in Scotland, it is imperative that Christian leaders appreciate the seriousness of the position we find ourselves in, and the necessity of setting aside denominational differences to speak with a united Christian voice. Such a voice has never been needed more than now, for it will only be when the members of Christ's Body proclaim and witness with one voice that Scotland will sit up and take notice.

Christian political engagement of any kind, however, is ultimately dependent on robust worshipping communities, for these supply and shape the Christian leaders who engage in political activity. If churches are to survive and thrive, they must rediscover their purpose as communities of virtue, where good citizens and neighbours are nurtured and formed. Without that nurturing and formation, the Church will not produce people who can further God's mission. Yet these communities also serve a wider purpose. That is because the Church, at its best, shows Scotland what it *should be* and what – when Christ returns – it *will be*. When it works, the Church is a community of unconditional care and love, in which the broken are comforted, the poor clothed and empowered and captives set free from the sin, shame and addiction. It is a place where people recover their purpose and worth, and discover their true identities. It is a place of hope, where we meet the future not with cynicism or resignation, but expectation and joy. While governments and NGOs speak much about human rights, dignity and equality, all too often this is mere rhetoric, masking a society which, for many, is indifferent, lonely and dehumanising. When it is faithful to its calling, the Church takes the rhetoric of abstract human rights and makes it concrete and real.

There is, then, a dialectical or reciprocal relationship between the public witness of the Church at national level and the local, day-to-day witness of congregations. As we have seen, local congregations shape and supply the Christian leaders who engage in public mission. Yet local congregations also provide the public pronouncements of the Church with weight and credibility. It is one thing to speak 'truth to power' as cosseted political radicals, quite another as a Church that serves poor, lonely, troubled Scots the length and breadth of the country. In a society organised on national lines, and with a reasonably high level of centralisation, the public witness of the Church also enhances the plausibility of local congregations. The Church's public witness can, if properly done, provide a higher profile and added resonance to the local activities of congregations. They make it clear that the Church is worth listening to, that it is making a difference across the country and is taken seriously by the government and civil society.

The importance of the public arena cuts both ways, however. While it provides the Church with opportunities to influence government and society, it also allows government and society to influence the Church in unhealthy ways. As such, in an interconnected Scotland where we are exposed to more information and alternative viewpoints than ever before, the Church must take whatever steps are necessary to preserve its identity and the integrity of its mission. This will, then, require a greater degree of *pillarisation*: creating strong Christian institutions, groups and networks that can insulate the Church from the worst effects of secular forces, and shape and form Scottish Christians into the likeness of Christ. This will be particularly necessary for Protestants, who currently lack the institutional framework of the Roman Catholic Church. We do not do this as an *alternative* to service and evangelism – a sad turning-inward that only thinks of itself – but as the *very means* to greater service and evangelism. For without our young people coming to and retaining, their faith, and without missional discipleship for every Church leader and member, God's mission to Scotland will wither and die. Yet with the preservation and multiplication of robust, confident and skilled communities of faith, in which Scots are loved, forgiven and discover their purpose, we will show our neighbours, our nation and our governments what they should be, and model what Scotland dreams of becoming.[27]

Conclusion

In this chapter, we have examined the public mission of the Scottish Church. We examined the biblical foundations for the Church's public activity, built on the twin pillars of the Lordship of Christ and his appointment of rulers to restrain vice and promote virtue. We then examined the public witness of the Scottish Church, noting divergences between different denominations and theological traditions and analysing their strengths and weaknesses. We concluded with an examination of the particular tasks that Scottish Christians are called to undertake in the public realm, and the politics of grace that should animate them. By shaping and supporting Christian leaders in every walk of life, the Church will extend God's influence over Scottish society, and awaken the seeds of common grace that God has placed throughout it. This activity will only effect large-scale change, however, if the Church can speak with one voice through a new inter-church body. Then, the Christians of Scotland, and the mission of God, will not be so easily ignored and the Kingdom will – more and more – extend and take root in our land.

Conclusion

A Contextual Missiology
for Scotland

*The Good News of the Kingdom will be preached through-
out the world as a testimony to the nations – and then the
end will come.*

In the days of Israel and Judah, there were prophets who spoke
good and prophets who spoke ill. Some spoke of God's favour
upon the nation, the righteousness of its rulers and the vic-
tories that awaited it, while others spoke of judgement and
decline, and the need to repent before the hour grew late.

In the Introduction to this book, I wrote of the desire to see
not with the eyes of the optimist, or of the pessimist, or of the
realist, but with the eyes of Christ. To see with Christ's eyes
is to see *double*: to see the depths of human sin, with all its
cruelty, stupidity and failure, and *yet* to believe that all things
will be made new, and that everything issues in good for those
who love God.

That is what I have tried to accomplish in these pages, as we
charted the movement from God's eternal heart to the Scotland of today. In Chapter 1, we saw the basis of mission in
God's desire to be for those who are not like him, the Son
and Spirit giving themselves to the world that they might be
witnesses to the Father and give him the glory. This self-giving
created a Church, which as Christ's Body, and animated by his
Spirit, now gives itself for the world, that through service and
evangelism the world might see and believe.

In Chapter 2, we saw how the Scottish Church interpreted
this mission, using power and law to shape the Scots into a
Christian people. The parish state led to the evangelisation of

the overwhelming majority of Scots, with schools, hospitals and universities establishing a fully encultured Christianity that furthered God's mission in important ways. Yet the political means used to accomplish this also gave rise to schisms and separations in the Body of Christ, with evangelism being largely conflated with the conversion of Scots from one form of Christianity to another. When added to the Reformed marks of the Church, an emphasis upon an educated ministry and a limited missional role for church members, God's mission to Scotland was unduly constrained, and unhelpful patterns established for the future.

Chapter 3 then charted the disintegration of the parish state, and the secularisation of Scotland. Industrialisation, class struggle, evangelicalism and patronage all played a role in the creation of the Free Church of Scotland, which directly led to secularisation and the replacement of the Church's social functions by the state. This reduced the social significance of the Church, and produced the necessary conditions for a collapse in the plausibility of the faith. When added to welfare security and affluence in the mid-twentieth century, Scots became freed from their historic dependence on community and elites, and began to adopt a variety of non-religious identities.

Chapter 4 examined these non-religious identities in more detail. We saw that welfare security and affluence, taken with consumerism, mean that the majority of Scots feel disconnected from history, community and even family. This frees them to develop worlds of meaning for themselves, borrowing from whatever sources they have access to. Yet lacking robust intellectual or social foundations, these identities are often fragile. Their instability requires a continuous struggle for liberation from shame, judgement and even nature itself, yet this struggle is never complete.

Chapter 5 then charted how this departure from Scotland's past manifests itself on a political level. We saw how British and Unionist identity was premised upon Protestantism and Empire, and how secularisation and decolonialisation removed two key foundations for the existence of the United Kingdom. In place of Protestant Unionism has arisen areligious nationalism. Following the collapse of Christianity and traditional communities focused on agriculture and heavy industry, nationalism provides a new source of identity for Scots, giving them an imagined community to be part of. With the advent of the Scottish Parliament, it is now the state and not the Church that is the safeguard of national identity, which is now increasingly tied up with progressive politics, and symbolised by the Rainbow Flag.

These social, economic and political changes give rise to the changed spiritual and religious landscape examined in Chapter 6. Despite arguments to the contrary, statistics show a wholesale collapse in Scottish Christianity across all available indicators, ranging from belief, to affiliation, to life events. While part of this collapse is related to intellectual scepticism, it is primarily due to comfortable indifference, which – with most of its material and emotional needs catered for – simply has no interest in considering the claims of Christ. This does not mean that 'spirituality' is not present in different forms, but – following the logic of religious individualisation – it is largely personal, and is disinterested in communal or institutional faith. Humanism is the perfect ritual counterpart to this spirituality, focusing on personal, rather than social or revealed, meaning. While Christianity is not totally spent in Scotland, and a minority of the population are open to faith, its potential is sapped by infighting and suspicion among the family and household of God.

Having examined the background and context of mission in contemporary Scotland, Chapter 7 turned to examine mission as *service*. We surveyed the pastoral care, material aid and community development that the Church is undertaking in obedience to Christ's commission to serve the least, and bring about the new creation. Yet following the Trinitarian logic of love as *self*-giving – which reveals both the giver and the glory of God – service cannot be neatly separated from evangelism, nor the Kingdom from the Church. The Church should not, therefore, rest complacent while the state takes over its work, or maintain an artificial, secular professionalism in the face of hurting people who need both care *and* Christ.

Because God's mission has a Church, Chapter 8 surveyed the ways in which Scottish Christians are attempting to evangelise their neighbours, and welcome them into the Church. We examined the importance of – and limits to – evangelism that is disconnected from a worshipping community. We then examined fresh expressions and church planting, noting the ways these new forms of Church are often healthier than some inherited forms. For this reason, the Scottish Church must invest in equipping and releasing the giftings of its members and give them permission to innovate and experiment. Nevertheless, there are cogent criticisms against an over-reliance on these forms of community, and the future of the Scottish Church will be a mixed ecology of different forms of Church.

God's mission is not only to individuals or communities, however, but to the nation as a whole. For that reason, Chapter 9 examined the Church's mission in the public square. We saw that the state has a legitimate, God-given authority, and can play an important role in the mission of God. Yet the churches are divided in what message they wish to convey to state and nation, leaving secular narratives to predominate. Nevertheless, the Church has an important treasure to offer in the politics of grace, and should declare God's vision of personal virtue, respectful speech and institutional neutrality to a nation afflicted by division, dehumanisation and unhelpful strains of identity politics.

In Sophocles' *Antigone*, the Chorus declares that nothing great enters the lives of mortals free and clear of ruin.[1] That has been the experience of the Scottish Church, which though forged in God's own heart, has – over 1,700 years of history – tried, and frequently failed, to live in obedience to its calling. The result of this is that we now find ourselves at the most serious crossroads since the Reformation, as we battle not only for survival, but for the soul of our nation.

But *why*? For even after the evidence is amassed, the arguments marshalled, the outcomes analysed, as I have written this work, I have been led, again and again, to the question of why the God who desires the salvation of all people would allow his name to go unloved and unregarded by the majority of Scots.

While we must be circumspect, and deeply humble, when discerning the providence of God, given the evidence examined in Parts 1 and 2 of this work, we should not be surprised by the spiritual state of contemporary Scotland. Jesus tells us explicitly that the rich will struggle to have faith and enter into the Kingdom. Through amassing more and more economic resources, often at the expense of the planet and the world's poor, and being satisfied with our multitudinous idols, few of us now feel that we need a Saviour. Jesus tells us that the world will only believe that God has sent him when it sees the unity and love of his Church. Yet with each schism the plausibility and social influence of Christianity declines, and when the world sees our disunity, pettiness and inability to perform our mission, it secularises our educational, therapeutic and philanthropic ministries and – not unreasonably – presumes that we have little more to offer.

What we are perhaps seeing in Scotland, then, worked out through centuries of economic progress and Church disunity, is the righteous judgement of God. Preferring consumerism, individual choice and personal satisfaction to sacrificial witness, Scotland has exchanged the glory of God for a lie, and is reaping the whirlwind that follows from it:

'The days are coming,' declares the Sovereign LORD,
   'when I will send a famine through the land –
not a famine of food or a thirst for water,
   but a famine of hearing the words of the LORD.
People will stagger from sea to sea
and wander from north to east,
searching for the Word of the LORD,
   but they will not find it.'

Yet while, for human beings, the situation we find ourselves in may seem impossible, for God, all things are possible, and through repentance, and prayer and study, God's Spirit will lead us from this exile to the new Scotland that he is preparing for us and for all people.

That exodus, however, begins from *within*: an exodus from false human hope and false human despair, and our conversion to the mind of Christ. By going deep into our tradition, and deep into the culture of contemporary Scotland, we must discover a new missiology to guide us through these days. This missiology will neither laud nor condemn our culture, but affirm what is good in it, reject what is false, and *tell a better story to our neighbours*, one that will reveal that their deepest needs and desires are met not with consumerism, or self-interest, or materialism, but with Christ, and Christ alone.

To that end, the following is offered as the beginning of a contextual missiology for contemporary Scotland.

God has a mission and that mission has a Church

God uses all things to further his will, yet the Church – as sign, foretaste and instrument of the Kingdom – is the primary means by which God exercises his mission to the world. This is not the Church's destiny by right, but by its election in Christ. While God's providence directs *all things* towards their end, he has not poured out his Spirit anywhere on earth as he has done in his Church. Neither has he called any other group as he has called the Church. The state, atheists and other religions may further his mission, particularly when they know something of him, or seek to live good and truthful lives. Yet without the Church, Scotland will not mirror the new creation. While Christ's Church includes the human, institutional aspects of Church life that we can see and touch and hear, he can only use our Church institutions if we constantly turn to him in faith. For that reason, we must confess our sin, collectively discern his will and be willing to lay behind our traditions, structures and cherished identities if he wills it.

God created Scotland and is working now to perfect it

Scotland and its government believe in progress and the ability to make our world better. So does God. He created Scotland, working with the Church to preserve its distinct culture and institutions over many centuries, and cares deeply for every person in it. He has planted communities in every part of the country to bear witness to the new Scotland he is creating. In this effort, God wants to work with all people of good will, utilising the gifts he created them with to advance his mission. By proclaiming and living out this message of activism and progress, the Church can tap into Scots' desire to build a fairer, kinder society.

In the context of our environmental crisis, a contextual missiology cannot exclude ecology. God has given the Church buildings, land and communities of faith in every part of Scotland, who – with good leadership and entrepreneurship – can be catalysts for creation care in every part of Scotland, being salt, yeast and light to galvanise and encourage their communities. If Christians understand their faith correctly, they will see that the scope of God's mission is cosmic in scale, and congregations can act as 'colonies of heaven' in the here and now, raising the plausibility of faith as their neighbours see God acting through them to transform the world.

Scots will only discover their true identity in Christ and his Church

We live in an age obsessed with identity, yet the majority of Scots hold a self-understanding that is incomplete or false. Scotland will only be perfected when Scots come to recognise that their true identity is found in Christ. Since birth, our neighbours have heard from themselves and others that they are not good enough, that they are worthless, that they are weak, that they are ugly, that they are failures. Yet the salvation our society offers only confirms their slavery. They are told that if they are successful enough, wealthy enough, beautiful enough or righteous enough, then they will finally have worth. Yet that worth is always just out of reach. Feeding off this sense of worthlessness, the market encourages them to part with their money so that they will have the possessions, appearance or lifestyle that will finally win them approval. Even if they are able to see through these lies, however, they can then fall into the alternative trap of *pride*, of thinking themselves superior to others, and trusting their own judgement above everyone else's.

This is not what our neighbours were created for. They were created in love, and through Christ have been given the opportunity to become sons and daughters of God. This is their true identity, and it gives them a God-given, unconditional worth that neither the judgement of others, nor their own judgement, can take away from them. Moreover, the Father created them with a specific set of characteristics and in relationship with him, and in imitation of Christ, Scots can discover who they are and what they were put on earth to do.

All Scots are given a purpose – and discover their freedom – in God's mission

By expanding the realm of personal freedom, the West has emptied nature and human life of intrinsic purpose. God gives Scots their purpose back. Through the gift of the Spirit, who works through our personalities, holy desires and experiences, and in the supportive community of the Church, Scots can rediscover their God-given purpose. Everyone – no matter their ability – has a part to play in God's Church, because the re-creation of Scotland requires every possible gifting and personality type. The calling of all people to discover their God-given purpose in the mission of God to Scotland has important implications for ministry and mission. Church leaders should seek to mobilise and train as many of their members as possible to discover and develop their giftings, and encourage them to exercise their initiative in seeking out and developing new missional opportunities. This is not a challenge to ordained ministry, but the *very reason* for ordained ministry. Clergy are set apart so that they can bless and sanctify other Christians, that those Christians might bless the world.

Service must be evangelistic and evangelism relational and loving

Secular Scotland often asserts a strict divide between Church and world. The Church sometimes replicates this divide, and must therefore leave behind the fruitless and unbiblical distinction between evangelism and service, accepting that they are two equal parts of God's mission to Scotland. Service to others should be authentic, which includes being open about our faith commitments. If we have understood our local contexts correctly, then every act of service increases the plausibility of faith, making it easier for our neighbours to believe the astounding claims that Christ makes through his Church. Likewise, as imperative as evangelism is, it should almost always take place in the context of loving relationships. Many Scots know what the Church claims about Jesus, but they are not always certain that they want to be part of what we're offering. Jesus is clothed in both law *and* grace, judgement *and* love, and aimless evangelism can sometimes do more harm than good.

The Church stands against the commodification of human goodness

The service of the Church is not only directed towards the good of our neighbours, however, but stands as a judgement against the increasing commodification of Scottish society. Our service is an act of faith, a *sacrifice*, which we offer freely as individual Christians and as congregations for the good of others. This stands in marked contrast to an ever-increasing range of services – from counselling, to Humanist life events, to New Age therapies and even some social enterprises – where relationships of concern and aid are conditional upon a *fee*. What should happen freely is still done, but only with an exchange of cash. This is not only a critique of particular service-providers, but of the entire capitalist system, which, as we have seen, is directly responsible for the collapse of community and the collapse of faith. The Church is a witness to a different reality, one in which all people, no matter their means, are loved unconditionally, and through the gift of our service are invited to participate in a new kind of community. We must be more conscious and vocal in proclaiming this counter-cultural reality, showing that Scots do not need to be conformed to this dying world, but can be transformed in the renewing of their minds.

The Church moves Scots from the abstract community of the nation to the concrete community of the Church

By creating cultures of service and witness that affirm the God-given worth and purpose of each person and which refuse to commodify human goodness, the Church demonstrates to state and nation what Scotland should become. While public life in Scotland is much concerned with equality and fairness, this equality and fairness often struggles to move beyond abstract human rights. Our laws and rhetoric declare the worth and dignity of each person, yet, as we have seen, this is not the experience of many Scots. That is because the state relies on law and – ultimately – force in order to effect change. Yet law and force alone cannot change the human heart. They lead only to resentment and hypocrisy, or the degradation and dehumanisation of unpopular groups in the cause of humanity and progress. True change comes from within, from the new life that comes with Christ, and the formation that happens in the community of the Church. Through the Church, Scots are shaped into faithful, virtuous citizens who bless their country in countless ways. When the Church truly acts as an agent of the Kingdom, its members and its worshipping communities become signs and foretastes of the perfected Scotland that our governments and countless activists agitate for, but will never fully attain.

Jesus gives us a politics of grace

Public life in Scotland is dominated by division over constitutional questions and, to a lesser extent, issues of sexuality and gender. These divisions lead even good people to believe and say terrible things about their neighbours, aided by social media platforms that dehumanise those with differing views. The Church must witness, in Benedict XVI's memorable words, to the *civilisation of love* that all Westerners are heir to.[2] We must witness to the fact there is something more than mere politics, that there are values and decencies that transcend our divisions, and that it is God – and not human beings – who is sovereign. The public ethic that must animate the Church is built upon the image of God (*imago Dei*) that each person bears. Human dignity is not founded on a social contract, the fiat of the state or the opinion of the crowd, but upon the love of God revealed in Jesus Christ. This dignity means that all – particularly minorities or those who suffer discrimination – must be listened to and allowed to speak freely. It also means that, when we disagree with others, we must honour them all the more, for fear that we would dishonour the divine image in them, and thereby dishonour God himself.

In a world of relativism, the Church stands for the objectivity of truth

A politics of grace is one part of the Church's public mission. It is the *form* that Christian truth takes. Yet without the *content* of that truth, our mission is incomplete. In a context where hedonism and materialism lead Scots to think that truth is whatever 'works' for the individual, and where critical theory reduces all truth claims to power struggles between warring groups, the Church must affirm more than ever the objectivity of truth. Truth does not depend on personal whim, nor on the desires of the powerful, but upon God's will for creation, revealed through his prophets, scribes, apostles and most fully in Jesus Christ. The Church must invest more in changing public perception regarding the compatibility of reason, science and faith, and the possibility of an objective moral truth grounded in Christ's witness of sacrifice, humility and forgiveness.

In all of these activities, the plausibility of the faith at local and national levels will depend on the Church telling a better story than our culture does. We must take what is good in our culture – an emphasis on dignity, wholeness, progress, reason and the search for one's authentic self – and show their true meaning, re-narrating them to point to Christ. This is not simply a *means* to bring people to salvation, but salvation itself, for salvation is not an escape from this world or its destruction, but the re-creation of human beings into the likeness of Christ.

The Identity and Marks of the Scottish Church

These are the elements of a contextual missiology that the Scottish Church must believe and enact if it is to respond properly to its context. Their adoption will help create local cultures of plausibility that resist the forces of secularisation and in which faith becomes real and God's name is glorified. Yet the success of the Church's mission is not only a matter of what it believes or does, but what *it is*.

What kind of Church, then, is best placed to further this contextual missiology, and how do we know if we, and our brothers and sisters across different denominations and forms of Church, *are* that Church?

As we have seen, the identity of the Church can be summed up in its *unity, holiness, catholicity and apostolicity*. This identity is shaped and structured by Christ and empowered and enabled by the Holy Spirit. In our Scottish context, it is the first part of the Church's identity that is sometimes most lacking: *unity*. The Church is *one* rather than many because of the sovereign will of God to engraft humanity into the Body of his Son. Just as there is only one Lord, into whom we are united through baptism and faith, so there is only one Church. As such, it is not unity of structures, or full uniformity in doctrine and practice, that makes the Church one, but *Jesus* and our participation *in him*. Unity, then, is something that is done *by Christ*, something which, to borrow a phrase, is done 'without us, against us, but finally for us'.[3] It is a spiritual fact that all Christians, whether they like it or not, are united with each other.

Christ identifies the unity of the Church as having a special role in his mission to the world. In John 17:22–23 he says:

> The glory that you have given me I have given them, so that they may be one, as we are one, I in them and you in me, that they may become completely one, so that the world may know that you have sent me and have loved them even as you have loved me.

Here, Jesus says that the *glory* – the fame, the attractiveness, the pride and joy – of the Church is that it is united in love, a unity and love that reflects the relationship between the Son and the Father. Crucially for what happened in Scotland, Jesus identifies this glory of unity and love as the *means* by which the world will know that Jesus has been sent by the Father. The unity of the Church, therefore, is not only morally desirable, but of great apologetic and missional importance. The sending of the Son by the Father in love is mirrored by the sending of the unified Church in love. Yet the opposite is also true. If the Church is *not* united, if the Church *does not* love itself as Father, Son and Spirit love each other, then it will fail to witness to Christ, and will fail in its mission. Without a reconciled Church, there cannot be a reconciled world.

This is not liberal ecumenism but biblical orthodoxy, something shown by the lives of the Church Fathers. Consider the life and ministry of Athanasius, known as the 'Father of Orthodoxy'. Athanasius was dogged in his defence of the Incarnation and the Trinity – the foundations of the Christian faith – at a time when the survival of those doctrines looked unsure. Having assumed the office of Bishop of Alexandria, he was exiled five times and was sometimes in fear of his life, as emperors, theologians and clergy attempted to force their heretical – Arian

– view of Christ upon the Empire. Indeed, he was so marginal at times, and accrued so many enemies in his defence of orthodoxy, that he had the nickname *Athanasius Contra Mundum*, 'Athanasius Against the World'. Yet if someone had suggested to the marginalised and persecuted Athanasius that the Church had become so apostate, so corrupted by false doctrine, that the righteous had no choice but to separate themselves from it, he would have rebuked them. He would have replied that there is only one Body of Christ, and to separate ourselves from the Church is to sever ourselves from Jesus, the living vine. That Body may have grown sick and gangrenous, yet that means we must move ever closer to it, fighting for it in the name of Christ. Athanasius, the Father of Orthodoxy, had to contend with the rejection of the most fundamental doctrines of the Christian faith, yet he remained in the Church and fought for it, and because he stayed and fought, he won it back for Christ.

Are we wiser than Athanasius? Are we holier than he was? If we are not, then we should have the humility to maintain and seek ever-greater unity, and if we believe *we are* as holy as he was, then we should do as he did.

Unity among Christians is one of the key means that Jesus identifies for the conversion of the world. When the members of the Church are united in love, the Body of Christ grows in strength and significance, and the living presence of Jesus is revealed to the world. Yet that is because unity is an aspect of *holiness*. Just as the Body is one because we are united in Christ, so it is holy because it lives in him. His righteousness covers it, and his Holy Spirit fills and sanctifies it. The holiness of the Church must stand as a witness against the affluence and consumerism that precipitated the loss of Scotland's faith, and an economic system that is now endangering the future of the planet itself. Holiness is not only a matter of possessing a greater amount of goodness than the world, however, but of being *different* from the world. The holy and the sacred is that which is set apart from the world for the sake of the world, and we, as saints, manifest our calling and mission by living lives that are different from other Scots'. This 'difference' has been the subject matter of this book, a difference that is central to the 'counter-cultural' model of mission that, as we saw, Bevans deems most appropriate for Western contexts.

We will only be different in what we do, however, when we are different in what we *believe*. The unity and holiness of the Scottish Church therefore depends on our faithfulness to the *catholic or universal faith* that was once and for all delivered to the saints. This is not agreement in all matters, but only on those matters that go to the substance of the faith. It is agreement on these matters, and not every matter, that makes one an orthodox Christian. Orthodoxy is sometimes thought to be indefinable, yet this is not the case. In the ancient creeds of the Church, the catholic or universal faith of the Church is summed up under the heads of Trinity, Incarnation, Atonement, Resurrection and Ascension, with the inspiration and authority of Scripture underpinning them all.[4] Many differences between orthodox Christians persist, yet given the missionary task facing us, acceptance of these fundamentals is enough to declare our unity, and allow us to cooperate on a wide variety of missional projects.

This brings us to the fourth aspect of the Church's identity: *apostolicity*. 'Apostolic' refers to the Church's fidelity to the catholic or universal faith taught by the apostles and their successors. Yet if we are faithful to the teaching and example of the apostles then we must do as they did, and plant and evangelise. We must understand that central to our identity as a Scottish Church is being called *out* of the world and set apart by Christ to be sent *to* the world in mission. Mission is not something that we *do* as Christians, but something that we *are* as Christians. Every Christian must serve and witness and evangelise as their gifts and charisms lead them, working together with our brothers and sisters of all denominations in the unity, holiness and catholicity of Christ's Body.

By directing the Scottish Church *outward*, apostolicity integrates the unity, holiness and catholicity of the Church, and regulates their function. When we keep God's mission to Scotland at the forefront of our hearts and minds, unity is saved from pettiness, holiness from condescension and catholicity from dogmatic self-righteousness. Mission not only saves Scotland – *it saves the Church*. It restores its likeness – marred by sin – to that of the Son, and enables the Church to be what it was created to be.

The identity of the Scottish Church, then, is one, holy, catholic and apostolic. Yet it is not only a question of knowing the identity of the Scottish Church. We must also know what it *looks* like, what it means *in practice* to be Christ's Church and how we can recognise the true Church in ourselves and in our neighbours. In short, we need to know what the *marks* of the Scottish Church are.

In previous chapters, we saw that, historically, the majority view among Scottish Christians was that the marks or notes of the Church could be seen in the preaching of the true Word, the right administration of the sacraments and discipline rightly ordered. For Episcopalian or Roman Catholic Scots, discipline also included a commitment to the historic episcopate or the Papacy. Unfortunately, because Christians sought *full* uniformity of doctrine, practice and discipline, a focus upon these marks led to endless schism and conflict.

While these marks were defined and described in a variety of ways, they nevertheless had a common focus upon the *internal* ordering and worship of the Church, rather than its external activities. In a Christendom context, this may have been appropriate, although it is doubtful whether the historic notes of the Scottish Church ever adequately expressed the fullness of its calling. In a post-Christendom context, however, a focus upon Word, Sacrament, discipline and structure is no longer adequate to identify the presence of Christ's Church. A church that does not attempt the evangelisation of the non-Christian culture it is situated in may still be Christ's Church, but it is a deficient Church. A church that is indifferent to creation, or indifferent to the social structures that enslave its neighbours, may still be a church of sorts, but cannot be said to be manifesting the fullness of God's intention for his people.

As such, in addition to the historic marks of the Church, we must, in our contemporary Scottish context, also add *missional* marks. In our contemporary context, 'missional' will mean those things recounted in Chapters 7 to 9, as well as the building blocks of a contextual missiology just given. This account of 'missional' is in line with wider ecumenical thinking. Although historically divided over the issue of social justice, since the creation of the Lausanne Covenant in 1974 and the Manila Manifesto in 1989, mainstream evangelicalism has accepted that evangelism, service and social responsibility belong together.[5] Likewise, in *Together Towards Life*, the more liberal World Council of Churches has accepted that evangelism is a legitimate form of mission alongside service and advocacy, and that the two are mutually complementary parts of the Spirit's work.[6]

This growing consensus concerning the integration of evangelism, service and the cosmic focus of mission is summarised well in the Five Marks of Mission of the Anglican Communion. Like the work of Lausanne and the World Council of Churches, the Five Marks are an attempt to achieve a balance between mission as service and mission as evangelism. The Five Marks of God's mission are:

- To proclaim the Good News of the Kingdom.
- To teach, baptise and nurture new believers.
- To respond to human need by loving service.
- To transform unjust structures of society, to challenge violence of every kind and pursue peace and reconciliation.
- To strive to safeguard the integrity of creation and sustain and renew the life of the earth.[7]

The difficulty with statements that address missional marks alone, however, is that they replicate the problems of the historic marks of the Scottish Church *in reverse*. Just as the historic marks focused too much on the internal life of the Church, so missional marks focus too much on the outward life of the Church. As we have seen in the foregoing, however, it is only when a proper integration of worship, discipleship, service and evangelism is achieved that mission is both effective and sustainable. Without this integration, the essence of the Church is separated from its actions, and its internal worship from its external mission. Just as God's being cannot be separated from his actions, nor Christ's divine and human natures from his work of salvation, so the missional marks of the Church cannot be separated from its ecclesiological marks.

To that end, and in the hope that the Scottish Church might renew its mind and actions for this day and age, I propose that the marks of the Scottish Church are:

- To glorify Father, Son and Holy Spirit in worship and prayer.
- To proclaim the catholic or universal faith.
- To celebrate the sacraments as signs and foretastes of the new creation.
- To teach, baptise and nurture new believers.
- To respond to human need by loving service.
- To transform unjust structures of society, to challenge violence of every kind and pursue peace and reconciliation.
- To strive to safeguard the integrity of creation, and sustain and renew the life of the earth.

These marks have two functions. First, they allow us to gauge whether our congregation, fresh expression or denomination is being the Church or not. This is important, because the loss of the Church's social functions and significance leaves many Christian leaders struggling to understand their purpose, leading to a collapse in morale, a sense of directionless and the adoption of activities that frustrate, rather than aid, the Kingdom. These marks remind us of what our core business is, and challenge us to be worthy of the calling to which we are called. The days of resting on historic laurels have long since vanished. If congregations and denominations do not engage in mission they will die, and perhaps rightly so.

This may sound cruel. Some churches, after all, may feel that they are unable to meet these marks – particularly the missional ones – in and of themselves. Yet no-one should be surprised or disheartened by this. The charisms of the Spirit, and the material blessings of the Father, were not distributed by Christ to a single congregation or denomination but *throughout* his Body, across *the whole* Scottish Church. In this, the Father displayed his will that his Church should seek ever closer unity, so that the fullness of the Body of Christ might be displayed, and Scotland might see and believe. This is where the second function of the Seven Marks of the Church comes into view: a basis for missional partnership. For if we, as congregations or as denominations, find that we are unable to properly fulfil these marks by ourselves, then we should seek to do so in collaboration with other Christians, whether within the same denomination or across denominations.

So what does this missional partnership look like in practice? It means, first, that other congregations in our locality are seen as potential partners rather than strangers or competitors. No longer does one congregation or denomination have the personnel, buildings, finance and skill set to reach the whole people of Scotland. As such, the first stage of recovering our missional identity as a united Scottish Church is to meet with other Christians in our area. We must get to know each other, and build or re-build our relationships. We then need, second, to pray together, and discern what God is doing in our communities. Third, once we have begun to discern God's will, we must be generous with what we have. If we as a denomination have spare buildings, why not develop a partnership with a church without a building? If we have healthy finances but few able-bodied people, why not work with a church that is people rich but money poor? The Father has given us everything we need, but sometimes it is only found in other churches!

Local, contextual mission will always be the most important element of the Church's witness to Scotland. Yet much can be done at regional and national level to facilitate this mission. Two of the most important activities are permission-giving and research. Significant theological differences continue to exist between Christian denominations and traditions in Scotland. While these are sometimes less important at a local level where relationships of trust exist, denominational leaders have an important role in exploring, and potentially removing, theological barriers. This is not about 'watering down' theological truth, but exploring whether perceived differences are more informed by historic animosities or mere terminology than fundamental divergences.

Part of the difficulty in fostering missional cooperation, however, is the absence of data and research into the missional context we find ourselves in. England boasts a number of bodies, such as the Church Army, Church Mission Society and Theos, who regularly undertake studies of English Christianity, and the mission field that is England. This allows English churches to have a clearer picture of their strengths, weaknesses and the missional opportunities available, creating a *shared picture of reality*. There are currently no missional research bodies in Scotland, which has a number of outcomes. First, denominational views of mission are formed largely by different theological positions rather than objective evidence. This effectively means that every denomination is undertaking ministry and mission in the dark, unsure as to what 'works' and therefore unsure where to prioritise resources. Second, this partial view of ourselves and our mission context encourages unilateral working. Without shared data and analysis, in important ways, Scottish Christians do not inhabit the same world. This means that they will frequently overestimate their own strengths and diminish the utility of working with others. If an inter-church research body were to be created, data and analysis could be generated that would allow us to move from dogma and anecdote to evidence, producing an accurate picture of our missional context, and highlighting areas of potential partnership. It would also share the financial burden of professional research across the whole of the Scottish Church, rather than each denomination replicating similar work.

All of these forms of unity should be facilitated and hosted by a new inter-church body such as the nascent Scottish Christian Forum, which will provide the structures for national missional cooperation. As we lean into God and each other, we will then worship, act and speak with ever-greater unity, and the significance and plausibility of the Scottish Church will rise to new levels.

The End of Mission

The Scottish Church will be unable to obey Christ's call to unity in mission, however, if it confuses its identity in Christ with its institutional identity, if it confuses *its* glory for the glory of the Lord. All we are able to do as individual Christians, congregations and denominations is to discern God's will for this day and age, and join as witnesses and participants in the drama of salvation in which *he* is the primary actor. That discernment begins with the worship and contemplation of his glory, and ends with the vision of the new creation that is breaking into the old. It neither begins nor ends with the preservation of historic feuds, theological systems, or denominational identities, but with God and with God alone.

For even now, the axe is at the foot of the tree, and any church that covets its inherited identity over Christ's call to unity in mission will sever itself from the universal Church and become a sect, a mere *denomination*: something of earth and not of heaven. Cut from the true vine, and cut from its branches, it will soon be fit for nothing, save to be thrown on to the fire and consumed.

Yet while tower and temple fall to dust, the true Church will never be consumed, save by the Spirit of the Living God. Founded on the throne of God itself, it cannot fail. So let us renew our confidence in the power and life and love of that God, and step from the ruined shadow of our sanctuaries into the light of day, that the Holy One of Israel might become, once more, *the Holy One of Scotland*.

For the hour is late, the day is ending and the King is approaching. So get up on a high mountain, O Zion! Proclaim the coming of the Holy One of Scotland! For Christ is coming once more, riding in poverty through the secular streets to redeem his people. He is riding in glory through Union Street and Princes Street, through Bearsden and Morningside, Govan and Niddrie. He comes to proclaim good news to the poor and freedom for the captives, to proclaim the year of the Lord's favour, that the people of Scotland might bring their hearts, their lives and their treasures into the Holy City, where loneliness and failure and despair shall be no more, and God will be all in all.

So let us repent of everything that is not of him, and commit ourselves to be Christ's disciples once more. That working in mission to the people of this land, we would be worthy – finally – of the high calling to which we are called. That we, as one Scottish Church, witnessing to the risen Christ through our worship, witness and sacrificial love might present the people of Scotland to the throne of the Father above, and with them, in the company of the angels and the saints, might adore him and the Son in the unity of the Holy Spirit, while countless ages run.

Amen! So let it be.
Come quickly, Lord Jesus – come!

Appendix

What Next?

Having come to the end of this book, you may be thinking – 'What Next? How can we move the task of mission forward and be the Church that Christ wants us to be?'

One option is to visit this book's companion website, **Mission in Contemporary Scotland** (missioninscotland.wordpress.com). This site hosts a community of people like you dedicated to exploring mission in contemporary Scotland, and contains resources, links and an evolving 'How To' guide to get you started in mission.

You may also like to purchase David Male's *How to Pioneer (Even If You Haven't a Clue)* (London: Church House Publishing, 2016). This is an excellent 'How To' guide, and is also supported by a range of accompanying materials.

What is offered below, however, are some concrete steps you can take to begin mission today. In fact, they are so easy, you can start the moment you put this book down!

Step 1 – Pray

All mission is God's mission, and all we can do is discern God's will and seek to further it. Yet how do we know God's will? Through Scripture and through prayer.

The first actions in prayer are to praise God for his glory, to thank him for all he has given, and to confess our sin and weakness. After we are 'right with God' in this way, we can begin to ask him what he wants us to do in our community, checking to see whether it is consistent with Scripture. Don't rush this stage. Indeed, don't even think of it as a discrete stage, but something – like water and sunlight in the growing of plants – that must be done constantly at every step.

Step 2 – Meet with Others

After you have some initial idea about what God might want you to do, seek out some like-minded Christians to speak about it. They may think it's wonderful and can be taken further right away, or that, while good, it requires more thought and exploration. If you are able to find at least one other person – and ideally more – who is able to journey with you and be part of a team, then that will make the task much easier.

Step 3 – Learn

After finding others to journey with you, learn more about your community and about the practice of mission. The following free resources can help you:

Church Army Research Unit (https://churcharmy.org)
Although written from an English context, the Church Army's Research Unit contains useful research on fresh expressions, Messy Church and a range of other missional projects.

Cinnamon Network (https://www.cinnamonnetwork.co.uk)
An organisation offering free advice and support for congregations as they seek to engage in needs- and asset-based community development.

Fresh Expressions Resourcing (https://fxresourcing.org)
A collection of videos, guides, and reflections to inspire you to develop a fresh expression of Church.

Resourcing Mission (https://www.resourcingmission.org.uk)
A useful range of Scotland-focused mission resources from the Church of Scotland.

Scottish Index of Multiple Deprivation (https://simd.scot)
An interactive map showing areas of deprivation and privilege across the country employing a number of indicators.

Statistics for Mission (https://www.churchofscotland.org.uk/resources/stats-for-mission)
The Church of Scotland's mission statistics resource, offering data on every parish in Scotland.

Step 4 – Seek Further Support

While you should seek to be entrepreneurial and take the initiative, it is courteous and often essential to inform your minister, priest, pastor or elders about your plans, and to ask for support. This may be practical support in terms of facilities, funds and so on, but may also be permission-giving depending on your church structures and tradition.

Step 5 – Consult

It is wise to consult with your community before you do anything. This helps gauge need and buy-in, and will give you essential local information that other more general sources will not provide. Your main task will be to ask specific questions that will help you assess the appropriateness of the project you have in mind. Yet it is also wise to ask more general questions about how respondents view the Church, and what they feel about spirituality and faith.

While consultation can be done through online questionnaires, because relationship-building is essential to mission, it is better to conduct face-to-face interviews. While you need to interview a variety of people, look particularly for those who are in the group you are targeting, along with those who are respected by the community or hold important offices.

Step 6 – Pilot

Once you have collected enough information, prayed through it and received any necessary permissions, start your project as a pilot! What that means is setting limitations on how you will run it before reviewing it. You need to run something long enough to give it a chance, but not so long as to seriously drain your team's energy or morale if you know something isn't working.

Step 7 – Refine

Having piloted your mission project, take time as a team to think through how it could be done better. If necessary, do more consultation. You may find that this allows it to keep flourishing, in which case keep going. You may find, however, that it has a fatal flaw that requires it to be stopped. In that case, head back to Step 1.

Step 8 – Thank God

No matter whether your mission project meets your expectations or not, thank God for the opportunity to try to make the world better, and to show something of his love and glory to others. Your worth is not dependent on whether you 'win' or 'fail', but only on that you are obedient, and that you do not bury the talents and insights that God has given you. May God bless you and your community richly as you try to serve him!

Bibliography

Aisthorpe, Steve, *Rewilding the Church*, Edinburgh: Saint Andrew Press, 2020.

Aisthorpe, Steve, *The Invisible Church*, Edinburgh: Saint Andrew Press, 2016.

Akomiah-Conteh, Sheila, 'New Churches in Glasgow 2000–2016', PhD diss., University of Aberdeen, Aberdeen, 2018, ProQuest Dissertations & Theses Global.

Allan, Tom, *The Face of My Parish*, London: SCM Press, 1954.

Alpha International, 'About', accessed 28.11.20, https://www.alpha.org.

Anglican Communion, 'Marks of Mission', accessed 28.10.20, https://www.anglicancommunion.org/mission/marks-of-mission.aspx.

Baggini, Julian, 'Loud But Not Clear', *The Guardian*, 13 April 2009, https://www.theguardian.com/commentisfree/2009/apr/13/atheists-christianity-religion-dawkins-bunting.

Ballard, Paul, 'Community and Christian Witness', in Paul Ballard, ed., *Issues in Church Related Community Work*, 26–30, Cardiff: University of Wales, 1990.

Bardgett, Frank D., *Devoted Service Rendered*, Edinburgh: Saint Andrew Press, 2002.

Barth, Karl, *Church Dogmatics*, Vol. 3.2, *The Doctrine of Creation*, eds G.W. Bromiley and T.F. Torrance, Edinburgh: T&T Clark, 1960.

BBC Sport, 'Australia End Player's Contract Over Anti-Gay Message', last modified 15 April 2019, https://www.bbc.co.uk/sport/rugby-union/47932231.

Bebbington, D.W., *Evangelicalism in Modern Britain*, London: Routledge, 1993.

Berger, Peter and Luckmann, Thomas, *The Social Construction of Reality*, Harmondsworth: Penguin, 1979.

Berger, Peter, *The Social Reality of Religion*, London: Penguin, 1973.

Bevans, Stephen B. and Schroeder, Roger, *Constants in Context*, Maryknoll, NY: Orbis Books, 2004.

Bevans, Stephen B., *Models of Contextual Theology*, Maryknoll, NY: Orbis Books, 2002.

Beveridge, Craig and Turnbull, Ronald, *Scotland After Enlightenment*, Edinburgh: Polygon, 1997.

Bloomberg, 'Scottish Family Party', accessed 16.12.20, https://www.bloomberg.com/graphics/2019-uk-general-election-results/parties/scottish-family-party/.

Bosch, David J., *Believing in the Future*, Valley Forge, PA: Trinity Press, 1995.

Bosch, David J., *Transforming Mission*, Maryknoll, NY: Orbis Books, 1991.

BPAS, 'Social Media, SRE and Sensible Drinking', last modified May 2018, https://www.bpas.org/media/3037/bpas-teenage-pregnancy-report.pdf.

Breen, Mike, *Building a Discipling Culture*, 3rd edn, United States: 3DM International, 2017.

Breen, Mike, *Multiplying Missional Leaders*, United States: 3DM International, 2014.

Bregman, Lucy, 'Psychotherapies', in Peter H. Van Ness, ed., *Spirituality and the Secular Quest*, 251–76, London: SCM Press, 1996.

Breitenbach, Esther, *Empire and Scottish Society*, Edinburgh: Edinburgh University Press, 2009.

Brendan Research, 'The Scottish Church and the COVID-19 Pandemic', accessed 28.4.21, https://www.brendanresearch.com/projects/sclf-acts-covid19.

Brierley Consultancy, 'Scottish Church Census 2016', last modified February 2017, https://www.brierleyconsultancy.com/scottish-church-census.

Brown, Andrew and Woodhead, Linda, *That Was the Church That Was*, London: Bloomsbury, 2016.

Brown, Callum G., *Becoming Atheist*, London: Bloomsbury, 2017.

Brown, Callum G., 'Each Take Off Their Several Way?', in Graham Walker and Tom Gallagher, eds, *Sermons and Battle Hymns*, 69–85, Edinburgh: Edinburgh University Press, 1991.

Brown, Callum G., 'Religion and Secularisation', in A. Dickson and J.H. Treble, eds, *People and Society in Scotland*, Vol. III, 48–75, Edinburgh: John Donald, 1992.

Brown, Callum G., *Religion and Society in Scotland Since 1707*, Edinburgh: Edinburgh University Press, 1997.

Brown, Callum G., *Religion and Society in Twentieth-Century Britain*, Harlow: Pearson, 2006.

Brown, Callum G., *The Strange Death of Christian Britain*, 2nd edn, London and New York: Routledge, 2009.

Brown, Stewart J., *Providence and Empire 1815–1914*, Harlow: Pearson Education, 2008.

Bruce, Steve, *A House Divided*, London: Routledge, 1990.

Bruce, Steve, *Religion in the Modern World*, Oxford: Oxford University Press, 1996.

Bruce, Steve, *Scottish Gods*, Edinburgh: Edinburgh University Press, 2014.

Bruce, Steve and Glendinning, Tony, 'What was Secularisation?', *British Journal of Sociology* 61, No. 1, 2010: 107–26.

Bruce, Steve and Voas, David, 'Religious Toleration and Organizational Typologies', *Journal of Contemporary Religion* 22, No. 1, 2007: 1–17.

Burleigh, J.H.S., *A Church History of Scotland*, Edinburgh: Hope Trust, 1988.

Calvin, John, *Institutes of the Christian Religion*, trans. Henry Beveridge, Peabody, MA: Hendrickson, 2009.

Cameron, James K., ed., *The First Book of Discipline*, Edinburgh: Saint Andrew Press, 1972.

Cheyne, A.C., *The Transforming of the Kirk*, Edinburgh: Saint Andrew Press, 1983.

Christians Against Poverty, 'Annual Report and Accounts 2018', accessed 28.11.20, https://capuk.org/downloads/finance/accounts_2018.pdf.

Church Army, 'Playfully Serious', last modified January 2019, https://www.churcharmy.org.uk/Publisher/File.aspx?ID=225713.

Church of England, 'Fresh Expressions of Church', accessed 12.12.20, https://www.churchofengland.org/about/fresh-expressions-church-england.

Church of England, *Mission-Shaped Church*, London: Church House Publishing, 2004.

Church of Scotland, 'About Us', accessed 14.7.20, https://www.churchofscotland.org.uk/about-us.

Church of Scotland, *Church Without Walls*, Edinburgh: Parish Education Publications, 2001.

Church of Scotland, *Understanding the Times*, Edinburgh: Saint Andrew Press, 1995.

Comte, August, *The Catechism of Positive Religion*, Cambridge: Cambridge University Press, 2016.

Cotter, Christopher R., 'A Discursive Approach to "Religious Indifference"', in Johannes Quack and Cora Schuh, eds, *Religious Indifference*, 43–64, Cham: Springer, 2017.

Cox, James T., *Practice and Procedure in The Church of Scotland*, 5th edn, Edinburgh: William Blackwood, 1964.

CPO, 'Who We Are', accessed 15.7.20, https://rcpolitics.org/who-we-are/.

Craig, Cairns, *Intending Scotland*, Edinburgh: Edinburgh University Press, 2009.

Craig, Carol, *The Scots' Crisis of Confidence*, Edinburgh: Big Thinking, 2003.

Croft, Steve, 'What Counts As a Fresh Expression?', in Louise Nelstrop and Martyn Percy, eds, *Evaluating Fresh Expressions*, 3–14, Norwich: Canterbury Press, 2008.

Darragh, James, 'The Catholic Population in Scotland 1878–1977', in David McRoberts, ed., *Modern Scottish Catholicism*, 211–47, Glasgow: Burns, 1979.

Davie, Grace, *Religion in Britain Since 1945*, Oxford: Blackwell, 1994.

Davies, Jon, 'War Memorials', *Sociological Review* 40, 1992: 116–18.

Davison, Andrew and Milbank, Alison, *For the Parish: A Critique of Fresh Expressions*, London: SCM Press, 2010.

Deneen, Patrick J., *Why Liberalism Failed*, Cambridge, MA: Yale University Press, 2019.

Denholm, Andrew, 'Student Ban on Pro-Life Groups at Strathclyde University is Dropped', *The Herald*, 31 October 2018, https://www.heraldscotland.com/news/17191395.student-ban-on-pro-life-groups-at-strathclyde-university-is-dropped/.

Destiny Edinburgh, 'Church Online', accessed 25.11.20, https://destiny edinburgh.com/locations/church-online.

Devine, Tom, *The Scottish Nation*, London: Penguin, 2012.

Donnelly, Mark, *Sixties Britain*, Abingdon: Routledge, 2005.

Dowie, Al, *Interpreting Culture in a Scottish Congregation*, Bern: Peter Lang, 2002.

Drake, Harold A., 'Church and Empire', in Susan Ashbrook Harvey and David G. Hunter, eds, *The Oxford Handbook of Early Christian Studies*, 446–64, Oxford: Oxford University Press, 2010.

Drane, John, *The McDonaldization of the Church*, London: Darton, Longman & Todd, 2000.

Drummond, Andrew L. and Bulloch, James, *The Victorian Church in Scotland 1843–1874*, Edinburgh: Saint Andrew Press, 1975.

Duffy, Judith, 'Rise in Number of Transgender Children in Scotland', *The Herald*, 12 April 2015, https://www.heraldscotland.com/news/13209521.rise-in-number-of-transgender-children-in-scotland/.

Durkheim, Émile, The *Elementary Forms of Religious Life*, trans. Karen Fields, New York: Free Press, 1995.

Eagleton, Terry, *Culture and the Death of God*, London: Yale University Press, 2014.

Ede, Paul, *Urban Eco-Mission*, Cambridge: Grove Books, 2013.

Edwards, Aaron, 'Secular Apathy and the Public Paradox of the Gospel', *International Journal of Public Theology* 13, No. 4, 2019: 413–31.

Engel, James F., *Contemporary Christian Communication*, New York: Thomas, 1979.

Faith Survey, 'Scottish Social Attitudes Survey 2016', accessed 28.12.20, https://faithsurvey.co.uk/download/ssa-religion.pdf.

Fergusson, David, 'Persons in Relation', *Journal of Practical Theology* 5, No. 3, 2012: 287–306.

Fergusson, David, 'Theology in a Time of War', in Andrew R. Morton, ed., *God's Will in a Time of Crisis*, 32–44, Edinburgh: CTPI, 1994.

Flett, John, *The Witness of God*, Grand Rapids, MI: William B. Eerdmans, 2010.

Flint, Robert, *Christ's Kingdom Upon Earth*, Edinburgh: William Blackwood, 1865.

Forge Scotland, *Pioneering in Scotland*, Glasgow: Forge Scotland, 2019.

Forrester, Duncan, 'The Church of Scotland and Public Policy', *Scottish Affairs* 4, 1993: 67–82.

Forsyth, Alexander, *Mission by the People*, Eugene, OR: Pickwick Publications, 2017.

Fraser, Liam Jerrold, *Atheism, Fundamentalism and the Protestant Reformation*, Cambridge: Cambridge University Press, 2018.

Fraser, Liam Jerrold, 'A Tradition in Crisis: Understanding and Repairing Division Over Homosexuality in the Church of Scotland', *Scottish Journal of Theology* 69, No. 2, 2016: 155–70.

Fraser, Liam Jerrold, 'The Scottish Ideal: Lay Education and Training in the Church of Scotland', *Theology in Scotland* 26, No. 2, 2019: 57–70.

Fukuyama, Francis, *Identity*, London: Profile Books 2018.

Gay, Doug, *Honey from the Lion*, London: SCM Press, 2013.

Gay, Doug, *Reforming the Kirk*, Edinburgh: Saint Andrew Press, 2017.

Gay, Doug, *Remixing the Church*, London: SCM Press, 2011.

Giddens, Anthony, *Modernity and Self-Identity*, Cambridge: Polity Press, 2001.

Gill, Robin, *The 'Empty' Church Revisited*, Aldershot: Ashgate, 2003.

Graham, Gordon, ed., *The Kuyper Centre Review Vol. 1*, Grand Rapids, MI: William B. Eerdmans, 2010.

Green, Chris, 'Nearly A Third of Scottish Men Believe Same-Sex Relationships are "Wrong"', *The i*, 28 December 2018, https://inews.co.uk/news/scotland/nearly-third-scottish-men-same-sex-relationships-wrong-240014.

Green, S.J.D., *The Passing of Protestant England*, Cambridge: Cambridge University Press, 2010.

Guder, Darrell L., ed., *Missional Church*, Grand Rapids, MI: Wm B. Eerdmans, 1998.

Hall, Stuart, ed., *Representation*, London: Routledge, 1997.

Harvey, John, *Bridging the Gap*, Edinburgh: Saint Andrew Press, 1987.

Harvie, Christopher, *No Gods and Precious Few Heroes*, 4th edn, Edinburgh: Edinburgh University Press, 2016.

Harvie, Christopher, *Scotland and Nationalism*, 2nd edn, London: Routledge, 1994.

Harvie, Christopher, *Scotland and Nationalism*, 3rd edn, London: Routledge, 1998.

Haskell, David Millard, Flatt, Kevin N. and Burgoyne, Stephanie,

'Theology Matters', *Review of Religious Research* 58, No. 4, 2016: 515–41.

HBSC Scotland, 'HBSC Briefing Paper', last modified May 2015, http://www.hbsc.org/publications/.

Health Scotland, 'Health Inequalities', last modified 14.2.19, http://www.healthscotland.scot/health-inequalities/measuring-health-inequalities.

Health Scotland, 'Mental Health and Wellbeing', last modified 17.6.20, http://www.healthscotland.scot/health-topics/mental-health-and-wellbeing/overview-of-mental-health-and-wellbeing.

Hegel, G.W.F., *Lectures on the Philosophy of Religion Vol. I*, trans. Peter C. Hodgson, Oxford: Oxford University Press, 2008.

Henderson, G.D., ed., *The Scots Confession of 1560*, Edinburgh: Saint Andrew Press, 1960.

Hense, Elisabeth, 'Present-Day Spiritualities', in Elisabeth Hense, ed., *Present-Day Spiritualities*, 1–17, Leiden: Brill, 2014.

Highet, John, *The Scottish Churches*, London: Skeffington, 1960.

Hirsch, Alan, *The Forgotten Ways*, 2nd edn, Ada, MI: Brazos Press, 2016.

Hoekendijk, J.C., *The Church Inside Out*, London: SCM Press, 1964.

World Council of Churches, 'Missionary Structure of the Congregation', in Michael Kinnamon and Brian E. Cope, eds, *The Ecumenical Movement*, 347–50, Grand Rapids, MI: William B. Eerdmans, 1997.

Hogg, Michael A. and Vaughan, Graham M., *Social Psychology*, 7th edn, Harlow: Pearson, 2014.

Holy See, *Catechism of the Catholic Church*, Vatican City: Libreria Editrice Vaticana, 2000.

Holy See, 'Redemptoris Missio', last modified 7.12.90, http://www.vatican.va/content/john-paul-ii/en/encyclicals/documents/hf_jp-ii_enc_07121990_redemptoris-missio.html.

Humanist Society of Scotland, 'Beliefs in Scotland 2018', last modified August 2018, https://www.Humanism.scot/what-we-do/news/beliefs-in-scotland-2018/.

Humanist Society of Scotland, 'Fair School Votes', accessed 27.11.20, https://www.Humanism.scot/fairschoolvotes/.

Hunt, Stephen, 'Some Observations on the Alpha Course', in Louise Nelstrop and Martyn Percy, eds, *Evaluating Fresh Expressions*, 161–74, Norwich: Canterbury Press, 2008.

Inglehart, Ronald, *Modernization and Postmodernization*, Princeton, NJ: Princeton University Press, 1997.

Jackson, Bob and Fisher, George, 'Everybody Welcome', last modified 23.4.20, https://www.dur.ac.uk/digitaltheology/ewo/.

JPIT, 'About Us', accessed 15.7.20, http://www.jointpublicissues.org.uk/about-us/.

Kasselstrand, Isabella, 'A Comparative Study of Secularisation in

Europe', PhD diss., The University of Edinburgh, 2013, ProQuest Dissertations & Theses Global.

Kasselstrand, Isabella, 'Traditions and Meaning-Making in Scottish Humanist Wedding Ceremonies', *Scottish Affairs* 27, No. 3, 2018: 273–93.

Kay, Jackie, 'The Long View', *The National*, 29 June 2019, https://www.thenational.scot/news/17738769.read-jackie-kays-moving-poem-scottish-parliament-celebration/.

Kernohan, R.D., 'Must the Kirk Die?', in Stewart Lamont, ed., *St. Andrews Rock*, 24–35, London: Bellew Publishing, 1992.

Kidd, Colin, *Union and Unionism*, Cambridge: Cambridge University Press, 2008.

King, Alex, *Memorials of the Great War in Britain*, Oxford: Berg, 1998.

King, Diane, 'US Preacher Could Take Legal Action', *The Scotsman*, 30 January 2020, https://www.scotsman.com/news/politics/us-preacher-could-take-legal-action-after-scottish-venue-axes-event-over-homo phobia-concerns-1-5083157.

Kirk, James, ed., *The Second Book of Discipline*, Edinburgh: Saint Andrew Press, 1980.

Knoblauch, Hubert, 'Popular Spirituality', in Elisabeth Hense, ed., *Present-Day Spiritualities*, 81–102, Leiden: Brill, 2014.

Lausanne Movement, 'Lausanne Covenant', accessed 30.12.20, https://www.lausanne.org/category/content.

Lausanne Movement, 'Manila Manifesto', accessed 30.12.20, https://www.lausanne.org/category/content.

Lee, Lois, 'Religion, Difference and Indifference', in Johannes Quack and Cora Schuh, eds, *Religious Indifference*, 101–22, Cham: Springer, 2017.

Lilla, Mark, *The Stillborn God*, New York: Alfred A. Knopf, 2007.

Lings, George, 'The Day of Small Things', last modified November 2016, https://www.churcharmy.org/Publisher/File.aspx?ID=204265.

Lovegrove, D.W., 'Pastoral Admonition', in Nigel M. de S. Cameron, ed., *Dictionary of Scottish Church History and Theology*, 647, Edinburgh: T&T Clark, 1993.

Luckmann, Thomas, *The Invisible Religion*, New York: Macmillan, 1967.

Luscombe, Edward, *The Scottish Episcopal Church in the Twentieth Century*, Edinburgh: General Synod Office, 1996.

Luther, Martin, *The Book of Concord*, Minneapolis, MN: Fortress Press, 2000.

Mackay, Emily, 'The Big Read – Chvrches', *NME*, 25 May 2018, https://www.nme.com/big-reads/nme-big-read-chvrches-punk-rock-joan-arc-pop-2302745.

MacKian, Sara, *Everyday Spirituality*, New York: Palgrave Macmillan, 2012.

Male, David, 'Who Are Fresh Expressions Really For?', in Louise Nelstrop and Martyn Percy, eds, *Evaluating Fresh Expressions*, 169–72, Norwich: Canterbury Press, 2008.

McCarthy, David, *Seeing Afresh*, Edinburgh: Saint Andrew Press, 2019.

McCrone, David, *The New Sociology of Scotland*, London: SAGE Publications, 2017.

McFarland, E.W., 'The Church of Scotland's Church Extension Movement 1946–61', *Twentieth Century British History* 23, No. 2, 2012: 192–220.

McKay, Johnston R., 'Is a Public Theology Possible?' in Johnston R. McKay, ed., *Christian Faith and the Welfare of the City*, 71–9, Largs: Centre for Theology and Public Issues, 2008.

McKay, Johnston R., 'Is the Kirk Still Relevant?', in Robert D. Kernohan, ed., *The Realm of Reform*, 57–68, Edinburgh: Handsel Press, 1999.

McKay, Johnston R., 'Reformed, but Still Reformable?', in Stewart Lamont, ed., *St. Andrews Rock*, 55–64, London: Bellew, 1992.

MacLaren, Duncan, *Mission Implausible*, Carlisle: Authentic Media, 2006.

McLeod, Hugh, *The Religious Crisis of the 1960s*, Oxford: Oxford University Press, 2007.

McPherson, Alexander, ed., *Westminster Confession of Faith*, Glasgow: Free Presbyterian Publications, 2003.

Meek, D.E., 'Scottish SPCK', in Nigel M. de S. Cameron, ed., *Dictionary of Scottish Church History and Theology*, 761–2, Edinburgh: T&T Clark, 1993.

Mental Health Foundation, 'Mental Health in Scotland', accessed 2.5.19, https://www.mentalhealth.org.uk/file/1750/download?token=TGrdFSpM.

Milbank, John, *Theology and Social Theory*, Oxford: Blackwell, 1990.

Mill, John Stuart, *On Liberty*, London: Penguin, 2006.

Morisy, Ann, *Beyond the Good Samaritan*, London: Mowbray, 1997.

Moynagh, Michael, *A Church for Every Context*, London: SCM Press, 2012.

Murray, Stuart, *Church After Christendom*, Milton Keynes: Paternoster, 2004.

Murray, Stuart, *Planting Churches*, Milton Keynes: Paternoster, 2008.

Murray, Stuart, *Post-Christendom*, Milton Keynes: Paternoster, 2004.

National Records of Scotland, 'Life Expectancy', last modified 24.9.18, https://www.nrscotland.gov.uk/news/2018/latest-estimates-indicate-life-expectancy-for-scotland-has-stalled.

National Records of Scotland, 'Scotland's Census 2011', accessed 27.11.20, https://www.scotlandscensus.gov.uk/documents/censusresults/release2a/rel2A_Religion_detailed_Scotland.pdf.

Newbigin, Lesslie, *The Gospel in a Pluralist Society*, London: SPCK, 2014.

Newbigin, Lesslie, *The Open Secret*, Grand Rapids, MI: William B. Eerdmans, 1995.

Newsroom, 'Community Spirit Rises', *Scottish Mail on Sunday*, 25 October 2020, https://www.pressreader.com/uk/the-scottish-mail-on-sunday/20201025/281805696423980.

Newsroom, 'Pro-Life Group Banned', *The Scotsman*, 23 November 2018, https://www.scotsman.com/education/pro-life-group-banned-from-joining-union-at-scottish-university-1-4834138.

Niebauer, Michael, 'Virtue Ethics and Church Planting', *Missiology* 44, No. 3, 2016: 311–26.

Offer, Avner, *The Challenge of Affluence*, Oxford: Oxford University Press, 2007.

Paas, Stefan, *Church Planting in the Secular West*, Grand Rapids, MI: William B. Eerdmans, 2016.

Pew Research, 'Global Views on Morality', last modified 15.4.14, https://www.pewglobal.org/2014/04/15/global-morality/table/pre marital-sex.

Pigliucci, Massimo, 'New Atheism and the Scientistic Turn in the Atheism Movement', *Midwest Studies in Philosophy* 37, No. 1, 2013: 142–53.

Piper, John, *Let the Nations Be Glad*, Grand Rapids, MI: Inter-Varsity Press, 2003.

Pirrie, Anne, 'The Disenchanted Assembly', *Scottish Affairs* 50, 2005: 71–85.

Randall, David J., *A Sad Departure*, Edinburgh: Banner of Truth, 2015.

Reasonable Faith, 'Testimonials', accessed 28.11.20, https://www.reasonablefaith.org/testimonials/.

Richter, Philip and Francis, Leslie J., *Gone for Good?*, London: Epworth Press, 2007.

Robertson, David, 'The Key to Understanding Contemporary Western Society', *The Wee Flea*, 14 May 2018, https://theweeflea.com/2018/05/14/the-key-to-understanding-contemporary-western-society-and-whats-happening-in-uk-politics-today/.

Rosen, Andrew, *The Transformation of British Life 1950–2000*, Manchester: Manchester University Press, 2003.

Sanctuary First, 'About Us', accessed 25.11.20, https://www.sanctuary first.org.uk/about.

Sanneh, Lumin, *Translating the Message*, Maryknoll, NY: Orbis 1991.

Sartre, Jean-Paul, *Existentialism and Humanism*, trans. Phillip Mairet, London: Methuen, 2013.

Savage, Sara, 'Fresh Expressions: The Gains and the Risks', in Louise Nelstrop and Martyn Percy, eds, *Evaluating Fresh Expressions*, 55–70, Norwich: Canterbury Press, 2008.

Schleiermacher, Friedrich, *Christian Faith*, Louisville, KY: Westminster John Knox Press, 2016.

Schmitt, Carl, *The Nomos of the Earth*, New York: Telos Press, 2003.

Schnabel, Landon and Bock, Sean, 'The Persistent and Exceptional Intensity of American Religion: A Response to Recent Research', *Sociological Science* 4, 2017: 686–700, https://www.scpo.scot/about-scpo/.

Scotland.org. 'Who Was St Andrew?', accessed 30.11.20, https://www.scotland.org/events/st-andrews-day/who-was-st-andrew?fbclid=IwAR2_21fb8NE2Gz-cWXG52T6uM2bT2v4dseKdPycO39hbEMn VAVUaRHyhBg4.

Scottish Catholic Education Service, 'Catholic Education', accessed 28.11.20, https://sces.org.uk/catholic-education/.

Scottish Government, 'Earnings', last modified 25.10.18, https://www2.gov.scot/Topics/Statistics/Browse/Labour-Market/Earnings.

Scottish Government, 'Guidance on Spiritual Care in the NHS in Scotland', last modified 20.1.09, https://www.gov.scot/publications/spiritual-care-chaplaincy/pages/2/.

Scottish Government, 'Inequality', last modified 28.3.19, https://www2.gov.scot/Topics/Statistics/Browse/Social-Welfare/IncomeInequality.

Scottish Government, 'Poverty and Income Inequality', last modified 22.3.18, https://www.gov.scot/publications/poverty-income-inequality-scotland-2014-17.

Scottish Government, 'Religion in Scotland', accessed 7.12.20, https://www.scotlandscensus.gov.uk/ods-web/data-visualisations.html.

Scottish Government, 'Religious Observance', last modified 30.5.17, https://www.gov.scot/publications/curriculum-for-excellence-religious-observance/.

Scottish Government, 'Scottish Household Survey', last modified 26.9.17, https://www.gov.scot/publications/scotlands-people-annual-report-results-2016-scottish-household-survey/pages/3/#Table3.2.

Scottish Government, 'Tackling Sectarianism and its Consequences in Scotland', last modified 29.5.15, https://www2.gov.scot/Publications/2015/05/4296/0.

Scottish Housing News, 'Foodbank Use in Scotland', last modified 6.1.20, https://www.scottishhousingnews.com/article/foodbank-use-in-scotland-rises-almost-80-in-five-years.

Scottish Trans Alliance, 'Equality Monitoring', accessed 26.11.20, https://www.scottishtrans.org/trans-rights/practice/equality-monitoring/.

SCPO, 'About SCPO', accessed 15.7.20, https://www.scpo.scot/about-scpo/.

Sissons, Peter L., *The Social Significance of Church Membership in the Burgh of Falkirk*, Edinburgh: The Church of Scotland, 1973.

Smith, Donald, *Freedom and Faith*, Edinburgh: Saint Andrew Press, 2013.

Smout, T.C., *A Century of the Scottish People*, London: Fontana, 1987.

Social Enterprise UK, 'What is it All About?', accessed 28.11.20, https://www.socialenterprise.org.uk/what-is-it-all-about/.

Sophocles, *The Three Theban Plays*, trans. Robert Fagles, London: Penguin Classics, 1984.

Steven, Morton, 'The Place of Religion in Devolved Scottish Politics', *Scottish Affairs* 58, 2007: 96–110.

Stonewall Scotland, 'Black History Month x Stonewall', accessed 27.11.20, https://www.stonewallscotland.org.uk/our-work/campaigns/black-history-month-x-stonewall.

Storrar, William, *Scottish Identity: A Christian Vision*, Edinburgh: Handsel Press, 1990.

Storrar, William, 'Three Portraits of Scottish Calvinism', in Robert D. Kernohan, ed., *The Realm of Reform*, 17–30, Edinburgh: Handsel Press, 1999.

Storrar, William, 'Understanding the Silent Disruption', in David Fergusson and D.W.D. Shaw, eds, *Future of the Kirk*, 21–36, St Andrews: University of St Andrews, 1997.

Sutherland, Liam T., 'One Nation Many Faiths', PhD diss., The University of Edinburgh, 2018, ProQuest Dissertations Publishing.

Taylor, Charles, *Sources of the Self*, Cambridge, MA: Harvard University Press, 1992.

Taylor, Charles, *The Ethics of Authenticity*, Cambridge, MA: Harvard University Press, 1992.

Teuton, Joanna, *Social Isolation and Loneliness in Scotland*, Edinburgh: NHS Health Scotland, 2018.

The Turning, 'Annual Report 2017', accessed 28.11.20, http://annualreport2017.theturning.eu/year-2/.

The Turning, 'Learning Report', accessed 28.11.20, http://theturning.eu/learning-review/.

Tiplady, Richard, 'Entrepreneurial Leadership Development in the Christian Church in Scotland', PhD diss., Glasgow Caledonian University, Glasgow, 2019, ProQuest Dissertations & Theses Global.

Torrance, David, 'Standing Up for Scotland', *Scottish Affairs* 27, No. 2, 2018: 169–88.

Trzebiatowska, Marta and Bruce, Steve, *Why Are Women More Religious Than Men?*, Oxford: Oxford University Press, 2012.

United Nations, 'Community Development', last modified 7.7.14, https://web.archive.org/web/20140714225617/http://unterm.un.org/DGAACS/unterm.nsf/8fa942046ff7601c85256983007ca4d8/526c2eaba978f007852569fd00036819?OpenDocument.

Van der Borght, Eduardus, *Theology of Ministry*, Leiden: Brill, 2007.

Vanity Fair, 'Tinder and the Dawn of the "Dating Apocalypse"', last modified 6.8.15, https://www.vanityfair.com/culture/2015/08/tinder-hook-up-culture-end-of-dating.

Vatican Radio, 'Construct a Civilization of Love', 22 August 2010, http://www.archivioradiovaticana.va/storico/2010/08/22/pope_bene dict_xvi_construct_a_civilisation_of_love/en1-417168.

Wagner, C. Peter, *Church Planting for a Greater Harvest*, Raleigh, NC: Regal Books, 1990.

Walker, Graham, 'The Religious Factor', in T.M. Devine and Jenny Wormald, eds, *The Oxford Handbook of Modern Scottish History*, 585–601, Oxford: Oxford University Press, 2012.

Walker, John, *Testing Fresh Expressions*, Farnham: Ashgate, 2014.

Walls, Andrew, *The Missionary Movement in Christian History*, Edinburgh: T&T Clark, 1996.

Ward, Pete, *Liquid Ecclesiology*, Leiden: Brill, 2017.

Weeks, Jeffrey, *Making Sexual History*, Cambridge: Polity Press, 2000.

Wells, Samuel, *A Future That's Bigger Than the Past*, Norwich: Canterbury Press, 2019.

Wells, Samuel, Rook, Russell and Barclay, David, *For Good*, Norwich: Canterbury Press, 2017.

Whitefield, George, *Letters, 1734–1742*, Edinburgh: Banner of Truth, 1976.

Wickham-Jones, M.E., 'The Church and Nation Committee of the Church of Scotland', in A. Elliott and Duncan B. Forrester, eds, *The Scottish Churches and the Political Process*, 69–72, Edinburgh: CTPI, 1986.

Wink, Walter, *Unmasking the Powers*, Philadelphia, PA: Fortress Press, 1986.

Wolffe, John, *God and Greater Britain*, London: Routledge, 1994.

World Council of Churches, 'Together Towards Life', accessed 28.10.20, https://www.oikoumene.org/sites/default/files/Document/Together_towards_Life.pdf.

Wright, Christopher J.H., *The Mission of God*, Nottingham: Inter-Varsity Press, 2006.

Notes

Introduction

1 'Scottish Church Census 2016', Brierley Consultancy, last modified February 2017, https://www.brierleyconsultancy.com/scottish-church-census, 4.

2 David McCrone, *The New Sociology of Scotland*, London: SAGE Publications, 2017, xxxix.

3 William Storrar, *Scottish Identity: A Christian Vision*, Edinburgh: Handsel Press, 1990, 215–16.

4 John Milbank, *Theology and Social Theory*, Oxford: Blackwell, 1990.

5 Callum G. Brown, *The Strange Death of Christian Britain*, 2nd edn, London and New York: Routledge, 2009, 16–47.

6 The concept of plausibility has previously been explored by Duncan MacLaren, *Mission Implausible*, Carlisle: Authentic Media, 2006.

Chapter 1 A Missional Theology

1 This is similar to that proposed by Bosch and Wright. See David J. Bosch, *Believing in the Future*, Valley Forge, PA: Trinity Press, 1995, 27–9; Christopher J.H. Wright, *The Mission of God*, Nottingham: Inter-Varsity Press, 2006, 33–47.

2 The lens of witness used here and throughout this work is derived from John Flett, *The Witness of God*, Grand Rapids, MI: William B. Eerdmans, 2010.

3 See Darrell L. Guder, ed., *Missional Church*, Grand Rapids, MI: William B. Eerdmans, 1998, 95.

4 Lesslie Newbigin, *The Open Secret*, Grand Rapids, MI: William B. Eerdmans, 1995, 110, 113, 150.

Chapter 2 The World That Was

1 Cf. Stuart Murray, *Church After Christendom*, Milton Keynes: Paternoster, 2004, 43.

2 Storrar, *Scottish Identity*, 11–14.

3 G.D. Henderson, ed., *The Scots Confession of 1560*, Edinburgh: Saint Andrew Press, 1960, Article XVIII, 44–5.

4 Tom Devine, *The Scottish Nation*, London: Penguin, 2012, 84.

5 See Henderson, *Scots Confession*, 51–2; James Kirk, ed., *The Second Book of Discipline*, Edinburgh: Saint Andrew Press, 1980, 213–16; Alexander McPherson, ed., *Westminster Confession of Faith*, Glasgow: Free Presbyterian Publications, 2003, 99–103.

6 J.H.S. Burleigh, *A Church History of Scotland*, Edinburgh: Hope Trust, 1988, 205.

7 Devine, *Scottish Nation*, 84.

8 Eduardus Van der Borght, *Theology of Ministry*, Leiden: Brill 2007, 10, 100–2.

9 John Calvin, *Institutes of the Christian Religion*, trans. Henry Beveridge, Peabody, MA: Hendrickson, 2009, IV 3.4.

10 See Kirk, *Second Book*, 187–90.

11 Calvin, *Institutes*, IV.3.4 and IV.3.8.

12 Van der Borght, *Ministry*, 132.

13 Kirk, *Second Book*, 163. Author's translation.

14 James K. Cameron, ed., *The First Book of Discipline*, Edinburgh: Saint Andrew Press, 1972, 104.

15 Henderson, *Confession*, 28, author's translation.

16 McPherson, *Westminster*, 377.

17 Frank D. Bardgett, *Devoted Service Rendered*, Edinburgh: Saint Andrew Press, 2002, 32.

18 D.E. Meek, 'Scottish SPCK', in *Dictionary of Scottish Church History and Theology*, ed. Nigel M. de S. Cameron, Edinburgh: T&T Clark, 1993, 761–2.

19 D.W. Bebbington, *Evangelicalism in Modern Britain*, London: Routledge, 1993, 1–19.

20 George Whitefield, *Letters, 1734–1742*, Edinburgh: Banner of Truth, 1976, 105.

21 See D.W. Lovegrove, 'Pastoral Admonition', in *Dictionary of Scottish Church History and Theology*, ed. Nigel M. de S. Cameron, Edinburgh: T&T Clark, 1993, 647.

Chapter 3 The Secularisation of Scotland

1 See e.g. Bebbington, *Evangelicalism*, 105–50.

2 Brown, *Death*, 16–47.

3 Storrar, *Scottish Identity*, 42.

4 Robert Flint, *Christ's Kingdom Upon Earth*, Edinburgh: William Blackwood, 1865, 71.

5 See e.g. Andrew L. Drummond and James Bulloch, *The Victorian Church in Scotland 1843–1874*, Edinburgh: Saint Andrew Press, 1975, 240–65; A.C. Cheyne, *The Transforming of the Kirk*, Edinburgh: Saint Andrew Press, 1983, 37–59.

6 Steve Bruce, *Scottish Gods*, Edinburgh: Edinburgh University Press, 2014, 11.

7 Brown, *Death*, 163–4.

8 Stewart J. Brown, *Providence and Empire 1815–1914*, Harlow: Pearson Education, 2008, 139–213.

9 S.J.D. Green, *The Passing of Protestant England*, Cambridge: Cambridge University Press, 2010, 309–11.

10 Callum G. Brown, *Religion and Society in Scotland Since 1707*, Edinburgh: Edinburgh University Press, 1997, 139–40.

11 Callum G. Brown, *Religion and Society in Twentieth-Century Britain*, Harlow: Pearson, 2006, 214–15.

12 Doug Gay, *Reforming the Kirk*, Edinburgh: Saint Andrew Press, 2017, 12.

13 John Highet, *The Scottish Churches*, London: Skeffington, 1960, 60–1.

14 Peter L. Sissons, *The Social Significance of Church Membership in the Burgh of Falkirk*, Edinburgh: The Church of Scotland, 1973, 133–5.

15 Sissons, *Falkirk*, 85–6.

16 Sissons, *Falkirk*, 163.

17 Callum G. Brown, *Becoming Atheist*, London: Bloomsbury, 2017.

18 Brown, *Becoming*, 175.

19 Hugh McLeod, *The Religious Crisis of the 1960s*, Oxford: Oxford University Press, 2007, 2.

20 See e.g. McLeod, *Crisis*, 2–10; Brown, *Death*, 170–92.

21 Brown, *Death*, 58–87.

22 McLeod, *Crisis*, 15.

23 T.C. Smout, *A Century of the Scottish People*, London: Fontana, 1987, 149–50.

24 Cf. Andrew Rosen, *The Transformation of British Life 1950–2000*, Manchester: Manchester University Press, 2003, 108–9; Brown, *Twentieth-Century Britain*, 215–16.

25 Ronald Inglehart, *Modernization and Postmodernization*, Princeton, NJ: Princeton University Press, 1997.

26 Avner Offer, *The Challenge of Affluence*, Oxford: Oxford University Press, 2007, 61–3 and 310.

27 Cf. Sara MacKian, *Everyday Spirituality*, New York: Palgrave Macmillan, 2012, 31–5.

28 McLeod, *Crisis*, 41–2 and 67–73.

29 See David Fergusson, 'Persons in Relation', *Journal of Practical Theology* 5, No. 3, 2012: 287–306.

30 See Edward Luscombe, *The Scottish Episcopal Church in the Twentieth Century*, Edinburgh: General Synod Office, 1996.

31 James Darragh, 'The Catholic Population in Scotland 1878–1977', in *Modern Scottish Catholicism*, ed. David McRoberts, Glasgow: Burns, 1979, 211–47 at 219.

32 Robin Gill, *The 'Empty' Church Revisited*, Aldershot: Ashgate, 2003, 184, 195.

33 John Harvey, *Bridging the Gap*, Edinburgh: Saint Andrew Press, 1987, 9.

34 Callum G. Brown, 'Religion and Secularisation', in *People and Society in Scotland Vol. III*, eds A Dickson and J.H. Treble, Edinburgh: John Donald, 1992, 48–75 at 75.

35 Callum G. Brown, 'Each Take Off Their Several Way?', in *Sermons and Battle Hymns*, eds Graham Walker and Tom Gallagher, Edinburgh: Edinburgh University Press, 1991, 69–85 at 82.

36 Johnston R. McKay, 'Is the Kirk Still Relevant?', in *The Realm of Reform*, ed. Robert D. Kernohan, Edinburgh: Handsel Press, 1999, 57–68 at 60.

Chapter 4 Social Context

1 'Life Expectancy', National Records of Scotland, last modified 24.9.18, https://www.nrscotland.gov.uk/news/2018/latest-estimates-indicate-life-expectancy-for-scotland-has-stalled.

2 'Health Inequalities', Health Scotland, last modified 14.2.19, http://www.healthscotland.scot/health-inequalities/measuring-health-inequalities.

3 'Earnings', Scottish Government, last modified 25.10.18, https://www2.gov.scot/Topics/Statistics/Browse/Labour-Market/Earnings.

4 'Inequality', Scottish Government, last modified 28.3.19, https://www2.gov.scot/Topics/Statistics/Browse/Social-Welfare/IncomeInequality.

5 'Poverty and Income Inequality', Scottish Government, last modified 22.3.18, https://www.gov.scot/publications/poverty-income-inequality-scotland-2014-17.

6 'Scottish Household Survey', Scottish Government, last modified 26.9.17, https://www.gov.scot/publications/scotlands-people-annual-report-results-2016-scottish-household-survey/pages/3/#Table3.2.

7 'Scottish Household Survey', Scottish Government, last modified 26.9.17, https://www.gov.scot/publications/scotlands-people-annual-report-results-2016-scottish-household-survey/pages/3/#Table3.2.

8 Joanna Teuton, *Social Isolation and Loneliness in Scotland*, Edinburgh: NHS Health Scotland, 2018.

9 'Community Spirit Rises', *Scottish Mail on Sunday*, last modified 25.10.20, https://www.pressreader.com/uk/the-scottish-mail-on-sunday/20201025/281805696423980.

10 'Mental Health in Scotland', Mental Health Foundation, accessed 2.5.19, https://www.mentalhealth.org.uk/file/1750/download?token=TG rdFSpM.

11 'Mental Health and Wellbeing', Health Scotland, last modified 17.6.20, http://www.healthscotland.scot/health-topics/mental-health-and-wellbeing/overview-of-mental-health-and-wellbeing.

12 Cf. John Drane, *The McDonaldization of the Church*, London: Darton, Longman & Todd, 2000, 19–20.

13 Charles Taylor, *The Ethics of Authenticity*, Cambridge, MA: Harvard University Press, 1992.

14 Jean-Paul Sartre, *Existentialism and Humanism*, trans. Phillip Mairet, London: Methuen, 2013.

15 Patrick J. Deneen, *Why Liberalism Failed*, Cambridge, MA: Yale University Press, 2019, 34.

16 Cited in Anthony Giddens, *Modernity and Self-Identity*, Cambridge: Polity Press, 2001, 195.

17 Charles Taylor, *Sources of the Self*, Cambridge, MA: Harvard University Press, 1992.

18 Mark Donnelly, *Sixties Britain*, Abingdon: Routledge, 2005, 29.

19 It is interesting to note that the Abortion Act 1967 began life as a Private Member's Bill of son of the manse David Steel.

20 'Global Views on Morality', Pew Research, last modified 15.4.14, https://www.pewglobal.org/2014/04/15/global-morality/table/premarital-sex.

21 'HBSC Briefing Paper', HBSC Scotland, last modified May 2015, http://www.hbsc.org/publications/.

22 'Social Media, SRE and Sensible Drinking', BPAS, last modified May 2018, https://www.bpas.org/media/3037/bpas-teenage-pregnancy-report.pdf.

23 'Tinder and the Dawn of the "Dating Apocalypse"', Vanity Fair, last modified 6.8.15, https://www.vanityfair.com/culture/2015/08/tinder-hook-up-culture-end-of-dating.

24 'Equality Monitoring', Scottish Trans Alliance, accessed 26.11.20, https://www.scottishtrans.org/trans-rights/practice/equality-monitor ing/; 'Health Care Needs Assessment of Transgender Services', Scottish Public Health Network, last modified May 2018, https://www.scotphn. net/wp-content/uploads/2017/04/2018_05_16-HCNA-of-Gender-Iden tity-Services-1.pdf.

25 Judith Duffy, 'Rise in Number of Transgender Children in Scot- land', *The Herald*, last modified 12.4.15, https://www.heraldscotland. com/news/13209521.rise-in-number-of-transgender-children-in-scot land/.

26 Giddens, *Modernity*, 34.

Chapter 5 Political Context

1 Christopher Harvie, *Scotland and Nationalism*, 2nd edn, London: Routledge, 1994, 12.

2 See Esther Breitenbach, *Empire and Scottish Society*, Edinburgh: Edinburgh University Press, 2009.

3 Christopher Harvie, *No Gods and Precious Few Heroes*, 4th edn, Edinburgh: Edinburgh University Press, 2016, 56–7.

4 Brown, *Religion and Society*, 139–40.

5 See Jon Davies, 'War Memorials', *Sociological Review* 40, 1992: 116–18.

6 Alex King, *Memorials of the Great War in Britain*, Oxford: Berg, 1998, 20–1.

7 Christopher Harvie, *Scotland & Nationalism*, 3rd edn, London: Routledge, 1998, 18, 23.

8 Colin Kidd, *Union and Unionism*, Cambridge: Cambridge Uni- versity Press, 2008, 2.

9 John Wolffe, *God and Greater Britain*, London: Routledge, 1994, 156–7.

10 Cf. Wolffe, *Greater*, 263–4.

11 Kidd, *Union*, 22.

12 Harvie, *No Gods*, 71.

13 Donald Smith, *Freedom and Faith*, Edinburgh: Saint Andrew Press, 2013, 72.

14 McCrone, *Sociology*, 45.

15 Cf. Terry Eagleton, *Culture and the Death of God*, London: Yale University Press, 2014, 42–3.

16 Francis Fukuyama, *Identity*, London: Profile Books 2018, 55.

17 Eagleton, *Culture*, 84–5.

18 Peter Berger and Thomas Luckmann, *The Social Construction of Reality*, Harmondsworth: Penguin, 1979: 142.

19 Émile Durkheim, The *Elementary forms of Religious Life*, trans. Karen Fields, New York: Free Press, 1995, 227.

20 Cf. David Torrance, 'Standing Up for Scotland', *Scottish Affairs* 27, No. 2, 2018: 169–88 at 186.

21 Eagleton, *Culture*, 54–5.

22 Craig Beveridge and Ronald Turnbull, *Scotland After Enlightenment*, Edinburgh: Polygon, 1997, 111–34.

23 Cairns Craig, *Intending Scotland*, Edinburgh: Edinburgh University Press, 2009, 3.

24 Craig, *Intending*, 11–12.

25 This line of thinking gave rise to Carol Craig's, *The Scots' Crisis of Confidence*, Edinburgh: Big Thinking, 2003.

26 See McCrone, *Sociology*, 17–24.

27 Cameron, *First Book*, 129–36.

28 Craig, *Intending*, 167.

29 'Who Was St Andrew?', Scotland.org, accessed 30.11.20, https://www.scotland.org/events/st-andrews-day/who-was-st-andrew?fbclid=IwAR2_21fb8NE2Gz-cWXG52T6uM2bT2v4dseKdPycO39hbEMnVAVUaRHyhBg4.

30 E.g. 'Fair School Votes', Humanist Society of Scotland, accessed 27.11.20, https://www.Humanism.scot/fairschoolvotes/; 'Black History Month x Stonewall', Stonewall Scotland, accessed 27.1.20, https://www.stonewallscotland.org.uk/our-work/campaigns/black-history-month-x-stonewall.

31 Peter Berger, *The Social Reality of Religion*, London: Penguin, 1973, 76–7.

32 Liam T. Sutherland, 'One Nation Many Faiths', PhD diss., The University of Edinburgh, 2018, 56, ProQuest Dissertations Publishing.

33 Cf. Fukuyama, *Identity*, 92; Giddens, *Modernity*, 209–31.

34 Jeffrey Weeks, *Making Sexual History*, Cambridge: Polity Press, 2000, 133.

35 See e.g. David Robertson, 'The Key to Understanding Contemporary Western Society', *The Wee Flea*, 14 May 2018, https://theweeflea.com/2018/05/14/the-key-to-understanding-contemporary-western-society-and-whats-happening-in-uk-politics-today/.

36 Chris Green, 'Nearly A Third of Scottish Men Believe Same-Sex Relationships are 'Wrong', *The i*, 28 December 2018, https://inews.co.uk/news/scotland/nearly-third-scottish-men-same-sex-relationships-wrong-240014.

37 Bruce, *Scottish Gods*, 230.

38 It should be noted, however, that the meanings of symbols such as the Rainbow Flag are not immutable, and can change very quickly. This was seen during the coronavirus pandemic, when the rainbow became a symbol of hope, and support for the NHS and other key workers. My thanks to David McCarthy for highlighting this point.

39 Cf. Steve Bruce, *Religion in the Modern World*, Oxford: Oxford University Press, 1996, 44.

40 Jackie Kay, 'The Long View', *The National*, 29 June 2019, https://www.thenational.scot/news/17738769.read-jackie-kays-moving-poem-scottish-parliament-celebration/.

41 Smith, *Freedom*, 38.

42 See Doug Gay, *Honey from the Lion*, London: SCM Press, 2013, for a theological defence of nationalism.

43 'Tackling Sectarianism and its Consequences in Scotland', The Scottish Government, last modified 29.5.15, https://www2.gov.scot/Publications/2015/05/4296/0.

44 Graham Walker, 'The Religious Factor', in *The Oxford Handbook of Modern Scottish History*, eds T.M. Devine and Jenny Wormald, Oxford: Oxford University Press, 2012, 585–601 at 596–7.

45 'Religious Observance', Scottish Government, last modified 30.5.17, https://www.gov.scot/publications/curriculum-for-excellence-religious-observance/.

46 Anne Pirrie, 'The Disenchanted Assembly', *Scottish Affairs* 50, 2005: 71–85.

47 All references are for 'Guidance on Spiritual Care in the NHS in Scotland', Scottish Government, last modified 20.1.09, https://www.gov.scot/publications/spiritual-care-chaplaincy/pages/2/.

48 Steve Bruce and David Voas, 'Religious Toleration and Organizational Typologies', *Journal of Contemporary Religion* 22, No. 1, 2007: 1–17 at 1.

49 BBC Sport, 'Australia End Player's Contract Over Anti-Gay Message', 15 April 2019, https://www.bbc.co.uk/sport/rugby-union/47932231.

50 For a discussion of the notion that non-Christians are better interpreters of Scripture than Christians, see Liam Jerrold Fraser, *Atheism, Fundamentalism and the Protestant Reformation*, Cambridge: Cambridge University Press, 2018, 162–73 and 219.

51 Cf. Thomas Luckmann, *The Invisible Religion*, New York: Macmillan, 1967, 111–14.

52 Newsroom, 'Pro-Life Group Banned', *The Scotsman* 23 November 2018, https://www.scotsman.com/education/pro-life-group-banned-from-joining-union-at-scottish-university-1-4834138; Andrew Denholm, 'Student Ban on Pro-Life Groups at Strathclyde University is Dropped', *The Herald*, 31 October 2018, https://www.heraldscotland.com/news/17191395.student-ban-on-pro-life-groups-at-strathclyde-university-is-dropped/; Diane King, 'US Preacher Could Take Legal Action', *The Scotsman*, 30 January 2020, https://www.scotsman.com/news/politics/us-preacher-could-take-legal-action-after-scottish-venue-axes-event-over-homophobia-concerns-1-5083157.

53 Gay, *Honey*, 65.

Chapter 6 Spiritual Context

1 All of these aspects need to be considered, as the privileging of church membership gives rise to skewed results. See Steve Bruce and Tony Glendinning, 'What was Secularisation?', *British Journal of Sociology* 61, No. 1, 2010: 107–26 at 111.

2 Bruce and Voas, 'Religious Toleration', 2.

3 McCrone, *Sociology*, 352.

4 McCrone, *Sociology*, 352.

5 'Religion in Scotland', Scottish Government, accessed 7.12.20, https://www.scotlandscensus.gov.uk/ods-web/data-visualisations.html.

6 'Religion in Scotland', Scottish Government, accessed 7.12.20, https://www.scotlandscensus.gov.uk/ods-web/data-visualisations.html.

7 'Religion in Scotland', Scottish Government, accessed 7.12.20, https://www.scotlandscensus.gov.uk/ods-web/data-visualisations.html.

8 'Scottish Social Attitudes Survey 2016', accessed 28.12.20, https://faithsurvey.co.uk/download/ssa-religion.pdf.

9 'Scottish Social Attitudes Survey 2016', accessed 28.12.20, https://faithsurvey.co.uk/download/ssa-religion.pdf.

10 Isabella Kasselstrand, 'Traditions and Meaning-Making in Scottish Humanist Wedding Ceremonies', *Scottish Affairs* 27, No. 3, 2018: 278.

11 See Grace Davie, *Religion in Britain Since 1945*, Oxford: Blackwell, 1994.

12 'Beliefs in Scotland 2018', Humanist Society of Scotland, last modified August 2018, https://www.Humanism.scot/what-we-do/news/beliefs-in-scotland-2018/.

13 Emily Mackay, 'The Big Read – Chvrches', *NME*, 25 May 2018, https://www.nme.com/big-reads/nme-big-read-chvrches-punk-rock-joan-arc-pop-2302745.

14 Church of Scotland, *Understanding the Times*, Edinburgh: Saint Andrew Press, 1995, 11.

15 Church of Scotland, *Times*, 13.

16 McCrone, *Sociology*, 367.

17 Murray, *After Christendom*, 231.

18 Church of Scotland, *Times*, 16.

19 Lois Lee, 'Religion, Difference and Indifference', in *Religious Indifference*, eds Johannes Quack and Cora Schuh, Cham: Springer, 2017, 105.

20 Christopher R. Cotter, 'A Discursive Approach to "Religious Indifference"', in *Religious Indifference*, eds Johannes Quack and Cora Schuh, Cham: Springer, 2017, 46–7.

21 Fraser, *Atheism*, 16–110.

22 Fraser, *Atheism*, 149–204.

23 E.g. Massimo Pigliucci, 'New Atheism and the Scientistic Turn in the Atheism Movement', *Midwest Studies in Philosophy* 37, No. 1, 2013: 152–3; Julian Baggini, 'Loud But Not Clear', *The Guardian*, 13 April 2009, https://www.theguardian.com/commentisfree/2009/apr/13/athe ists-christianity-religion-dawkins-bunting.

24 'Scotland's Census 2011', National Records of Scotland, accessed 27.11.20, https://www.scotlandscensus.gov.uk/documents/censusresults/ release2a/rel2A_Religion_detailed_Scotland.pdf.

25 Fraser, *Atheism*, 73–87; Steve Bruce, *A House Divided*, London: Routledge, 1990, 25.

26 Fraser, *Atheism*, 188–204.

27 Martin Luther, *The Book of Concord*, Minneapolis, MN: Fortress Press, 2000, 386.

28 Leonard Cohen, 'Steer Your Way', *The New Yorker*, 13 June 2016, https://www.newyorker.com/magazine/2016/06/20/steer-your-way-by-leonard-cohen.

29 Hubert Knoblauch, 'Popular Spirituality', in *Present-Day Spiritualities*, ed. Elisabeth Hense, Leiden: Brill, 2014, 81–102 at 82.

30 MacKian, *Everyday*, 1.

31 Elisabeth Hense, 'Present-Day Spiritualities', in *Present-Day Spiritualities*, ed. Elisabeth Hense, Leiden: Brill, 2014, 1–17 at 1.

32 Hense, 'Present-Day', 5.

33 MacKian, *Everyday*, 26.

34 Cited in MacKian, *Everyday*, 34.

35 MacKian, *Everyday*, 2–4, 51, 60.

36 Drane, *McDonaldization*, 6–7.

37 Andrew Brown and Linda Woodhead, *That Was the Church That Was*, London: Bloomsbury, 2016, 182.

38 Inglehart, *Modernization*, 285.

39 Marta Trzebiatowska and Steve Bruce, *Why Are Women More Religious Than Men?*, Oxford: Oxford University Press, 2012, 65.

40 Trzebiatowska and Bruce, *Why Are Women*, 77.

41 Trzebiatowska and Bruce, *Why Are Women*, 75–6.

42 Lucy Bregman, 'Psychotherapies', in *Spirituality and the Secular Quest*, ed. Peter H. Van Ness, London: SCM Press, 1996, 251–76 at 251–4.

43 Isabella Kasselstrand, 'A Comparative Study of Secularisation in Europe', PhD diss., The University of Edinburgh, 2013, 131–3, ProQuest Dissertations & Theses Global.

44 Bruce, *Scottish Gods*, 183–4.

45 Kasselstrand 'Traditions and Meaning-Making', 287–90.

46 Luckmann, *Invisible Religion*, 50–3.

47 In so doing, Humanism achieves much of the 'religion of humanity' argued for by August Comte in the nineteenth century. See August

Comte, *The Catechism of Positive Religion*, Cambridge: Cambridge University Press, 2016.

48 Carl Schmitt, *The Nomos of the Earth*, New York: Telos Press, 2003, 103.

49 Philip Richter and Leslie J. Francis, *Gone for Good?*, London: Epworth Press, 2007.

50 Steve Aisthorpe, *The Invisible Church*, Edinburgh: Saint Andrew Press, 2016, 137.

51 Brierley, 'Church Census', 14.

52 Brierley, 'Church Census', 27.

53 'Scotland's Census 2011', National Records of Scotland, accessed 27.11.20, https://www.scotlandscensus.gov.uk/documents/censusresults/release2a/rel2A_Religion_detailed_Scotland.pdf.

54 See Liam Jerrold Fraser, 'A Tradition in Crisis: Understanding and Repairing Division Over Homosexuality in the Church of Scotland', *Scottish Journal of Theology* 69, No. 2, 2016: 155–70.

55 See David J. Randall, *A Sad Departure*, Edinburgh: Banner of Truth, 2015.

56 The phrase comes from Storrar, although is used here in a different sense. See William Storrar, 'Understanding the Silent Disruption', in *Future of the Kirk*, eds David Fergusson and D.W.D. Shaw, St Andrews: University of St Andrews, 1997, 21–36.

57 Brierley, 'Church Census', 50.

58 Brierley, 'Church Census', 52.

59 Brierley, 'Church Census', 52.

60 Brierley, 'Church Census', 53.

61 Brierley, 'Church Census', 54.

62 Brierley, 'Church Census', 54.

63 Friedrich Schleiermacher, *Christian Faith*, Louisville, KY: Westminster John Knox Press, 2016.

64 See Fraser, *Atheism*, 238–44 for more description of theological liberalism.

65 Bruce, *House Divided*, 131–45.

66 McLeod, *Crisis*, 83–101.

67 Johnston R. McKay, 'Is a Public Theology Possible?', in *Christian Faith and the Welfare of the City*, ed. Johnston R. McKay, Largs: Centre for Theology and Public Issues, 2008, 71–9 at 78.

68 Bruce, *House Divided*, 109–13.

69 McLeod, *Crisis*, 209.

70 Landon Schnabel and Sean Bock, 'The Persistent and Exceptional Intensity of American Religion: A Response to Recent Research', *Sociological Science* 4, 2017: 686–700.

71 David Millard Haskell, Kevin N. Flatt and Stephanie Burgoyne, 'Theology Matters', *Review of Religious Research* 58, No. 4, 2016: 515–41 at 535.

72 Haskell, Flatt and Burgoyne, 'Theology Matters', 535–7.
73 MacLaren, *Implausible*, 161.
74 See Fraser, *Atheism*, 84.

Chapter 7 Service

1 'Foodbank Use in Scotland', Scottish Housing News, last modified 6.1.20, https://www.scottishhousingnews.com/article/foodbank-use-in-scotland-rises-almost-80-in-five-years.

2 'Annual Report and Accounts 2018', Christians Against Poverty, accessed 28.11.20, https://capuk.org/downloads/finance/accounts_2018.pdf.

3 Ann Morisy, *Beyond the Good Samaritan*, London: Mowbray, 1997, 7–8.

4 'The Scottish Church and the COVID-19 Pandemic', Brendan Research, accessed 28.4.21, https://www.brendanresearch.com/projects/sclf-acts-covid19.

5 'Community Development', United Nations, last modified 7.7.14, https://web.archive.org/web/20140714225617/http://unterm.un.org/DGAACS/unterm.nsf/8fa942046ff7601c85256983007ca4d8/526c2ea ba978f007852569fd00036819?OpenDocument.

6 Morisy, *Samaritan*, 17–18.

7 See Paul Ede, *Urban Eco-Mission*, Cambridge: Grove Books, 2013.

8 'What is it All About?', Social Enterprise UK, accessed 28.11.20, https://www.socialenterprise.org.uk/what-is-it-all-about/.

9 Further arguments for the use of social enterprises by churches can be found in Samuel Wells, *A Future That's Bigger Than the Past*, Norwich: Canterbury Press, 2019.

10 Murray, *Church After Christendom*, 228.

11 Quoted in Paul Ballard, 'Community and Christian Witness', in *Issues in Church Related Community Work*, ed. Paul Ballard, Cardiff: University of Wales, 1990, 26–30 at 27.

12 Murray, *Church After Christendom*, 228.

13 Ballard, 'Christian Witness', 26.

14 See e.g. G.W.F. Hegel, *Lectures on the Philosophy of Religion Vol. I*, trans. Peter C. Hodgson, Oxford: Oxford University Press, 2008.

15 Cited in David Fergusson, 'Theology in a Time of War', in *God's Will in a Time of Crisis*, ed. Andrew R. Morton, Edinburgh: CTPI, 1994, 32–44.

16 Harvey, *Bridging*, 85.

17 J.C. Hoekendijk, *The Church Inside Out*, London: SCM Press, 1964, 38.

18 World Council of Churches, 'Missionary Structure of the Congregation', in *The Ecumenical Movement*, eds Michael Kinnamon and Brian E. Cope, Grand Rapids, MI: William B. Eerdmans, 1997, 347–50.

19 Michael Moynagh, *A Church for Every Context*, London: SCM Press, 2012, 337.

Chapter 8 Evangelism

1 See e.g. 'Redemptoris Missio', The Holy See, last modified 7.12.90, http://www.vatican.va/content/john-paul-ii/en/encyclicals/docu ments/hf_jp-ii_enc_07121990_redemptoris-missio.html, para. 33.

2 See Stephen B. Bevans, *Models of Contextual Theology*, Maryknoll, NY: Orbis Books, 2002, 107.

3 The Holy See, *Catechism of the Catholic Church*, Vatican City: Libreria Editrice Vaticana, 2000, 237–8.

4 'Catholic Education', Scottish Catholic Education Service, accessed 28.11.20, https://sces.org.uk/catholic-education/.

5 See http://streetchurchedinburgh.co.uk for more information.

6 See Aaron Edwards, 'Secular Apathy and the Public Paradox of the Gospel', *International Journal of Public Theology* 13, No. 4, 2019: 413–31.

7 'Annual Report 2017', The Turning, accessed 28.11.20, http://annualreport2017.theturning.eu/year-2/.

8 'Learning Report', The Turning, accessed 28.11.20, http://theturning.eu/learning-review/.

9 The author is a member of GTN's Steering Board.

10 Cf. MacLaren, *Implausible*, 95–9.

11 'Testimonials', Reasonable Faith, accessed 28.11.20, https://www.reasonablefaith.org/testimonials/.

12 'About', Alpha International, accessed 28.11.20, https://www.alpha.org.

13 David Male, 'Who Are Fresh Expressions Really For?', in *Evaluating Fresh Expressions*, eds Louise Nelstrop and Martyn Percy, Norwich: Canterbury Press, 2008, 169–72.

14 Stephen Hunt, 'Some Observations on the Alpha Course', in *Evaluating Fresh Expressions*, eds Louise Nelstrop and Martyn Percy, Norwich: Canterbury Press, 2008, 161–74 at 174.

15 Stefan Paas, *Church Planting in the Secular West*, Grand Rapids, MI: William B. Eerdmans, 2016, 262.

16 Cf. Male, 'Really For?', 174.

17 See Berger and Luckmann, *Construction*, 172–8; Berger, *Reality*, 54–6.

18 E.W. McFarland, 'The Church of Scotland's Church Extension

Movement 1946–61', *Twentieth Century British History* 23, No. 2, 2012: 192–220 at 209.

19 Harvey, *Bridging*, 15, 18–19. Cf. McFarland, 'Church of Scotland's Extension Movement', 219.

20 Van der Borght, *Ministry*, 415.

21 Murray, *After Christendom*, 136–7; Alan Hirsch, *The Forgotten Ways*, 2nd edn, Ada, MI: Brazos Press, 2016, 139.

22 Tom Allan, *The Face of My Parish*, London: SCM Press, 1954, 32–7.

23 See Church of Scotland, *Church Without Walls*, Edinburgh: Parish Education Publications, 2001.

24 See Liam Jerrold Fraser, 'The Scottish Ideal: Lay Education and Training in the Church of Scotland', *Theology in Scotland* 26, No. 2, 2019: 57–70 at 64–5 for more analysis of CWW's lack of progress within the Kirk.

25 Church of England, *Mission-Shaped Church*, London: Church House Publishing, 2004, 90.

26 Church of England, *Mission-Shaped*, 100.

27 The closest the report gets to a single definition is when, interestingly, it discusses fresh expressions as an example of church planting. See Church of England, *Mission-Shaped*, 29–34.

28 See Steve Croft, 'What Counts As a Fresh Expression?', in *Evaluating Fresh Expressions*, eds Louise Nelstrop and Martyn Percy, Norwich: Canterbury Press, 2008, 3–14 at 10.

29 Church of England, *Mission-Shaped*, 44.

30 'Fresh Expressions of Church', Church of England, accessed 12.12.20, https://www.churchofengland.org/about/fresh-expressions-church-england.

31 Cf. Stuart Murray, *Planting Churches*, Milton Keynes: Paternoster, 2008, 8.

32 Paas, *Secular West*, 2.

33 Murray, *Planting*, 20–45.

34 John Piper, *Let the Nations Be Glad*, Grand Rapids, MI: Inter-Varsity Press, 2003, 17.

35 Moynagh, *Context*, 354.

36 Hirsch, *Forgotten*, 178–80.

37 Lesslie Newbigin, *The Gospel in a Pluralist Society*, London: SPCK, 2014, 227.

38 Stephen B. Bevans and Roger Schroeder, *Constants in Context*, Maryknoll, NY: Orbis Books, 2004, 277–9.

39 Guder, *Missional*, 244–62.

40 R.D. Kernohan, 'Must the Kirk Die?', in *St. Andrews Rock*, ed. Stewart Lamont, London: Bellew Publishing, 27.

41 Cf. Hirsch, *Forgotten*, 230.

42 Paas, *Secular West*, 40.

43 Hirsch, *Forgotten*, 154–55.

44 Moynagh, *Context*, 357.

45 Andrew Walls, *The Missionary Movement in Christian History*, Edinburgh: T&T Clark, 1996, 27.

46 Lumin Sanneh, *Translating the Message*, Maryknoll, NY: Orbis 1991, 36–48.

47 Bevans, *Models*, 50.

48 David J. Bosch, *Transforming Mission*, Maryknoll, NY: Orbis Books, 1991, 21.

49 Hirsch, *Forgotten*, 149.

50 Doug Gay, *Remixing the Church*, London: SCM Press, 2011, 63–40.

51 Stuart Hall, ed., *Representation*, London: Routledge, 1997, 2–4.

52 Pete Ward, *Liquid Ecclesiology*, Leiden: Brill, 2017, 68.

53 Ward, *Liquid*, 69.

54 Gay, *Remixing*, 116–17.

55 See Gay, *Remixing*, 92–3.

56 Bevans, *Models*, 101.

57 Bevans, *Models*, 102.

58 David McCarthy, *Seeing Afresh*, Edinburgh: Saint Andrew Press, 2019, 16–17 and 130–48.

59 Murray, *After Christendom*, 21–2 and 203–7.

60 Sara Savage, 'Fresh Expressions: The Gains and the Risks', in *Evaluating Fresh Expressions*, eds Louise Nelstrop and Martyn Percy, Norwich: Canterbury Press, 2008, 55–70 at 56–7.

61 Mike Breen, *Building a Discipling Culture*, 3rd edn, United States: 3DM International, 2017, 5–6.

62 Breen, *Discipling*, 11–18.

63 See James F. Engel, *Contemporary Christian Communication*, New York: Thomas, 1979.

64 Al Dowie, *Interpreting Culture in a Scottish Congregation*, Bern: Peter Lang, 2002, 162–3.

65 Dowie, *Congregation*, 190.

66 A truth found in sources as different as the Preamble to ordination vows in the Church of Scotland and the writings of Hirsch. See James T. Cox, *Practice and Procedure in The Church of Scotland*, 5th edn, Edinburgh: William Blackwood, 1964, 369–70, and Hirsch, *Forgotten*, 187.

67 See 1 Corinthians 12.

68 Hirsch, *Forgotten*, 127.

69 Mike Breen, *Multiplying Missional Leaders*, United States: 3DM International, 2014, 3–4.

70 See Richard Tiplady, 'Entrepreneurial Leadership Development in the Christian Church in Scotland', PhD diss., Glasgow Caledonian University, Glasgow, 2019, ProQuest Dissertations & Theses Global.

71 Hirsch, *Forgotten*, 152.

72 Hirsch, *Forgotten*, 127.

73 See Fraser, 'Scottish Ideal', 61; Alexander Forsyth, *Mission by the People*, Eugene, OR: Pickwick Publications, 2017, 193–9.

74 Hirsch, *Forgotten*, 128–33.

75 Cf. Paas, *Secular West*, 471.

76 See McCarthy, *Afresh*, 158–63.

77 Guder, *Missional*, 202.

78 Andrew Davison and Alison Milbank, *For the Parish: A Critique of Fresh Expressions*, London: SCM Press, 2010.

79 Michael Niebauer, 'Virtue Ethics and Church Planting', *Missiology* 44, No. 3, 2016: 311–26 at 312.

80 Davison and Milbank, *Parish*, 54.

81 Davison and Milbank, *Parish*, 1–27.

82 Sheila Akomiah-Conteh, 'New Churches in Glasgow 2000–2016', PhD diss., University of Aberdeen, Aberdeen, 2018, 280–1 and 287–92, ProQuest Dissertations & Theses Global.

83 Paas, *Secular West*, 121.

84 Milbank and Davison, *Parish*, 71–2.

85 Michael A. Hogg and Graham M. Vaughan, *Social Psychology*, 7th edn, Harlow: Pearson, 2014, 395–418.

86 Paas, *Secular West*, 38–9.

87 Paas, *Secular West*, 151.

88 Johnston R. McKay, 'Reformed, but Still Reformable?', in *St. Andrews Rock*, ed. Stewart Lamont, London: Bellew, 1992, 61–4.

89 Hirsch, *Forgotten*, 165.

90 Paas, *Secular West*, 178.

91 Moynagh, *Context*, 81.

92 Cf C. Peter Wagner, *Church Planting for a Greater Harvest*, Raleigh, NC: Regal Books, 1990, 11; Murray, *Planting*, 1–4.

93 Bob Jackson and George Fisher, 'Everybody Welcome', last modified 23.4.20, https://www.dur.ac.uk/digitaltheology/ewo/.

94 'Scottish Church and the COVID-19 Pandemic'.

95 'Church Online', Destiny Edinburgh, accessed 25.11.20, https://destinyedinburgh.com/locations/church-online.

96 'About Us', Sanctuary First, accessed 25.11.20, https://www.sanctuaryfirst.org.uk/about.

97 See McCarthy, *Afresh*, 177.

98 For examples see McCarthy, *Afresh*, 33–73 and Forge Scotland, *Pioneering in Scotland*, Glasgow: Forge Scotland, 2019.

99 Brierley, 'Church Census', 4.

100 Akomiah-Conteh, 'New Churches in Glasgow', 280.

101 George Lings, 'The Day of Small Things', Church Army, last modified November 2016, https://www.churcharmy.org/Publisher/File.aspx?ID=204265, 81–129.

102 Moynagh, *Context*, 79; Steve Aisthorpe, *Rewilding the Church*, Edinburgh: Saint Andrew Press, 2020, 105–6.

103 Murray, *Planting*, 73–7.

104 Lings, 'Small Things', 81–129, and Church Army, 'Playfully Serious', last modified January 2019, https://www.churcharmy.org.uk/Publisher/File.aspx?ID=225713.

105 John Walker, *Testing Fresh Expressions*, Farnham: Ashgate, 2014, 203–5.

106 The first phrase comes from Rowan Williams and the second is based on Aisthorpe's *Rewilding the Church*.

107 See Aisthorpe, *Invisible Church*, 20.

Chapter 9 Public Witness

1 Harold A. Drake, 'Church and Empire', in *The Oxford Handbook of Early Christian Studies*, eds Susan Ashbrook Harvey and David G. Hunter, Oxford: Oxford University Press, 2010, 446–64 at 448–57.

2 The unpreparedness of the Church for this task is the subject of Mark Lilla's useful work *The Stillborn God*, New York: Alfred A. Knopf, 2007.

3 Drake, 'Church and Empire', 458–9.

4 McPherson, *Westminster*, 99–103.

5 Samuel Wells, Russell Rook and David Barclay, *For Good*, Norwich: Canterbury Press, 2017, 1–18.

6 See e.g. Murray, *Post-Christendom*, 245–50.

7 For an introduction see Gordon Graham, ed., *The Kuyper Centre Review Vol. 1*, Grand Rapids, MI: William B. Eerdmans, 2010.

8 See Morton, *God's Will*.

9 William Storrar, 'Three Portraits of Scottish Calvinism', in *The Realm of Reform*, ed. Robert D. Kernohan, Edinburgh: Handsel Press, 1999, 17–30.

10 Formerly known as the Church and Nation Committee and now transitioning to become the Faith Impact Forum.

11 'About Us', The Church of Scotland, accessed 14.7.20, https://www.churchofscotland.org.uk/about-us.

12 See Brown, 'Religion and Secularisation', 75.

13 M.E. Wickham-Jones, 'The Church and Nation Committee of the Church of Scotland', in *The Scottish Churches and the Political Process*, eds A. Elliott and Duncan B. Forrester, Edinburgh: CTPI, 1986, 69–72 at 70.

14 Wickham-Jones, 'Church and Nation', 70–1.

15 Duncan Forrester, 'The Church of Scotland and Public Policy', *Scottish Affairs* 4, 1993: 67–82.

16 'About Us', JPIT, accessed 15.7.20, http://www.jointpublicissues. org.uk/about-us/.

17 'About SCPO', SCPO, accessed 15.7.20, https://www.scpo.scot/ about-scpo/.

18 'Who We Are', CPO, accessed 15.7.20, https://rcpolitics.org/ who-we-are/.

19 Compare https://rcpolitics.org/what-is-catholic-social-teaching/ and https://www.eauk.org/resources/what-we-offer/reports/what-kind-of-society.

20 Morton Steven, 'The Place of Religion in Devolved Scottish Politics', *Scottish Affairs* 58, 2007: 96–110 at 104.

21 Steven, 'Place of Religion', 102 and 106.

22 Steven, 'Place of Religion', 97–8.

23 Bruce, *Scottish Gods*, 223–7.

24 'Scottish Family Party', Bloomberg, accessed 16.12.20, https:// www.bloomberg.com/graphics/2019-uk-general-election-results/par ties/scottish-family-party/.

25 Walter Wink, *Unmasking the Powers*, Philadelphia, PA: Fortress Press, 1986.

26 John Stuart Mill, *On Liberty*, London: Penguin, 2006, 60–1.

27 Gay, *Honey*, 65.

Conclusion

1 Sophocles, *The Three Theban Plays*, trans. Robert Fagles, London: Penguin Classics, 1984, 92.

2 Vatican Radio, 'Construct a Civilization of Love', 22 August 2010, http://www.archivioradiovaticana.va/storico/2010/08/22/pope_bene dict_xvi_construct_a_civilisation_of_love/en1-417168.

3 Karl Barth, *Church Dogmatics*, Vol. 3.2, *The Doctrine of Creation*, eds G.W. Bromiley and T.F. Torrance, Edinburgh: T&T Clark, 1960, 532. My thanks to Paul Nimmo for his help with this reference.

4 The most important of these creeds are the Nicene-Constantin-opolitan and the Chalcedonian. Almost all Scottish churches affirm these catholic or universal creeds.

5 Both documents can be accessed at https://www.lausanne.org/cat egory/content.

6 'Together Towards Life', World Council of Churches, accessed 28.10.20, https://www.oikoumene.org/sites/default/files/Document/To gether_towards_Life.pdf.

7 'Marks of Mission', Anglican Communion, accessed 28.10.20, https://www.anglicancommunion.org/mission/marks-of-mission.aspx.

Index of Names and Subjects